Allen Kent:
INFORMATION ANALYSIS AND RETRIEVAL

Robert S. Taylor:
THE MAKING OF A LIBRARY

Herman M. Weisman:
INFORMATION SYSTEMS, SERVICES, AND CENTERS

Jesse H. Shera:
THE FOUNDATIONS OF EDUCATION FOR LIBRARIANSHIP

Charles T. Meadow:
THE ANALYSIS OF INFORMATION SYSTEMS, Second Edition

Stanley J. Swihart and Beryl F. Hefley:
COMPUTER SYSTEMS IN THE LIBRARY

F. W. Lancaster and E. G. Fayen:
INFORMATION RETRIEVAL ON-LINE

Richard A. Kaimann:
STRUCTURED INFORMATION FILES

Thelma Freides:
LITERATURE AND BIBLIOGRAPHY OF THE SOCIAL SCIENCES

Manfred Kochen:
PRINCIPLES OF INFORMATION RETRIEVAL

Dagobert Soergel:
INDEXING LANGUAGES AND THESAURI: CONSTRUCTION AND
MAINTENANCE

Robert M. Hayes and Joseph Becker:
HANDBOOK OF DATA PROCESSING FOR LIBRARIES, Second Edition

Andrew E. Wessel:
COMPUTER-AIDED INFORMATION RETRIEVAL

Lauren Doyle
INFORMATION RETRIEVAL AND PROCESSING

Charles T. Meadow:
APPLIED DATA MANAGEMENT

Andrew E. Wessel
THE SOCIAL USE OF INFORMATION—OWNERSHIP AND ACCESS

**The Social Use
of Information—
Ownership and Access**

The Social Use
of Information—
Ownership and Access

Andrew E. Wessel

A WILEY-INTERSCIENCE PUBLICATION

JOHN WILEY & SONS
NEW YORK • LONDON • SYDNEY • TORONTO

Library of Congress Cataloging in Publication Data:

Wessel, Andrew E
    The social use of information—ownership and access.

    (Information sciences series)
    "A Wiley-Interscience publication."
    Includes bibliographical references and index.
    1. Information storage and retrieval systems.
2. Computers.   3. Freedom of information.   I. Title.

Z699.W452   029.7   76-18211
ISBN 0-471-93377-5

Printed in the United States of America

10 9 8 7 6 5 4 3 2 1

Information Sciences Series

Information is the essential ingredient in decision making. The need for improved information systems in recent years has been made critical by the steady growth in size and complexity of organizations and data.

This series is designed to include books that are concerned with various aspects of communicating, utilizing, and storing digital and graphic information. It will embrace a broad spectrum of topics, such as information system theory and design, man-machine relationships, language data processing, artificial intelligence, mechanization of library processes, non-numerical applications of digital computers, storage and retrieval, automatic publishing, command and control, information display, and so on.

Information science may someday be a profession in its own right. The aim of this series is to bring together the interdisciplinary core of knowledge that is apt to form its foundation. Through this consolidation, it is expected that the series will grow to become the focal point for professional education in this field.

Preface—
An Open Invitation

This book is addressed to those who wish to continue their participation in the making of informed decisions. There are more than enough critical decisions to be made but, within our societies, there are not enough informed people helping to make them.

This book is not predominantly technical. The problems to be considered are far too important and complex to be resolved by technology alone. We are confronted with a mixture of interrelated problems; human, social, political, economic, and technological. All these aspects are involved in any attempt to provide, through the use of automated information retrieval technology, more equitable access to that form of power known as information.

Yet any serious discussion of the policies and effects associated with the development and implementation of automated information retrieval processes requires a reasonable degree of comprehension of the technology. Chapters 2 and 6 attempt to provide this. These, and other chapters, also describe some new techniques and methods. The imminent second generation of software, much needed to provide broader access to automated information retrieval capabilities, is presented. Some of this new technology has not previously been made public.

Those who may not be even remotely interested in technology are, nonetheless, encouraged to attempt these chapters. As the rest of the book makes clear, managers, administrators, legislators, and the public generally will be called on to make some rather profound decisions. The thrust of the developing information retrieval technology will require decisions, informed or not.

For those interested in additional material and more detailed discussion of the technical grounds for some of the positions taken, frequent references are made to *Computer-Aided Information Retrieval.** This book, hereafter referred to as CAIR, deals with the problems of providing effective computer aids to the processes of document analysis, description, indexing, and file entry. Computer aids for search and search request formulation are also discussed. The new and different discussion of these problems permits the present book to stand, or perhaps fall, on its own.

We are concerned with some of the increasingly controversial and difficult problems associated with obtaining enough useful information for more people to make better decisions. In particular, we focus on the recent and growing role of computers in providing information for those with access to automated information retrieval capabilities. We are not concerned with "how to make decisions" or in general, what decisions should be made. We urge that one very important and specific decision must be made: To provide more equitable public access to the information available in the growing and already massive computerized files.

We describe the means and methods required to achieve broader and more equitable public access. Chapter 7 offers a recommended and detailed implementation program. Chapter 8 continues this discussion providing additional information and speculation as to the economic and political aspects. Chapter 9 deals with alternative approaches to the solution of the human and social problems identified in Chapters 1, 3, 4, and 5.

Technological comprehension, and managerial, executive, and legislative skills are the necessary ingredients for making wise and humane decisions. So are such old-fashioned but badly needed qualities as good sense, will, perseverance, courage, and humor. Yet all these characteristics can fail us through lack of information; timely, relevant, and complete enough information. Thus our main concern is to broaden access to better information.

* Andrew E. Wessel, *Computer-Aided Information Retrieval,* Wiley-Interscience Division, John Wiley & Sons, Inc., New York, 1975.

Those who may share this concern are invited to continue the discussion already begun. However, this is an invitation to more than a necessary public discussion. To isolate and clarify the key issues and processes pertinent to broadening public access to automated information retrieval are but the first steps. We explore as well the next: how to ensure that more of us obtain reliable access to these newer capabilities.

The American bicentennial is a celebration of the democratic processes, however imperfectly functioning, anywhere. The parades and speeches are already underway; it is time to do what we can to see to it that these same democratic processes function less imperfectly everywhere.

ANDREW E. WESSEL

Munich, West Germany
March 1976

Acknowledgments

To those good friends and colleagues who have drawn my attention to the many articles, reports, and items I could not have discovered myself, I apologize for not being able to list them all.

To Noel Isotta and W. A. Martin, both of the Space Documentation Service, European Space Agency, I extend credit for their contributions to and implementation of many of the ideas explored in this book. To the Space Documentation Service and the European Space Agency, my thanks for support during the last 2 years and for their permission to publish on matters I developed under their auspices. The views expressed in this book, however, are my own responsibility and should not be attributed to any of the persons or organizations mentioned.

I am grateful to Betty Oldroyd, Chief Librarian and Head of Scientific and Technical Information Service, European Space Research and Technology Center, who not only supplied me with many citations, but also provided me with the perspectives of modern librarianship. I also thank Phyllis Kaplan, an American librarian, who shared her views with me.

To Art Hoffman, Public Affairs Counselor, United States Mission to the European Communities, I extend my appreciation for his insights into the needs and problems of fulfilling the needs for public information.

Thanks are also given to Oscar Firschein, Principal Investigator, Lockheed Research Laboratory, who supplied me with current data on the DIALIB experiment.

Marie Marcks' drawings are truly worth "more than a thousand words."

H. Eberhard Seelbach, Dr. Erwin Kayser Threde & Co.,

produced the computer programs, which in turn ingeniously produced the extensional tables.

Hermann Graml and Klaus Wimmer, Siemens AG, obtained many references for me and provided significant aid to my wife, Hildegard G. Wessel, in producing the German translation, *Information im Dienste der Gesellschaft,* Hermann Luchterhand Verlag, simultaneously published with this English version. Ann Campbell aided in the proofreading and with the preparation of the index, tables, and charts. All helped with the lengthy collaborative processes that resulted in both the English and German manuscripts. Which brings me, most gratefully, to my wife.

A. E. W.

Note for the
American Edition

This book is the result of a close collaboration with my wife, Hildegard G. Wessel, who produced a German draft translation of the initial English draft. These drafts, both English and German, were together compared, edited, and then the final manuscripts completed. This process, a lengthy collaborative effort, had more than the expected merits. Rhetoric and verbal 'fireworks' which hide weak arguments, often do not 'translate'. Shallow thinking is shown to be what it is; sometimes with a delightful clarity. Should it be found that this book has less rhetoric and more clarity and reasoned discussion than what normally may be expected these days, a small degree of what my wife has contributed would be indicated.

ANDREW E. WESSEL

Munich, West Germany
March, 1976

Contents

Chapter 4

The Need for Access   **83**

Chapter 5

Some Binary Digits Were Missing—A Contemporary Tale   **107**

Chapter 6

**Second-Generation Computer Software for a Public
Information Retrieval System**   **113**

Chapter 8

A Question of Nationalities and Costs   179

Chapter 9

Alternatives   200

Chapter 10

The Distribution of Information   232

**The Social Use
of Information—
Ownership and Access**

Chapter One

Cassandra's Trojan Horse

Doomsayers are unwelcome folk. Even when clearheaded and precise, no one really wants to pay attention to announcements of tomorrow's disasters if what we can do today makes little difference. Had Cassandra the wit to describe exactly Odysseus' stratagem for obtaining the easy entry of his Greek soldiers, her reception among the Trojans would not have been greatly improved. There was no way out for Troy. At the least we want one way out per doom, else there is little point in spreading alarm.

The contemporary situation with regard to the ownership of and access to automated information systems somewhat resembles the insidious entry of a Trojan Horse within our midst. It is as if we are unknowingly permitting all the intelligence and craft of the legendary Odysseus to be given to those with power enough already, leaving ourselves even more empty-handed in comparison. This is alarming indeed, and should be so regarded. It is rather easy to state existing policy with regard to the development and implementation of automated information retrieval systems: Everybody pays for the costs of development; few benefit from the implementation. The effects of such a policy ought to be alarming to those who opt for a more democratic and equitable social use of information.

There is a way out. To find it we must explore the capabilities of computer technology as applied to the tasks of obtaining and extracting for us information of great social utility. We also have to consider the social impact of this technology and, in particular, the relevant policies with regard to its development and application. Those who simply wish to "join the system" are similar in certain respects to those who prefer to blow it up. They need far less understanding and analysis of alternatives than those who wish to change the system. As we shall see there are some viable alternatives; we can change both the existing policy as well as the technology to which the policy is addressed. In fact we shall find that the desirable technical modifications are very much related to any attempt to modify policy.

We need to delineate more carefully the problems of ownership and access and to consider certain issues previously identified. Alarms have already been sounded; sometimes appropriately and sometimes not.

We have heard much concerning the "privacy issue" and the problems of preventing erroneous or destructive information concerning individuals from accumulating in governmental or private data banks (1). These issues are important. They focus on how we can protect ourselves from computers. Yet however we eventually work out procedures and methods of protecting ourselves from computers, they will still exist and be owned and used. This is to say that some organizations and groups will own, have access to, and control the information within computerized information files and, given current policy, only some and not many others.

Recognizing this fact is the beginning of understanding the broader issues involved in the ownership, access to, control, and use of automated information retrieval systems. These issues do not affect only a relatively few wronged individuals or infringe on some individual rights, as is the case with personal privacy versus computer files. The question of the control and availability of information involves matters at the heart of our social and political fabric; it effects everyone's "individual" rights. One might even speculate that the much touted "privacy issue" may well be functioning as a lightning rod muting public discussion of the broader social issues and focusing attention away from what would make a significant difference to the so-called "establishments" or "power elites."

Yet perhaps a more basic reason for the relative sparsity of public discussion of these central issues is technological. It is true that computer technology has made it possible to store vast amounts and kinds of information in automated data banks. The next 10 years will see even more widespread application of computers in this direction. At the same time, however, conventional computer systems have done rather poorly in helping us get the information we want and need out again, except for certain special kinds of cases.

In CAIR a distinction was made between well-structured data and ill-structured or mixed information (2). Conventional computer systems work rather efficiently with well-structured data, such as is found within airline reservation systems, banking and accounting systems, and process control systems. Automated information retrieval is at the moment relatively inefficient and costly when applied to the more generalized problems of information storage and retrieval (3).

Recent developments in computer software and expected growth in random access computer storage capacities and capabilities are beginning to change this picture. The effectiveness of automated information retrieval will increase and its costs decrease. The means to structure more varied kinds of information well enough to permit more useful recall in terms of user needs are becoming available along with the necessary computer software. These developments will in turn produce more widespread and generalized applications of computers to information storage and retrieval. It is in these more generalized capabilities to store and retrieve information that both the newer power and dangers of computers arise.

Who will benefit from this technology? Given current development and implementation policies only certain, select elements within society will own, have access to, and control the utilization of our automated information retrieval systems. Executive government agencies, industrial giants and conglomerates, major corporations, military organizations, some of the larger labor unions, some politicians, some institutes and leading universities already benefit from the existing computer technology. Those now on such a list will remain there, reaping yet more power from the coming technology. Unimaginable amounts and kinds of information, vital to the lives of billions of people throughout the varying social strata in our world, will be available—but not for everyone capable of and wanting to use such information for their legitimate purposes.

Our legitimate needs for information can be quite specialized and perhaps grandiose; they can be also exceedingly ordinary and specific. "For the many occasions in ordinary life where information exists of great utility, information necessary to the achievement of results important and beneficial to our endeavors, the knowledge that such information exists, its location, and the means by which it can be obtained are too often only haphazardly available, if at all. The list of typical problems requiring such often hard-to-get information is endless. Helping our children with the "new" mathematics or to gain admission to schools and universities, keeping our tables furnished with foods at rational prices, paying our taxes in accordance with the regulations taking advantage of the same "expert" advice available to business executives, selecting the right doctor for the patient in our family, finding the right lawyer for our legal problems or better, knowing enough to avoid legal problems in advance, determining our insurance requirements, knowing how to select candidates for public office and whom to vote for among such candidates, evaluating the performance of elected officials . . . are just some of the areas illustrating the informational needs pertaining to contemporary life. We are all "experts" in something with a rather good feel for the information we need and how to obtain it within the fields of our expertise. But we are overwhelmed with information requirements and irrelevant information even as experts. And we are all "babes in the informational wilderness" with regard to all the other important aspects of our lives. Whatever the political and economic infrastructures may be of the society in which we live (perhaps with certain unhappy exceptions), the question of whether we are citizens or slaves to ignorance may depend upon our ability to obtain and use the available information" (4).

The issue is not only how little- or well-satisfied may be such concerns of individual citizens. The very "shape" of society is being altered. It is already established that politicians with access to computer files fare better in their bids for re-election than those without such access. It is already known that corporations with access to computer files are doing better economic planning, product development, and market assessment than those without. We certainly have become aware that government agencies with computer files can marshal a better case to justify their positions and decisions than those without, and than those who must evaluate such positions in the legislative branches.

Imagine a society in which all schools and libraries were owned by certain private corporations, industrial groups, government executive agencies, military agencies, and the like. Such societies have existed and do exist. Furthermore, let admission or access to those schools and libraries be controlled by the organizations that own them. Lastly, let the structure of the information available and the goals/values inherent in such structuring be similarly controlled. Many of us in the so-called Western World would find such a society intolerable. We might well consider such a society a new Dark Age.

We need not equate the importance of schools and libraries to that of automated information systems. We need only note the already known results of our current development and implementation policy as to automated information systems. The ownership of these systems, the control of their informational structures and purposes, the control of access and utilization are all occurring in such a manner as to make these uncomfortable suppositions concerning our society more real than imaginary.

Yet the current policies applicable to this new technology may not result in what could be appropriately described as a new Dark Age. The Dark Ages have been characterized as a society where information felt to be relevant was stored in monasteries, preserved and guarded by monks, and accessible to few. In this regard, we have much to ponder and compare. Decision-making in the Dark Ages, however, was decentralized. Throughout this period there were certain places where a relative degree of freedom persisted and access to information and power was less limited. Today the means to communicate and control both broadly and deeply are available to those with information and power. The scattered colonies of monks were relatively remote from Rome. They performed their services and preserved the heritage of the past in their various ways. They often had little direct effect on their environment beyond a few leagues. They sometimes offered, in differing degrees, places to hide and thrive. We may be heading for a society too well-lit for anyone to find a place to hide.

A more detailed discussion of the potential impact of automated information retrieval technology on the shape of our society is warranted. Unlike Troy, our fall is far from inevitable. Computer technology combined with modern communications does not in itself imply complete and totalitarian control. In fact the newer technology could lead in quite the opposite direction, toward more informed democratic decision-making and relevant public participation in the resolution of the many pervasive problems in contemporary life. We must consider certain features of this technology and certain aspects of its current development policy. There are, in particular, some quite critical "timing" considerations. Certain technological development and implementation steps must be taken rather soon or our freedom of action, our ability to change direction or influence matters will become severely limited by economic, technological, and socio-political factors. At present we may still determine the direction of this technological implementation, determine more equitably who will have access to the coming automated information retrieval systems, how such access will be achieved, what information will be made available, and how to make our retrieval capabilities more responsive to a broader public. We can still develop reasonably good cost estimates for various alternative ways to accomplish greater and more useful public access before the cost of any alternative other than our existing policy offers begins to cost too much.

The direction our society takes in the next few years with regard to automated information systems will importantly effect our options for changing existing development and implementation policy. We have observed that these current development and implementation policies have done a great deal for a few and hardly anything directly for the rest of us. We have indicated a list of the benefited few. To date, a catalog of those without such resources includes legislative branches of government, local parliaments and councils, individual businessmen, workers, "intellectuals," students, and often, their teachers, government employees, "ordinary" citizens, consumers. We need a reliable answer to the question of whether technology can provide useful access to automated information systems for such groups and for the public generally. We would want to know how useful such access might be, who would really use it, and how much it would really cost. And we need to know whether certain brute force solutions make any sense. For example, does it accomplish anything other than confusion simply to open existing computer files structured for specific users to the public or even selected public groups? This is one "solution" to be considered; there are others.

Actually we shall discover that there are many apparent "ways out." But many will change little if anything, others may be foolish or worse, and perhaps only a few worth taking. We must isolate and describe these few preferred alternatives to existing policies for development and implementation of automated information retrieval systems. Furthermore, we present the case for their implementation at least experimentally, describe what will be involved in any such attempt, and argue, quite strongly, that we can do what needs to be done.

We now leave Cassandra and proceed, hopefully with the craft and art of Odysseus, in our explorations of quite complicated and interconnected social, technological, economic, and political concerns. If the result is our own Trojan Horse for the public, placed inside the camp of the political, industrial, and technological establishments, so be it. We will have paid for our admission tickets.

NOTES

1. Arthur R. Miller, *The Assault on Privacy—Computers, Data Banks and Dossiers,* The University of Michigan, 1971; F. Gruenberger, *Computers and the Social Environment,* Melville Publishing Company, Los Angeles, 1972; L. J. Hoffman, *Security and Privacy in Computer Systems,* Melville Publishing Company, Los Angeles, 1973.

2. A. E. Wessel, *Computer-Aided Information Retrieval* (CAIR) Melville Publishing Company, Los Angeles, 1975.

3. Ibid.

4. CAIR, p. 4.

Chapter Two

The Technological Potential

As the United States observes the bicentennial year of 1976, the electronic computer will be only in its 30th year of existence. Yet even the birthdate of the modern computer is a bit cloudy. If the mysterious British computer, "Colossus," antedated the University of Pennsylvania's ENIAC we might have to point to an earlier date than 1946 (1). The application of computers to any kind of generalized information retrieval probably occurred in the early 1960s. Any serious attempt at automated information retrieval had to await the development of the transistor and diode as replacements for the vacuum tube, and of disk storage to supplement tapes. To achieve fast enough response times to permit on-line interaction and direct feedback of search results, disk storage had to be combined with very large random access core storage. The third generation of computer systems had to become available before such systems as INSPEC, NASA-RECON, or DIALOG, handling millions of documents, became feasible (2).

It is important to note that we are considering rather new phenomena, however omnipresent computers may seem. We are at the beginning of a process the end of which can only be suggested. This fact has significance. First, as with all new phenomena, there are conflicting opinions as to what it all may mean. Second, the range of the possible, from the point of view of the technically feasible, is yet unclear. And last, the formative stage is now at hand; options that will be closed a bit later are open now. Chapter One hinted at the first and last of these three themes, which are expanded in later chapters. But first this chapter offers a close look at the technically feasible, both at present and in the short-term future.

2.1 COMPUTER STORAGE CAPABILITIES

Automated information retrieval systems are supposed to store large numbers of documents (millions) within computer files. They do not. Although it is possible to store literally the texts of millions of documents and other information carriers, using tape or disk storage, this is too costly and results in unacceptable search times and system responses. Both tape and disk storage are peripheral storages supplementing the internal core or computer working store. The internal computer store is random access, which means that any piece of information stored there can be reached and processed by the computer as readily as any other. It is in the core or computer working storage that internal processing takes place, where comparisons, counts, and other similar programmed operations occur. Such programmed operations are performed incredibly quickly. But to date, such random access internal computer storage cannot handle the texts of millions of documents.

Existing disk storage capabilities permit a significant degree of "focused" access to the material stored there. Unlike tape stores, one can search disks not only by individual disk, but also by disk track. A great deal of sequential search, such as reading a tape from beginning to end to find a desired piece of information, can be avoided. Computer software techniques have been developed to take advantage of this capability. (3). Even so there are limits imposed by the physical characteristics of disk storage and the complexities involved in the computer programs that must keep track of where data is stored on disks. Transfers between disks and internal computer working storage can mount, producing very long wait times for system responses. Until new developments take place in internal random access stores permitting very much larger capacities, or peripheral stores are developed permitting significant processing of data to occur there, full text storage of millions of documents remains a dubious possibility.

2.2　TEXTUAL ENTRY AND STORAGE CAPABILITIES

There is yet another factor making full text storage uneconomical. We have no sensible way to enter such huge amounts of data other than manually, by punching computer cards or paper tapes. Devices capable of producing magnetic tape often require some form of predominantly manual production in the data entry processes; it all amounts to one form or other of keyboard entry and all the errors associated with such processes. This is also very expensive. Until developments that provide us with "error-free" text entry devices are available, such as trouble-free and inexpensive optical readers, full text document storage will be reserved for limited and very special applications (4).

One opinion may be as good as any other with regard to when such developments permitting feasible full text storage and entry may be accomplished. We offer the view that it will take quite a while. Perhaps one recent example may be illustrative. Shortly after the laser became almost a household object (that is to say, was promoted from its status as a science fiction gadget), the idea to "pack" one image after the other onto the same tiny spot of microfilm and to "read" such images via a laser controlled light source was suggested (5). There were other forms of this concept, all of which proposed to pack quite densely large numbers of information bearing images on film. Such densely packed film elements could then constitute the building blocks of a new form of random access storage for computers. The increase in effective core storage would be fantastic; billions of items could be stored. Even some respectable engineers began contemplating the construction of electronic "brains." This kind of radical increase in quantity of information, theoretically directly processable, might well lead to a qualitative jump in computer capabilities. If we could only find some feasible means to fill such a store, the term "think-tank" might take on a new meaning.

Typically, as with most new technology, there were a few problems, foreseen and unforeseen, in the implementation. The basic idea is interesting enough. Information is greatly reduced in size and stored as tiny images superimposed one on top of the other on film. Each such image is picked up (retrieved) by "reversing" the light beam with which it was stored. Each "twist" or "focus" of the laser (or other controlled light source) can place a given image on the film and similarly retrieve it. We can achieve as much "density" of information storage images as we have "twists" or "focusing" possibilities.

There are several serious technical problems, however, with such an approach. First, film is easy to scratch, destroying a great deal of information. It also gets "dusty." The smaller the film area for storing the packed images, the more information can be lost or destroyed. Second, electromechanical devices to handle the film have to be very carefully made and precisioned. Things have to be moved, either the light source or the film or perhaps both. Again the smaller the image area and the "sharper" the focus points and "twists," the more precision we need. The difference between lines drawn on blackboards by electrical engineers and physicists and the capabilities of mechanical engineers working with physical substances becomes rather large. Precision in concept can often not be implemented without blurring in the real world of hardware. (6). We simply are not sure what image will be picked up or exactly where it may be stored, nor are we sure how good a "picture" we are going to have of the images, however and wherever they are stored.

There are some software problems as well. We have to keep records somewhere in the computer as to where on the film to look and precisely how deep within the densely packed images on a given spot of film is every piece of information. And as files change or changes are made within files, a feature quite relevant to computer-aided information retrieval (7), we have to be able to both make such changes and keep track of them.

These and other problems are some of the reasons why we are still waiting for the development of usable massive capacity random access computer storage. We have many interesting ideas in our laboratories, one of which involves a solid state device and magnetic fields known as "magnetic bubble memory chips" (8). As yet, however, there has been no significant change in the available large memories. Two more years is as good a guess as 10 before such massive random access memories become feasible. For the moment, we must content ourselves with a discussion of existing capabilities; they are impressive enough.

2.3 AUTOMATED INFORMATION RETRIEVAL SYSTEMS—BASIC CHARACTERISTICS

Various existing or developing programming "solutions" and storage manipulative techniques may treat the basic characteristics that follow differently. They may be combined, transformed, or otherwise structured within the computer. Nonetheless, the conceptual framework presented below is felt to be both sound and necessary for general comprehension.

The general kinds of automated information retrieval systems considered here have the following features.

a. Document Identification Schemata

Documents are stored in the form of short document identification schemata rather than in full text form. These document identification schemata contain the means to indicate the locations of the document texts in external microfilm or other library files. A document accession number is almost always part of the document identification schemata. In addition, titles and authors are often listed along with other bibliographic data. Sometimes short abstracts and/or content descriptors are present. The file containing such document schemata is generally called a direct or linear file. Document schemata may have the addresses of textual field elements computer-stored elsewhere in what are called textual files.

b. Descriptor Identification Schemata

Descriptors purport to tell us what kind of document it is they describe and what the document is about. Often a separate file for descriptor identification schemata (in which the descriptors, their identifying or computer coded forms, their textual elements, and other relevant information, such as hierarchical place or thesauri rules pertaining to them, are stored) supplements the linear or direct file for document schemata. Sometimes addresses in the descriptor identification schemata file exist pointing to other computer files. The descriptors themselves may be terms or phrases selected from the textual material, derived from such textual expressions, and/or expressions constructed in various ways to form a thesaurus or thesauri for various informational fields.

c. The Inverted File

Automated search usually occurs within the inverted file. The inverted file consists of formulas containing a short form of a descriptor identification schema concatenated with short forms of the document identification schemata to which the given descriptor has been associated. Thus for any descriptor identification schema "A," all the document identification schemata to which "A" has been assigned are connected in often very long formulas (i.e., A + document numbers 23, 29, 356, 374, ... 5007, 9845, 23956, ... 895375, ...). For most applications, computer addresses of the schemata replace the schemata themselves within the inverted file. Often complex structuring exists involving the use of ISAM files that permit focused access to inverted and other computer files by means of such computer addresses (9).

Automated search essentially involves locating the descriptor formulas stipulated by the given search questions, comparing in the computer core the document "strings" attached to the specified descriptors, and constructing the search result for display or printout to the requestor of the search. While the comparisons are made in the computer working core, the descriptor/document-string formulas are stored on tape or disk files. Tape files are too slow except for batch processing search, although often the files are "passively" stored on tape and placed on disk prior to on-line system operation. System response times are essentially determined by the times required to access the disks and transfer the appropriate formulas to the computer working core where comparisons are made. But disk files and ingenious computer programming make on-line interactive search possible; not, however, overwhelmingly good at present!

d. Batch Processing Search

Batch processing and on-line, interactive search exist as available options for most automated information retrieval systems. With batch processing, the original requestor of the search is seldom if ever involved in the computer search. A search center is set up. Search requests from various sources come into this center. These requests are then reformulated by search middlemen into search questions the computer can understand. They are "batched," that is, run through the computer in "efficient" lots. The results are then delivered to the original requestor of the search by all known forms of communication including messenger, teletype, airmail, and slow boat. There is almost always a significant delay between the original request and the computer result intended to satisfy that request. Feedback to aid in reformulation of search requests is seldom available and almost never timely enough. And the original search requestor usually has no idea of what occurred during the computer search processes. A result is obtained, useful or not; take it or leave it.

e. *Interactive Search*

On-line interactive search systems offer the search requestor and/or the search middleman the opportunity to obtain direct feedback as a result of the initially formulated search question. If abstracts or other general information have been stored within or connected to the document identification schemata attached to the inverted file formulas, additional information concerning the search result can be directly obtained from the computer. Otherwise, and normally, only document titles and limited bibliographic data are available with the list of document accession numbers retrieved. (Additional computer files are required to provide such additional information.) However, based on search result size, plus some hints as to document content, the searcher can decide to reformulate his search request in terms of broader or more restrictive search questions as he sees fit. Often thesauri, collections of acceptable descriptors with varying amounts and kinds of explanatory information as to descriptor usage and meaning, are available for on-line display. This, too, can offer aid to the searcher in formulating and reformulating his search request. Lastly, of course, the searcher may use the retrieved document accession numbers to obtain the actual documents (or copies) from external files. This provides yet another input to the decision whether to reformulate search requests or rest content with what has already been obtained.

2.3.1   Some Typical Search Result Characteristics

Search results obtained using on-line interactive search systems are usually more satisfactory than with older batch-processing systems, particularly with regard to retrospective search. For selective dissemination, where document citations are distributed according to user profiles on a regular spaced interval basis under contract, batch processing is usually the appropriate method. Yet the actual search result quality both for systems offering retrospective search and selective dissemination, although difficult to determine, does not indicate superior performance. Important citations are often missed and the percentage of irrelevant or useless citations is high. Recall relevancy is seldom better than 60% and is often worse, sometimes as low as 20%. This means that from four to eight out of every ten citations obtained via computer search are irrelevant or useless. The percentage of missed documents might well be similar (10); that is, at best we seem to be missing about four out of every ten citations we should ideally obtain. To obtain better recall and relevancy, some search centers with interactive search systems have introduced a significant degree of manual screening between the actual computer-generated search results and their customers. As many as $3\frac{1}{2}$ hrs are spent per search request of manual screening of the computer output in at least one such search center (11). However one looks at it, the cost of either prescreening by search centers or postscreening by users, in addition to the automated retrieval costs, may mean that for many users such systems are worth less than they cost (12). In any event, for results such as these, automated information retrieval simply costs too much at present for very widespread application. However, there are some changes taking place of great relevance to our investigations.

2.3.2   Some Newer and Nontypical Features

On-line, interactive search systems have begun to offer computer aids to searchers in formulating and reformulating their search requests. These aids involve such features as displayable thesauri, direct feedback of search results, and, sometimes, additional data concerning the search result beyond simply listing citations obtained. With the exception of the displayable thesauri, most existing automated retrieval systems fail to provide any aids to those responsible for indexing or describing the documents in the first place. This means that whatever aids to search may exist, the ability to obtain relevant and full recall of information from computer files remains dependent on the validity of manual indexing.

For data banks consisting of well-structured or preformated and quantified data, this dependency on manual indexing is not too serious. Either such data is sufficiently "self" described and comprehended by potential searchers or normally it can be made so. It is one thing to request information about the numbers of items on hand in a warehouse for which an automated inventory system exists and satisfy our reasonable expectation that the answer will be both relevant and valid. It begins to become quite another thing when requesting information from even census data banks (13), or when requesting information concerning medical case histories and clinical records. As soon as we have a mix of users with their sundry retrieval interests combined with a mix of informational materials, search results to date indicate that both search requestors and indexers need far more help than they have so far been given. Computer aids offering this kind of help have recently become available (14). We describe two forms of these newer features, which have just left the laboratory development stages, and suggest yet a third that can be applied directly to most existing systems. Our discussion of the technological features of automated information retrieval systems will then have been sufficient for us to proceed to a more informed discussion of the major themes of this book.

2.3.2.1 *Computer-Aided Indexing* One way to improve the quality of search results obtained with automated retrieval systems is to attempt to improve indexing quality. The hope for fully automated solutions to the indexing problems has not yet been substantiated (15). Attempts to program computers to apply statistical frequency techniques, modern linguistic models, semantic factoring, and logical apparatus to textual material have failed in general to produce the means to describe such material sufficiently well and consistently so as to permit accurate formulation of search requests. Search requests can be formulated using natural language expressions and programming computers to search textual material for occurrences of such expressions. However, the results of such searches have proved disappointing to most users. There may or may not be "standard" syntactical ways with which we express ourselves. But there are no "standard" semantic or pragmatic ways to express syntactically our relevant informational needs, nor are there such standard ways with which the textual material to be searched is created by all the many and varied producers of information. Or if there are such "standards" in heaven, on earth, or in the laboratory, most humans happily seem to fail to interpret or use them in a sufficiently standardized fashion.

Neither the continued failures of sophisticated, fully automated techniques nor those of unstructured natural language description exhaust the alternatives available for providing better indexed information and, thereby, better search results. The very same computer manufacturers who provided us with on-line, interactive search systems could and should have provided us with interactive indexing systems. Instead of concentrating on the attempt to replace the human indexer and document analyst by machines, human indexers and their problems should have been the focus of development. These human problems and concerns are, after all, our problems. No one has proposed very seriously to do away with the human formulation of search requests. No one seems to feel that machines, with any degree of confidence, can tell us what we want and need to know. Certainly for any authority that purports to tell us what we ought to want and need to know counter-authorities exist, as well as countervailing common sense. But it seems that the "apparatniks," whether computer technologists, linguistic experts, or library scientists, have attempted the assumption of sufficient authority to eliminate the human indexer or, at the least, to tell the indexer how to behave. It is not surprising that the necessary capabilities never backed up the presumed authority.

Computer-aided indexing takes another tack. It attempts to help human indexers do better what they do best; to choose the most appropriate descriptors for indicating the content and the characteristics of the textual material in documents and other information carriers. To provide such help, at least one additional computer file is required. To continue the list begun in Section 2.3, computer-aided interactive indexing requires these additional features.

f. A Direct File for Documents and Descriptors

A direct file consisting of formulas in which each document identification schema is connected to the string of descriptor identification schemata assigned to the document. Again computer addresses will often be used in place of such identification schemata. These addresses indicate where such schemata can be found in other computer files. Most, but not all, of the existing search only retrieval systems use one form or other of such direct files. These are used in such systems primarily as inputs for creation of the inverted file, through which computer searches are conducted. Although the direct file constitutes a kind of "double-storing" of information already in the inverted file, information that forms the basis of significant computer aids is far more easily extracted from the direct file. For example, should an indexer considering a given document wish to know what the pattern of descriptor assignments has been for any other document or document group, the direct file can be directly accessed by document or documents to obtain this information.

g. Other Special Accessory Files

These would consist of various kinds of relevant information attached to "documents," such as abstracts, document classifica-. tions, bibliographic data, user profiles, or specified user rankings of the documents, and so forth. Such special files are needed also for "descriptors," where textual explanations and rules may be associated with descriptors. When both inverted and direct files exist along with these kinds of special accessory files, the computer can offer significant guidance to human indexers. This computer guidance should include:

1. Displaying the relevant thesauri structures, explanations, rules, and associations applicable to the descriptors considered by the indexer as possible choices for assignment to a document. In this manner thesauri can utilize rather complicated structuring methods, and human indexers need not study or memorize them. When stored in computers and triggered by the initial descriptor selections of human indexers, just those relevant thesauri expansions of the given descriptors can be displayed as a function of the indexers' choices.

2. Computer-suggested lists of potentially relevant descriptors based on the initial descriptor choices of the indexer. Such computer suggested lists can be "weighted" to conform to indexing patterns established by expert committee consensus indexing. They can emphasize indexing practices of certain selected indexers and not others. They can "defer" to more recent indexing rather than older. And such "weighting" principles need not be exclusive; they can be combined and changed over time, and be influenced by search test results. Such computer-suggested lists function by searching the computer files to determine the most closely related descriptors to those that the indexer has selected as initial choices for assignment to the document being indexed. They provide a means to increase consistency and completeness of indexing. Each indexer receives computer guidance, which can be based on the practices and choices of all indexers including the indexer being guided. Such computer-suggested descriptors are a function of the individual indexer's initial choices; in addition, the suggestion algorithms "learn" or are influenced by the individual indexer's selection from the suggested lists.

3. Computer-suggested or mandatory fill-in formats. Based on the selection of given descriptors, the computer can suggest or require that other descriptors or qualifying expressions be chosen by the indexer. Formats for bibliographic description or other specialized formats can be displayed to indexers on entry of documents for indexing with computer-offered multiple choice descriptor lists. Various forms of standard operating indexing procedures can be similarly offered as computer guidance, depending on organizational requirements or other factors. These too may change over time as a result of search tests and other user feedback.

Such capabilities have quite profound implications when one considers various means to permit public access to automated information retrieval systems. Once the appropriate files have been built and on-line interactive guidance is available for indexers, the very same kinds of guidance become available to searchers as well. In both ways search results can be improved sufficiently to achieve broader and better use of the information stored within automated retrieval systems. We turn to some newer search aids now becoming available.

2.3.2.2 Newer Aids to Search Automated information retrieval systems with the newer features f and g providing computer aids for indexers can also offer similar computer aids to searchers. We shall illustrate one form of the preceding kinds of computer guidance applied to search request formulation. By means of displayable thesauri or other descriptor lists, and whatever other means may be available, a few descriptors are selected by a searcher. These descriptors may be combined with "AND," "OR," or "NOT" in most contemporary systems to form a search question. The computer then searches its files to determine which documents satisfy the given search question and which documents have the descriptors so assigned in the logical combination stipulated. Now suppose the searcher was interested in all documents to which descriptors "A" AND ("B" OR "C") had been assigned. (Note that either "bracketing" to show the strength of the connectives is possible or standard interpretations are used.) All documents listed with an "A" descriptor schema in the inverted file would be transferred to the computer core. Usually this is accomplished one by one, but for our purposes such detail is irrelevant. So then would all documents listed with descriptor "B" and descriptor "C" be transferred. Those documents that appear in the list obtained with "A" would be compared in core with those obtained with "B." Documents appearing in both lists would be set up for display. Then the "C" list of documents would be compared with the "A" list. Additional documents would, perhaps, now be obtained and added to those to be displayed. On completion of such operations, the search result would be made available to the searcher.

The search result would be a list of document citations found. Most existing automated information retrieval systems (features *a* through *e*) provide little if any additional information. Perhaps the total number of citations found would be offered either before displaying the citation list or simultaneously with such a display. The document titles or a bit more bibliographic information might be available on request from the computer. Occasionally abstracts of the citations listed are available. But here we have essentially exhausted the capabilities of conventional systems. The searcher is then left to his own resources to determine whether he should refine his search request or seek to obtain the documents cited from external sources for his inspection and screening. This represents the "normal" situation with automated information retrieval systems. However, there is no requirement to accept such an abnormality as "normal."

Automated information systems with a special direct and other accessory files (features *f* and *g*) can do more. Along with the search result obtained in the previous example, by using these special files additional information can be offered to the searcher. A suggested list of descriptors most strongly related to those in the original search question can be obtained by computer comparisons of just those descriptors attached to the documents first cited. These suggested descriptors could then be used to reformulate the search request. If the search result size had been too small, such descriptors could expand the search request formulation. Had the original search result been too large, descriptors could be selected from those suggested to refine the original search request formulation. In either case, the searcher does not have to know or to browse through thousands of descriptors; he can simply select from those suggested by the computer as a function of his original descriptor search choices. Furthermore, the descriptors suggested by the computer can be influenced by another choice made by the searcher. By rejecting citations when their titles indicate lack of utility relative to the purpose of the search, the "base" of documents in the special direct file used to construct the computer-suggested list can be transformed. This decision to filter may be indicated by noting the original search result size. There are many variations to this basic theme. Our example is only illustrative; yet it does indicate that far more aid can be obtained from automated information systems than we have so far been offered conventionally.

Such capabilities do exist. They have been programmed and tested by various users (16). However it will not be easy for systems based on search only software simply to add the required features to provide such aids (17). Yet it is precisely these features that can make widespread public usage of automated information systems practical and worth the cost. In Chapter 1 we touched on this topic as one of the three themes covered by this book. While automated information systems remain in the formative stage of development and implementation, awareness of "public" requirements still can influence their characteristics. If this is not soon accomplished, it will be difficult and costly later to transform such systems so that the interests and needs of the public can be satisfied. A minimum understanding of the technology involved is thus essential for those who wish to change current implementation policies. We should be aware both of the interests and needs of the public and the technological feasibility of incorporating satisfactory solutions within the current and continuing development of automated information systems. Otherwise, it will be all too easy for those who may so wish to argue that "public access is too costly." Public access need not be too costly if we "do our homework." Luckily, and at the current stage of development, we can do a bit more.

2.3.2.3 Worthwhile Modifications to Existing Systems The purpose of the kind of computer-aided indexing described above is not merely to improve the general quality of search recall. It is of course one of our aims, and the computer aids described above attempt to achieve this as well. Our principal purpose, however, is to make it possible for a much wider variety of searchers to understand sufficiently well what took place during the indexing process. Rather than attempting the impossible—to index documents with every conceivable user interest in mind and to do this coherently and consistently—we suggest another approach. By using thesauri and computer-aided indexing, and focusing on the needs and requirements of selected user groups and informational fields, we also make explicit what has occurred during the indexing processes. And we make comprehension of these indexing procedures available to all searchers and users by the suggested on-line search aids to be provided by information retrieval systems. This approach offers us one of the keys to achieving useful public access, and is discussed in later chapters. Here we have again underscored the importance of establishing the appropriate characteristics of information retrieval systems by beginning to indicate what characteristics are appropriate.

We have also noted the importance of timing in the incorporation of such desirable features within the developing information retrieval systems. For those now considering the application of computer technology to their information retrieval problems, to begin with computer-aided indexing should make sense. It is the preferred approach for those confronted with the task of achieving

well-indexed documents for their own files. Computer-aided indexing will not be more costly than purely manual methods; it is likely
to be far less costly. The indexing quality will be significantly better, as we have indicated. Furthermore, all the evidence to date
indicates that similar conclusions as to cost and quality apply to a
comparison between computer-aided indexing and fully automated
indexing.

Of course, it might be thought that there are drawbacks. The
fact is that the benefits of computer-aided indexing will accrue to
everybody. It will provide better search results for those who own
or have developed their own automated information retrieval
systems. It will also make plausible more meaningful public utilization of the very same files and automated information retrieval
systems. Though this consequence may frighten certain individuals
and groups, it is well to spell it out.

We also return to this topic. But we must now concern ourselves
with the problems inherent in systems based on already indexed
documents. No one wants to reindex the hundreds of thousands, or
even millions, of documents that have been described by manual
indexing over the years. We have observed that most automated
information systems extant will not easily incorporate the computer-aided indexing technology now available. Their file structures
and software are fitted to a search only approach. The question for
such systems containing files of large numbers of already, though
poorly, indexed documents is whether any useful modifications are
practical. And in keeping with our themes, would such modifications, if practical, be useful not only to those now having access to
such systems but to a wider public?

We answer this question by showing how certain modifications
can be made and what they are. We describe a solution to handling
"old" files containing conventionally indexed documents. However,
it must be admitted that our solution is novel and is just now in the
processes of testing and implementation. Any such modifications
would require convincing tests obtained with existing systems. Such
testing is now underway and will be completed toward the end of

1976 in Frascati, Italy, by the European Space Agency (formerly ESRO)—Space Documentation Service (18). The required batch processing computer programs have been completed (see Chapter 6, Section 6.3, p. 123). Initial results permit a considered opinion to be offered now; these modifications will be worth their costs. They are practical and require only the conventional files normally available with search only systems. They provide means to extract from such files information already present but not now sufficiently used. Most multiuser, conventional, search only systems are based on software, which would create overly long response times for on-line extraction of this information. Therefore, we suggest that batch processing programs be used for this purpose. Running the batch processing programs does not cause complications within the on-line search software. The results of the batch processing programs are a set of tables that would be stored on disks (or even tapes) and called into the computer core when needed for on-line look-up. Thus the aids to be suggested provide on-line search aids without requiring reindexing and without rebuilding or interfering with search only system software.

We shall go into some detail here for three reasons. We want to show that better search result quality is obtainable even with existing conventional automated information retrieval systems. We want to indicate that such better search result quality, and the search aids that produce it, make possible meaningful public usage of such systems. Last, we want to offer the nontechnical reader interested in these topics some further insight concerning the relevant technology.

2.3.2.3.1 EXTENSIONAL RELATIONSHIPS The special direct or linear file (f), which is structured so as to permit on-line feedback of computer-suggested descriptors in addition to those initially selected by the searcher or indexer, does not exist as such in most conventional automated search systems. However, we have observed that this special file is essentially a double-storing of information already existent within the inverted file. The information has been reordered to permit on-line interaction with indexers and searchers and, in combination with other specially ordered files (*g*), provides significant computer aids to system users.

For most conventional systems, the attempt to introduce such specially ordered files within existing software and file structures would be an almost impossible procedure. It is simpler to reprogram the conventional systems starting from ground zero. Furthermore, to introduce computer-aided indexing and its associated requirements for on-line file changes would strain the multiuser operational software to its breaking point or produce unacceptable system response times. Again total reprogramming, for the most part, would be required.

Whether worthwhile and practical modifications to existing systems can be accomplished resolves to the question of whether feasible ways can be found to extract the information already in conventional files but not now used in search only operations. Without significant reordering and resultant new file creation, we must resort to batch processing programs to extract such information. If successful, these programs could produce tables containing the extracted information, which could then be stored as separate files within conventional systems. One could then build "table look-up," on-line options without disturbing existing file structures and software normally used for on-line search.

We have noted that the inverted files consist of formulas in which each descriptor is connected with the documents to which it has been applied. Such a list of documents attached to a descriptor represents the descriptor's extension within the document files. The descriptor extensions have been produced by indexers either by applying thesauri descriptors to documents or by indicating expressions that occur within document texts. (Sometimes a combination of both methods of indexing has produced the extensions of the descriptors within the document files.) However they are produced, such extensions exist within the files of conventional automated retrieval systems. Furthermore, descriptors can be related according to their extensions. Such extensional relationships would be a function of similarities among the lists of documents associated with the descriptors.

This concept of extensional relations may offer the means to improve the search recall obtained with conventional systems. Let us indicate how this might work.

Any given descriptor "A" may be extensionally related to any other descriptor "B" on the basis of the amount of overlap that occurs within their respective document lists. For example, if 25% of the documents to which A is associated have also been associated with B, we could say that B lies within the R-25% group of descriptors so related to A; and so on for any other descriptors in the inverted file we wish to consider as sufficiently interesting. One can raise the percentage to 50%, 75%, or higher, and even lower than the 25% of the example. Furthermore, we may choose to consider only descriptors applicable to more than 5 or 10% of the total number of documents in our files. We can select descriptors according to their thesauri status, whether they are proper names in some free-text list, or any other definable aspect. But the point is that all such limitations, which are not merely a matter of programming practicality and computer run times, may well be based on the later analyses of the extensional relationships as they may exist within our files. More importantly, such limitations could be based on their utility with regard to obtaining better search recall.

Consider a very simple search request for all documents to which two descriptors apply, for example, "air pollution" and "motor vehicles." The resultant list of documents cited would contain just those documents to which both descriptors applied. Now consider a group of documents to which the descriptors "exhaust emissions," "leaded gasoline," and "motor vehicles" applied but the descriptor "air pollution" had not been assigned as an index term or had not appeared as a phrase in the texts. (Perhaps the term "smog" had been used instead, or any other alternative to "air pollution," or suppose "air pollution" had been regarded as too general a term to be applied to the particular documents.) Certainly many of these documents would be quite relevant to the search request. And perhaps expert search question formulators might have selected some of the descriptors necessary to obtain some of these documents. Simple broadening of the search question could pick up the desired documents, say by asking for "air pollution" or "motor vehicles." But this would result in a great many irrelevant citations. With conventional systems one must aim for completeness of recall with great skill and knowledge of perhaps thousands or tens of thousands of descriptors, complex thesauri, and/or with the complicated art of expert search formulators; and one still cannot avoid a great deal of irrelevant recall.

By making use of the extensional relationships we do not reduce our dependency on such knowledge, skill, and art. But rather than possessing such search formulation specialties ourselves, to some extent we attempt to store such knowledge and information within the computer in forms useful to ourselves.

If we had tables of the extensional relations for descriptors, such as in our example, and if such tables were available to us for computer look-up, we might well discover the required additional descriptors in the R-30–60% groups of descriptors so related to "air pollution" and/or "motor vehicles." At the least the computer could display on request such R-groups of descriptors related to those in our original search question. We could then accept or reject any such computer-suggested descriptors and obtain just those document citations associated with the descriptors accepted. The additional citations would be just those documents picked up by the accepted descriptors that were not already picked up by our original search question. The relevancy of these additional citations would very likely be similar to that obtained by far more skillful and knowledgeable search question formulation experts. It might well be even better. We could, for example, weight the importance of the descriptors in our original search question by varying the percentages required to form the given R-groups. We might say, for example, that we want the R-30% group for "air pollution" and the R-50% group for "motor vehicles." Such techniques are not currently available even to highly skilled searchers with conventional systems.

To provide a realistic illustration of the possibilities offered by this extensional relationship method, some computer printouts selected from the initial runs on the Space Documentation Service–European Space Agency computer follow (19). These computer runs had not been expected to provide anything more significant than a working test of the computer programs. As such, preediting of the list of terms treated as descriptors was limited. For these runs all terms were taken as they were from document titles. A short "stop list" was used to reject unwanted terms. However the requirement that terms chosen for further analysis must have had at least ten occurrences within the titles was the basic means used to limit the number of terms considered. Computer runs scheduled for late 1976 will cover free text descriptors in recent vintage National Aeronautics and Space Agency (United States) Space Technology Abstracts (STAR ABSTRACTS). For these runs, the descriptor lists were manually edited to remove unwanted prepositions and other such high-frequency grammatical entities of little use as indexing or search descriptors. Misspelled terms were corrected and rectification of plural/singular entries was accomplished. Thus some "garbage" will be noticed in the printouts that follow. What is striking, however, is that such "garbage," and the restriction to terms in titles only, did not prevent the demonstration of the power of the concept of descriptor extensional relationships. These first computer printouts show us far more than had been expected. They may someday be regarded as a historic demonstration of a most important breakthrough.

The first printouts come from computer runs through the AGRIS (Agricultural Information Worldwide—United Nations) file, one newly available through SDS in Europe and containing, at the time, 6000 documents. From these 6000 titles, 1173 terms were found with at least 10 occurrences within the titles. To make a search request through such a file, one must formulate a search question(s) that corresponds somehow to both the conceptual request in mind and the available search terms or descriptors. Even when "natural language search" is available, one still has to choose the "natural language" terms or phrases that correspond to the question in mind. There is no guarantee that the "natural language" of the documents desired is identical to any one person's "natural vocabulary;" nor are the "natural language vocabularies" of the documents the same from document to document or from document writer to document writer. To aid the searcher, primitive thesauri are available. These list the descriptors or terms in alphabetic order (or some other simple ordering method), sometimes combined with some form of hierarchical descriptor ordering. The searcher then scans the thousands of such descriptor possibilities choosing those that seem closest in correspondence to the concepts in mind.

For instance, suppose one wanted documents about "agricultural planning." A reasonable seeming correspondence might be thought to occur when one discovers the terms "agricultural" and "planning" in the AGRIS term list. Combining such terms with "AND," the resultant search would produce five document citations from the AGRIS file based on search of titles only at the time of these printouts. At least nine other equally plausible documents obtainable via search through titles only would be missed, plus many other possibly relevant citations. We can tell this within a few decimal points by just looking at the extensional tables. These same tables also tell us, without having to first initiate a computer search, how to obtain these missing, and probably relevant, citations. We can determine precisely how to formulate the appropriate search question. It is equally interesting that such search request formulation, unlike simply using an "OR" instead of an "AND," will not pick up many irrelevant citations. Without extensional relationship tables, we are indeed restricted to such simpler search question reformulation possibilities by the lack of any useful information as to how to reformulate search questions.

Figure 1 (see pp. 34–35) is the first page of the computer printout showing the tables. Each term, listed in alphabetical order, is given with its 20 most related (extensionally) terms. The related terms are listed in four columns of five terms each, in accordance with the strength of their relationship to the term in question. The numbers of terms related, in accordance with specified relational percentages, are found on the bottom line for each term. For example, "Agrarian," the first term in the tables, has the term "Reform" extensionally related to it at the 60% level, with "Economics" as the twentieth most related term at the 13.33% level. The number of terms related to "Agrarian" at the various percentage levels shows 1 term at 60%, 1 term at 40%, 16 terms at 20%, 2 terms at 10%, and 15 terms related at levels less than 10%. On the top are the number of documents to which the term in question has been assigned and the total number of extensionally related terms. To the right is an internal descriptor address.

"Agricultural" is the second term listed in Figure 1. "Planning" does not even appear among the first 20 extensionally related terms. ("Planning" is extensionally related to "Agricultural" but toward the weaker end of the list, as we shall note in Figure 2. "Planning" is simply one of the weaker of the 266 extensionally related terms to "Agricultural.")

"Agriculture," the third term listed in Figure 1, is another story. "Planning" does appear among the first 20 extensionally related terms (at the 7.964% level). "Agriculture" is also the second highest listed term related to "Agricultural." The data from such tables could be presented to the searcher by the computer on-line based on the initial selection of "Agricultural." An appropriate search question could then be formulated.

Let us go through this process more slowly. Our searcher wishes documents concerning agricultural planning. With this in mind, the AGRIS terms "Agricultural" and "Planning" are chosen from the alphabetical term list. The searcher, on being informed that extensional relationship tables are available, requests a look at "Agricultural." Figure 1, or that part of it where "Agricultural" is listed with its related terms, is displayed on console. The searcher notes that "Planning" is not listed among the 20 most related terms. He

```
AGRIS   THESAURUS ANALYSIS   20.8.1975

    AGRARIAN                              15   DOCUMENTS ASSIGNED TO

*   % 60,00   REFORM                      20,00   AGRICULTURAL
*   % 40,00   ED                          20,00   AMERICA
*   % 26,66   CHANGE                      20,00   BASED
*   % 26,66   LAND                        20,00   EXPERIENCE
*   % 26,66   STRUCTURE                   20,00   FAO
******              >90%         >80%        >70%      1 >60%

    AGRICULTURAL                         123   DOCUMENTS ASSIGNED TO

*   % 13,82   DEVELOPMENT                 10,56   DEVELOPMENTS
*   % 13,00   AGRICULTURE                 9,756   ANNUAL
*   % 12,19   PRODUCTION                  9,756   SELECTED
*   % 11,38   ED                          9,756   TRAINING
*   % 11,38   REVIEW                      7,317   COOPERATIVE
******              >90%         >80%        >70%         >60%

    AGRICULTURE                          113   DOCUMENTS ASSIGNED TO

*   % 45,13   REVIEW                      30,97   ED
*   % 43,36   TRAINING                    16,81   FR
*   % 42,47   ANNUAL                      15,04   DEVELOPMENT
*   % 42,47   DEVELOPMENTS                14,15   AGRICULTURAL
*   % 42,47   SELECTED                    14,15   SP
******              >90%         >80%        >70%         >60%

    AIR                                   22   DOCUMENTS ASSIGNED TO

*   % 18,18   POLLUTION                   9,090   CHANGE
*   % 13,63   DRYING                      9,090   EFFECTS
*   % 13,63   SPRAY                       9,090   FLOW
*   % 9,090   AEDES                       9,090   FOREST
*   % 9,090   BETWEEN                     9,090   FORMATION
******              >90%         >80%        >70%         >60%

    ALFALFA                               69   DOCUMENTS ASSIGNED TO

*   % 52,17   SCIENCE                     7,246   SEED
*   % 52,17   TECHNOLOGY                  5,797   CONTROL
*   % 8,695   BREEDING                    5,797   L
*   % 8,695   MEDICAGO                    5,797   PEA
*   % 7,246   SATIVA                      4,347   APHID
******              >90%         >80%        >70%         >60%

    ALGAE                                 10   DOCUMENTS ASSIGNED TO

*   % 30,00   ARGENTINA                   10,00   BETWEEN
*   % 30,00   SPECIES                     10,00   CALCIUM
*   % 20,00   BROWN                       10,00   CARBON
*   % 20,00   NEW                         10,00   CONCENTRATION
*   % 20,00   1                           10,00   CONTAINING
******              >90%         >80%        >70%         >60%

    ALKALOID                               9   DOCUMENTS ASSIGNED TO

*   % 22,22   LOW                         11,11   BREEDING
*   % 22,22   PLANTS                      11,11   CHLOROPHYLL
*   % 22,22   STUDIES                     11,11   CONTENT
*   % 22,22   TOBACCO                     11,11   DISTRIBUTION
*   % 11,11   BEARING                     11,11   EFFECT
******              >90%         >80%        >70%         >60%
```

Figure 1

34

```
   35  DESCRIPTORS RELATED TO    1037  DESCRIPTOR ADDRESS

20,00  FR                       20,00  ROLE
20,00  LATIN                    20,00  SETTLEMENT
20,00  MARKETING                20,00  SP
20,00  PROJECT                  13,33  DEVELOPMENT
20,00  RESEARCH                 13,33  ECONOMICS
 >50%      1 >40%       >30%     16 >20%     2 >10%>     15

  266  DESCRIPTORS RELATED TO    1038  DESCRIPTOR ADDRESS

7,317  RESEARCH                 4,878  ECONOMIC
6,504  EDUCATION                4,878  EXPERIENCE
6,504  FR                       4,878  PROJECT
5,691  LAND                     4,878  SP
5,691  POLICY                   4,878  1972
 >50%        >40%       >30%        >20%     6 >10%>    260

  202  DESCRIPTORS RELATED TO    1039  DESCRIPTOR ADDRESS

11,50  EXTENSION                6,194  WORKER
8,849  EDUCATION                5,309  PRACTICAL
7,964  NEW                      5,309  RURAL
7,964  PLANNING                 5,309  SCHOOL
6,194  USE                      5,309  TECHNICAL
 >50%      5 >40%     1 >30%        >20%     5 >10%>    191

   89  DESCRIPTORS RELATED TO    1040  DESCRIPTOR ADDRESS

9,090  INCORPORATION            9,090  SOYBEAN
9,090  L                        9,090  SURFACE
9,090  MILK                     9,090  TEMPERATURE
9,090  OBSERVATION              9,090  TYPE
9,090  PEANUT                   9,090  1
 >50%        >40%     >30%          >20%     3 >10%>     86

  173  DESCRIPTORS RELATED TO    1015  DESCRIPTOR ADDRESS

4,347  CHILE                    4,347  PRODUCTION
4,347  CULTURE                  4,347  RECORDS
4,347  EFFECTS                  4,347  RELATIONSHIP
4,347  FEEDING                  4,347  RESISTANCE
4,347  NEW                      4,347  USE
2 >50%       >40%      >30%         >20%       >10%>    171

   45  DESCRIPTORS RELATED TO    1016  DESCRIPTOR ADDRESS

10,00  CULTURE                  10,00  EXPERIMENTAL
10,00  DIFFERENT                10,00  FACTORS
10,00  DISTRIBUTION             10,00  FOOD
10,00  EL                       10,00  FORMATION
10,00  ENVIRONMENTAL            10,00  GENERA
 >50%        >40%     2 >30%      3 >20%    40 >10%>

   18  DESCRIPTORS RELATED TO    1041  DESCRIPTOR ADDRESS

11,11  EFFECTS                  11,11  SHEEP
11,11  FLORA                    11,11  STRAIN
11,11  METABOLISM               11,11  4
11,11  NEW
11,11  RUMEN
 >50%        >40%      >30%       4 >20%    14 >10%>
```

Figure 1 (*Continued*)

35

notes that "Agriculture" is so listed, as are perhaps other terms of interest to him, such as "Development," the most-related term, and "Research," "Policy," and "Economic" all of which may lead the searcher towards AGRIS terms corresponding to the notion he has in mind. If the searcher now checks "Agriculture," the term "Planning" appears among the 20 terms most closely related; 7.946% of the 113 documents to which "Agriculture" has been assigned via title have "Planning" also. There are 9 such documents. (The absolute numbers could have been given instead of percentages, but for various other experimental purposes percentages were chosen, resulting in decimal document totals that we here treat as whole numbers.)

Now let us look at "Planning" in Figure 2 (see pp. 38–39) assuming that the extensional relationship table for this term had next been requested. It is true that "Agricultural" does appear among the 20 most closely related. (Note that the strength of extensional relationships is not reciprocal.) The percentage is 10.63%, lower than "Agriculture" with 19.14%, the second highest on the list. The searcher now has two important facts. First, the term "Agriculture" is more strongly related to "Planning" than is "Agricultural." Second, by combining, as might normally be expected, "Agricultural" with "Planning," only about five citations would result. 10.63% of the 47 documents for which "Planning" has occurred in titles have "Agricultural" also in the titles. There are five such documents (or 4.996 given our usage of percentages rather than whole document numbers.) If the searcher chooses "Agriculture" as well for his search question, at least 10 citations will be picked up. (These may overlap the five using "Agricultural" or they may be 10 quite different document citations.) And the searcher has had a second indication that "Agriculture" should be used as well as, or in place of, "Agricultural." "Agriculture" is the second closest related term to "Planning." Just in case the searcher wants a "triple" check, he can return to the term "Development" suggested as likely in the first display (Figure 1 under "Agricultural," closest related term.)

Figure 3 (see pp. 40–41) shows the extensional relational table for "Development," the fourth term down. Here, "Agricultural" and "Agriculture" have the same percentage, 7.359% extensional relationship to "Development". Each has 17 documents in common with "Development." These 17 documents are probably not the same 17. For the third time, the idea that "Agricultural" and "Agriculture" are often used indiscriminately by document title makers is suggested. Furthermore, it should now be clear to the searcher concerned with agricultural planning that title makers have more often preferred to use the separate terms "Planning" and "Agriculture" in their titles than to concatenate "Agricultural Planning." As the title makers wrote the documents as well, this is quite relevant information for the searcher.

This example was selected simply by choosing to begin with the first table printout page and selecting the second term found there. Similar examples can be found on every page of the printouts. Such extensional relationship tables also show us precisely what is going on within our files with regard to descriptor usage and assignment patterns. These tables do not show us directly how documents should have been or ought to be indexed, or in this case, titled. The tables show us in deed how such documents have been described, in this case, how terms are used in titles. Such information when presented within easily comprehended formats can be used to formulate better search questions. Extensional tables can be constructed for any document files however indexed. Free text, natural language, and/or thesauri descriptors all show whatever extensional relationships they have in fact throughout the files. It appears that through these methods significant computer-generated aids are becoming available to help searchers achieve a more meaningful correspondence between concepts and search descriptors.

Extensional relationships depend on one fundamental factor: the manner by which, and the patterns with which indexing terms appear throughout the files. The use of these extensional tables depends on another relevant factor: human choice and selection from among the terms suggested within the extensional tables. One

AGRIS THESAURUS ANALYSIS 20.8.1975

```
PLANNING                                    47   DOCUMENTS ASSIGNED TO

*    % 21,27   MANAGEMENT             14,89   WATER
*    % 19,14   AGRICULTURE            12,76   BASIC
*    % 14,89   AT                     12,76   MEETING
*    % 14,89   ISSUE                  12,76   PAPERS
*    % 14,89   PROBLEM                12,76   RESOURCE
******               >90%      >80%        >70%         >60%

    PLANT                                   156   DOCUMENTS ASSIGNED TO

*    % 8,974   L                       7,692   STUDIES
*    % 7,692   AS                      7,051   DEVELOPMENT
*    % 7,692   CELL                    7,051   NEMATODE
*    % 7,692   GROWTH                  7,051   RICE
*    % 7,692   SOIL                    7,051   2
******               >90%      >80%        >70%         >60%

    PLANTATION                               19   DOCUMENTS ASSIGNED TO

*    % 15,78   GRANDIS                10,52   FOREST
*    % 15,78   PINE                   10,52   NEMATODE
*    % 10,52   ARGENTINA              10,52   PINUS
*    % 10,52   CONTROL                10,52   STATE
*    % 10,52   EUCALYPTUS             10,52   STUDIES
******               >90%      >80%        >70%         >60%

    PLANTING                                 30   DOCUMENTS ASSIGNED TO

*    % 16,66   EFFECT                 10,00   GROWTH
*    % 16,66   L                      10,00   INFLUENCE
*    % 13,33   PLANT                  10,00   METHODS
*    % 10,00   DENSITY                10,00   TREE
*    % 10,00   EFFECTS                10,00   YIELD
******               >90%      >80%        >70%         >60%

    PLANTS                                  145   DOCUMENTS ASSIGNED TO

*    % 11,03   SOME                    7,586   EFFECTS
*    % 9,655   RICE                    6,896   WATER
*    % 8,965   STUDIES                 6,896   1
*    % 8,275   GROWTH                  6,206   NITROGEN
*    % 7,586   EFFECT                  6,206   TOMATO
******               >90%      >80%        >70%         >60%

    PLASMA                                   16   DOCUMENTS ASSIGNED TO

*    % 37,50   LEVELS                 18,75   PROTEIN
*    % 25,00   DURING                 12,50   ACID
*    % 18,75   CATTLE                 12,50   CHICKEN
*    % 18,75   EFFECT                 12,50   CONCENTRATION
*    % 18,75   EWE                    12,50   FATTY
******               >90%      >80%        >70%         >60%

    POLICY                                   18   DOCUMENTS ASSIGNED TO

*    % 38,88   AGRICULTURAL           22,22   BASIC
*    % 27,77   AT                     22,22   MANAGEMENT
*    % 27,77   DEVELOPMENTS           22,22   MEETING
*    % 27,77   ISSUE                  22,22   SUBMITTED
*    % 27,77   PAPERS                 22,22   WATER
******               >90%      >80%        >70%         >60%
```

Figure 2

```
  140   DESCRIPTORS RELATED TO    1775   DESCRIPTOR ADDRESS

12,76   SUBMITTED                8,510   DEVELOPMENTS
10,63   AGRICULTURAL             8,510   DEVELOPMENT
10,63   ED                       6,382   ANNUAL
10,63   FARM                     6,382   FISHERIES
10,63   LAND                     6,382   FR
 >50%        >40%        >30%       1 >20%      14 >10%>   125

  454   DESCRIPTORS RELATED TO    1776   DESCRIPTOR ADDRESS

6,410   EFFECT                   5,128   EFFECTS
6,410   INFLUENCE                5,128   PARASITIC
6,410   YIELD                    5,128   PRODUCTION
5,769   BETWEEN                  5,128   PROTECTION
5,769   1                        5,128   RESPONSE
 >50%        >40%        >30%          >20%      >10%>    454

   74   DESCRIPTORS RELATED TO    1777   DESCRIPTOR ADDRESS

10,52   VARIATION                5,263   BLACK
5,263   APHIDS                   5,263   BRAZIL
5,263   APPLE                    5,263   CHEMICAL
5,263   BASED                    5,263   COFFEE
5,263   BASIC                    5,263   COLOMBIA
 >50%        >40%        >30%          >20%      11 >10%>    63

  115   DESCRIPTORS RELATED TO    1778   DESCRIPTOR ADDRESS

6,666   BEAN                     6,666   DEVELOPMENT
6,666   BRAZIL                   6,666   FOREST
6,666   CROPS                    6,666   FREQUENCY
6,666   CULTURE                  6,666   HIGH
6,666   DEPTH                    6,666   METHOD
 >50%        >40%        >30%          >20%      10 >10%>   105

  391   DESCRIPTORS RELATED TO    1779   DESCRIPTOR ADDRESS

5,517   AS                       4,827   LIGHT
5,517   DISTRIBUTION             4,827   MINERAL
5,517   SOIL                     4,827   VIRUS
4,827   CONDITIONS               4,137   BETWEEN
4,827   LEAF                     4,137   CONTENT
 >50%        >40%        >30%          >20%       1 >10%>   390

   79   DESCRIPTORS RELATED TO    1780   DESCRIPTOR ADDRESS

12,50   FREE                     6,250   ACIDS
12,50   HORMONE                  6,250   AMINO
12,50   LIPID                    6,250   AT
12,50   SERUM                    6,250   BEEF
12,50   SHEEP                    6,250   BETWEEN
 >50%        >40%       1 >30%       1 >20%      13 >10%>    64

   77   DESCRIPTORS RELATED TO    1781   DESCRIPTOR ADDRESS

16,66   AGRICULTURE              16,66   TRAINING
16,66   ANNUAL                   11,11   APPLICATION
16,66   MORE                     11,11   DEVELOPMENT
16,66   REVIEW                   11,11   ECONOMICS
16,66   SELECTED                 11,11   ED
 >50%        >40%       1 >30%       9 >20%      16 >10%>    51
```

Figure 2   (*Continued*)

39

```
AGRIS   THESAURUS ANALYSIS   20.8.1975

    DETERMINATION                        66  DOCUMENTS ASSIGNED TO

*    % 15,15   METHOD                 7,575  MILK
*    % 12,12   ACID                   7,575  NITROGEN
*    % 10,60   METHODS                7,575  SOME
*    % 9,090   QUANTITATIVE           7,575  TOTAL
*    % 7,575   CONTRIBUTION           7,575  1
******            >90%          >80%         >70%          >60%

    DETERMINING                          23  DOCUMENTS ASSIGNED TO

*    % 26,08   METHOD                13,04  QUALITY
*    % 17,39   APPLICATION            8,695  ANALYSIS
*    % 13,04   EVALUATION             8,695  ASPECT
*    % 13,04   FACTORS                8,695  AT
*    % 13,04   ITS                    8,695  MEASUREMENT
******            >90%          >80%         >70%          >60%

    DEVELOPING                           21  DOCUMENTS ASSIGNED TO

*    % 52,38   COUNTRIES              9,523  ACID
*    % 23,80   PRODUCTION             9,523  CHANGE
*    % 19,04   ANIMAL                 9,523  CHILE
*    % 19,04   ED                     9,523  COAST
*    % 19,04   EDUCATION              9,523  COMPARATIVE
******            >90%          >80%         >70%          >60%

    DEVELOPMENT                         231  DOCUMENTS ASSIGNED TO

*    % 11,25   ED                     6,926  FR
*    % 8,658   1                      6,926  MANAGEMENT
*    % 7,359   AGRICULTURAL           6,493  FOREST
*    % 7,359   AGRICULTURE            6,493  1973
*    % 7,359   FISHERIES              6,060  MEETING
******            >90%          >80%         >70%          >60%

    DEVELOPMENTS                         60  DOCUMENTS ASSIGNED TO

*    % 80,00   AGRICULTURE           53,33  ED
*    % 78,33   ANNUAL                26,66  FR
*    % 78,33   REVIEW                26,66  SP
*    % 78,33   SELECTED              21,66  AGRICULTURAL
*    % 78,33   TRAINING              20,00  EXTENSION
******            >90%        1 >80%       4 >70%          >60%

    DEVICE                               13  DOCUMENTS ASSIGNED TO

*    % 23,07   MEASURING              7,692  AUTOMATIC
*    % 15,38   BLOOD                  7,692  BOLLWORM
*    % 7,692   ACTIVITY  ACT ACTION   7,692  COLLECTION
*    % 7,692   APPLICATION            7,692  CONSTANT
*    % 7,692   AQUATIC                7,692  COTTON
******            >90%          >80%         >70%          >60%

    DIET                                 30  DOCUMENTS ASSIGNED TO

*    % 26,66   EFFECT                13,33  GROWING
*    % 20,00   AS                    13,33  RATS
*    % 20,00   PROTEIN               13,33  REARING
*    % 16,66   ARTIFICIAL            13,33  STUDIES
*    % 13,33   FED                   10,00  CATTLE
******            >90%          >80%         >70%          >60%
```

Figure 3

40

```
  205   DESCRIPTORS RELATED TO     1264   DESCRIPTOR ADDRESS

6,060   CHROMATOGRAPHY            4,545   CHLORIDE
6,060   SOILS                     4,545   DAIRY
4,545   ANIMAL                    4,545   GAS
4,545   APPLICATION               4,545   PROTEIN
4,545   CARBOHYDRATE              4,545   RAPID
  >50%          >40%       >30%          >20%      3 >10%>    202

  131   DESCRIPTORS RELATED TO     1265   DESCRIPTOR ADDRESS

8,695   NITROGEN                  8,695   USE
8,695   NOTE                      8,695   YIELD
8,695   PRODUCTS                  4,347   ACID
8,695   SOIL                      4,347   AGE
8,695   TEST                      4,347   APPROACH
  >50%          >40%       >30%      1 >20%      5 >10%>    125

   65   DESCRIPTORS RELATED TO     1266   DESCRIPTOR ADDRESS

9,523   DISTRIBUTION              9,523   PESTICIDE
9,523   FIVE                      9,523   SP
9,523   FR                        9,523   STUDY
9,523   INDUSTRIAL                9,523   SYSTEMS
9,523   MEXICO                    4,761   APPROACH
1 >50%          >40%       >30%      1 >20%      3 >10%>     60

  508   DESCRIPTORS RELATED TO     1267   DESCRIPTOR ADDRESS

6,060   PROCEEDINGS               5,627   HUMID
6,060   REVIEW                    5,627   INFLUENCE
6,060   TECHNICAL                 5,627   PROGRAMMING
5,627   AMERICAN                  5,627   TROPICS
5,627   EFFECT                    5,194   FEBRUARY
  >50%          >40%       >30%          >20%      1 >10%>    507

  100   DESCRIPTORS RELATED TO     1268   DESCRIPTOR ADDRESS

15,00   DEVELOPMENT               10,00   RURAL
13,33   EDUCATION                 10,00   SCHOOL
13,33   WATER                     10,00   WORKER
11,66   NEW                       8,333   POLICY
10,00   PRACTICAL                 6,666   ENVIRONMENT
1 >50%          >40%       >30%      4 >20%      8 >10%>     82

   42   DESCRIPTORS RELATED TO     1269   DESCRIPTOR ADDRESS

7,692   EFFICIENCY                7,692   INCREASING
7,692   EQUIPMENT                 7,692   INOCULATION
7,692   FISH                      7,692   INSECTS
7,692   FUNGI                     7,692   K
7,692   HELIOTHIS                 7,692   LARGE
  >50%          >40%       >30%      1 >20%      1 >10%>     40

  132   DESCRIPTORS RELATED TO     1270   DESCRIPTOR ADDRESS

10,00   FATTENING                 6,666   ACIDS
10,00   HIGH                      6,666   BEEF
10,00   LOW                       6,666   COMPOSITION
10,00   MOISTURE                  6,666   CONTENT
10,00   WHEAT                     6,666   EFFECTS
  >50%          >40%       >30%      3 >20%     12 >10%>    117
```

Figure 3   (*Continued*)

41

cannot and does not achieve fully automated indexing by these methods (20). This is probably why these valuable aids to human searchers and indexers had not been previously developed.

There are many more ways to use these extensional tables for direct aid to searchers and also for thesauri refinement and development, which can provide still better aids to searchers and indexers. These methods themselves and the extent of their utility in developing search and indexing tactics and strategies are only now being explored. But again, examples from the first computer runs can indicate some of the potential range of computer support to these critical information retrieval processes.

It was deemed pertinent to conduct the program tests on a second and larger file. A file of scientific information, the ISI file, produced by the Institute for Scientific Information, Philadelphia, Pa., was used for a second program test run. The same "ground rules" obtained; a short and not very "deep" stop list was combined with the requirement for at least a 10-time occurrence of terms in titles. However, this time 50,000 documents were involved with their titles, of which 4462 terms occurred at least ten times. Without such restrictions, the number of terms would roughly equal the number of documents and some such cut-off would soon have to be applied (21).

The following figures illustrate one exceedingly important fact. Once the extensional tables have been produced, a simple application of a sorting routine can arrange the information available in many different useful ways. The tables from the AGRIS file listed the terms in alphabetical order, each associated with other terms extensionally related. Figure 4 (see pp. 44-45), for the ISI file, shows the terms listed in accordance with their "relatedness." Terms with the highest extensional relationships to other terms throughout the file begin the table listing.

"Flameless" through "Jahn" are the five most extensionally related terms. The strengths of the relatedness and the terms to which they are related are made evident within the same printout format used for the AGRIS tables. The 700 most highly related terms were so listed in these printouts from the ISI file. Any specified "cut-off" number could, of course, have been selected. Figure 5 (see pp. 46–47) shows the last five highly related terms of these 700. Note the strong relatedness percentages hover around 30% in Figure 5, whereas 100% relationships were shown in Figure 4.

To further underline the point and power of simply using a sorting routine to arrange the extensional relationship tables, terms can be ordered in other ways as well. For example, terms can be listed in accordance with the identity of the term most related to them. The listing can be set up to group terms by the fact that they each have the same term ranked highest in relationship.

Figure 6 (see pp. 48–49) shows seven terms grouped around their highest related term, "Approximation." Not shown are three additional terms, "Best," "Intervals," and "Rational" with the same highest related term, "Approximation," but similarly grouped on adjacent printout pages. The printout format again remains the same as the AGRIS printouts with the further extensional relationships, document assignment numbers, and so forth, shown for these grouped terms.

Figure 7 (see pp. 50–51) offers seven terms grouped around their highest related term, "Boundary." Again other terms listed in adjacent printout pages ("Conditions," "Computational," "Turbulent," and "Fluctuating") included in this group are not shown here.

As a last example Figure 8 (see pp. 52–53) shows terms grouped around "Catalyst" with the term "grouped" by "Cataly*sis*" listed on top for possible inclusion in the "Catalyst" group. Not shown are the two other terms grouped by "Catalyst" and one additional term suggested for this group, "Epoxidation," as its highest related term is "Cataly*zed*."

Groupings according to other patterns found among the extensional relationships are obtainable. One could group by first, second, and third-highest related terms or any other such stipulated pattern or combinations thereof, including relational strength per

```
          T.S.I.THESAURUS ANALYSIS   22.8.1975

     FLAMELESS                               11   DOCUMENTS ASSIGNED TO

*    %100,00   ABSORPTION                27,27  WATER
*    %100,00   ATOMIC                    18,18  CARBON
*    % 63,63   DETERMINATION             19,18  GRAPHITE
*    % 36,36   CADMIUM                   18,18  MERCURY
*    % 36,36   SPECTROMETRY              18,18  TUBE
******             2 >90%         >80%           >70%      1 >60%

     PREMOUNTED                               8   DOCUMENTS ASSIGNED TO

*    %100,00   BEARING                   12,50  MACHINED
*    % 75,00   PLAIN                     12,50  METAL
*    % 25,00   ELEMENT                   12,50  MOLDED
*    % 25,00   ROLLING                   12,50  PLASTIC
*    % 12,50   BALL                      12,50  PRESSED
******             1 >90%         >80%        1  >70%         >60%

     MULTIWIRE                               14   DOCUMENTS ASSIGNED TO

*    % 92,85   PROPORTIONAL              14,28  FAST
*    % 71,42   CHAMBER                   14,28  READOUT
*    % 28,57   IMAGING                   14,28  SYSTEM
*    % 21,42   COUNTER                    7,142 AMPLIFIER
*    % 14,28   DETECTOR                   7,142 ANODE
******             1 >90%         >80%        1  >70%         >60%

     BREEDER                                 18   DOCUMENTS ASSIGNED TO

*    % 94,44   REACTOR                   11,11  FISSION
*    % 55,55   FAST                      11,11  FUELS
*    % 22,22   COOLED                    11,11  LIQUID
*    % 22,22   GAS                       11,11  PLUTONIUM
*    % 11,11   CONCEPT                   11,11  TECHNOLOGY
******             1 >90%         >80%           >70%         >60%

     DICHROISM                               44   DOCUMENTS ASSIGNED TO

*    %100,00   CIRCULAR                  11,36  SPECTRA
*    % 50,00   MAGNETIC                   9,090 ACIDS
*    % 18,18   COMPLEXES                  6,818 ACTIVITY
*    % 11,36   ABSORPTION                 6,818 COBALT
*    % 11,36   OPTICAL                    6,818 ION
******             1 >90%         >80%           >70%         >60%

     DIELS                                   11   DOCUMENTS ASSIGNED TO

*    %100,00   ALDER                     18,18  CONDITIONS
*    % 45,45   REACTION                  18,18  FURAN
*    % 27,27   REACTIONS                 18,18  LEWIS
*    % 18,18   ADDUCT                    18,18  MALEIC
*    % 18,18   ANHYDRIDE                  9,090 ACID
******             1 >90%         >80%           >70%         >60%

     JAHN                                    23   DOCUMENTS ASSIGNED TO

*    %100,00   TELLER                    13,04  CUBIC
*    % 47,82   EFFECT                    13,04  DYNAMIC
*    % 17,39   CO2                       13,04  STATES
*    % 17,39   ZNS                       13,04  T
*    % 13,04   COMPLEX                   13,04  TRANSITIONS
******             1 >90%         >80%           >70%         >60%
```

Figure 4

44

```
   47  DESCRIPTORS RELATED TO    2564  DESCRIPTOR ADDRESS

18,18  1                         9,090  COPPER
9,090  ACID                      9,090  DETECTION
9,090  AIR                       9,090  ESTIMATION
9,090  CHROMATOGRAPHY            9,090  EXTRACTION
9,090  CONDITIONS                9,090  FILAMENT
  >50%         >40%      2 >30%      1 >20%       5 >10%>       36


   12  DESCRIPTORS RELATED TO    4130  DESCRIPTOR ADDRESS

12,50  ROLLER
12,50  UNITS



  >50%         >40%        >30%      2 >20%       8 >10%>

   53  DESCRIPTORS RELATED TO    3613  DESCRIPTOR ADDRESS

7,142  APERTURE                  7,142  CONTENT
7,142  CAPACITANCE               7,142  DATA
7,142  CHARACTERISTIC            7,142  DELAY
7,142  CIRCUITS                  7,142  DETECTED
7,142  COMPUTER                  7,142  DETERMINATION
  >50%         >40%        >30%      2 >20%       4 >10%>       45

   46  DESCRIPTORS RELATED TO    1477  DESCRIPTOR ADDRESS

11,11  THERMODYNAMICS            5,555  CHLORIDES
11,11  URANIUM                   5,555  COOLING
5,555  ALLOYS                    5,555  EQUATIONS
5,555  ASSEMBLIES                5,555  EXCHANGES
5,555  CHLORIDE                  5,555  FUEL
1 >50%         >40%        >30%      2 >20%       8 >10%>       34

  158  DESCRIPTORS RELATED TO    2115  DESCRIPTOR ADDRESS

6,818  L                         4,545  IMPURITIES
4,545  ANTIFERROMAGNETIC         4,545  INDUCED
4,545  BETA                      4,545  IONS
4,545  CHELATES                  4,545  MANGANESE
4,545  EFFECT                    4,545  SCHIFF
1 >50%         >40%        >30%        >20%       4 >10%>      152

   44  DESCRIPTORS RELATED TO    2119  DESCRIPTOR ADDRESS

9,090  ACIDS                     9,090  BONDS
9,090  ADDITION                  9,090  CATALYZED
9,090  ADDITIONS                 9,090  COMPOUNDS
9,090  ALDEHYDE                  9,090  CONJUGATED
9,090  ALPHA,BETA-UNSATURATED    9,090  CONVERSION
  >50%       1 >40%        >30%      1 >20%       6 >10%>       35

  104  DESCRIPTORS RELATED TO    3143  DESCRIPTOR ADDRESS

8,695  BAND                      8,695  DISTORTED
8,695  COOPERATIVE               8,695  EPR
8,695  COUPLING                  8,695  EXCITED
8,695  CO2                       8,695  INTERACTION
8,695  DEPENDENCE                8,695  ION
  >50%       1 >40%        >30%        >20%       8 >10%>       94
```

Figure 4   (*Continued*)

45

```
    I.S.I.THESAURUS ANALYSIS  22.8.1975

   PHOSPHIDE                             24  DOCUMENTS ASSIGNED TO

*    % 37,50  GALLIUM               12,50  X
*    % 33,33  INDIUM                 8,333  ATOMS
*    % 16,66  METAL                  8,333  BANDS
*    % 12,50  ARSENIDE               8,333  EPITAXY
*    % 12,50  FIELD                  8,333  LIQUID
******              >90%        >80%       >70%        >60%

   RESONANCE                            656  DOCUMENTS ASSIGNED TO

*    % 38,26  MAGNETIC              10,51  C
*    % 30,94  NUCLEAR                7,621  PROTON
*    % 17,98  ELECTRON               7,317  1
*    % 13,41  SPIN                   5,945  PARAMAGNETIC
*    % 11,12  SPECTRA                5,792  SPECTROSCOPY
******              >90%        >80%       >70%        >60%

   REORIENTATION                         16  DOCUMENTS ASSIGNED TO

*    % 31,25  MOLECULAR            12,50  RESONANCE
*    % 31,25  SPIN                   6,250  AMMONIUM
*    % 12,50  MAGNETIC               6,250  ANGULAR
*    % 12,50  NUCLEAR                6,250  ANISOTROPIC
*    % 12,50  PHASE                  6,250  AXIS
******              >90%        >80%       >70%        >60%

   OSMIUM                                13  DOCUMENTS ASSIGNED TO

*    % 30,76  DETERMINATION        15,38  SPECTROPHOTOMETRIC
*    % 30,76  RUTHENIUM              7,692  ADSORPTION
*    % 15,38  ACID                   7,692  ALLOYS
*    % 15,38  COMPLEXES              7,692  ALLYL
*    % 15,38  LIGAND                 7,692  AMPEROMETRIC
******              >90%        >80%       >70%        >60%

   INDOLE                                27  DOCUMENTS ASSIGNED TO

*    % 33,33  DERIVATIVE           11,11  REARRANGEMENT
*    % 33,33  SYNTHESIS              7,407  ACIDS
*    % 11,11  ALKALOID               7,407  ALPHA
*    % 11,11  COMPOUNDS              7,407  AZIDE
*    % 11,11  REACTIONS              7,407  BENZENE
******              >90%        >80%       >70%        >60%

   NERVE                                 33  DOCUMENTS ASSIGNED TO

*    % 30,30  AUDITORY             12,12  TONE
*    % 30,30  FIBERS                 9,090  ACTIVITY
*    % 12,12  AFTER                  9,090  CELLS
*    % 12,12  FACTOR                 9,090  COCHLEAR
*    % 12,12  GROWTH                 9,090  DISCHARGE
******              >90%        >80%       >70%        >60%

   AL2O3                                 59  DOCUMENTS ASSIGNED TO

*    % 33,89  SYSTEM               10,16  MGO
*    % 32,20  SIO2                   8,474  ALPHA
*    % 15,25  CATALYST               8,474  EFFECTS
*    % 13,55  H2O                    8,474  SOLID
*    % 10,16  FORMATION              8,474  STRENGTH
******              >90%        >80%       >70%        >60%
```

Figure 5

46

```
 103  DESCRIPTORS RELATED TO     3956  DESCRIPTOR ADDRESS

8,333  MAGNETIC                  8,333  STRUCTURAL
8,333  PHASE                     8,333  SYSTEM
8,333  PHOSPHORUS                8,333  V
8,333  RAY                       8,333  VALENCE
8,333  SPECTRAL                  8,333  1
   >50%        >40%    2 >30%       >20%      4 >10%>    97


1236  DESCRIPTORS RELATED TO     4425  DESCRIPTOR ADDRESS

5,487  RADICAL                   3,810  GAMMA
5,182  COMPLEXES                 3,658  STRUCTURE
4,420  INVESTIGATION             3,506  THEORY
3,810  CYCLOTRON                 3,353  ANALYSIS
3,810  FIELD                     3,353  EFFECT
   >50%        >40%    2 >30%       >20%      4 >10%>   1230


  67  DESCRIPTORS RELATED TO     4406  DESCRIPTOR ADDRESS

6,250  BARRIER                   6,250  CRYSTAL
6,250  BI                        6,250  DEPENDENCE
6,250  BUCKLING                  6,250  DEUTERIUM
6,250  C                         6,250  DIPOLE
6,250  CORRELATION               6,250  DISTRIBUTION
   >50%        >40%    2 >30%       >20%      4 >10%>    61


  66  DESCRIPTORS RELATED TO     3827  DESCRIPTOR ADDRESS

7,692  ANNUAL                    7,692  CO
7,692  ATTACK                    7,692  COMPOSITION
7,692  CATALYTIC                 7,692  COMPOUNDS
7,692  CATION                    7,692  COORDINATED
7,692  CATIONIC                  7,692  COVERING
   >50%        >40%    2 >30%       >20%      4 >10%>    60


  95  DESCRIPTORS RELATED TO     2985  DESCRIPTOR ADDRESS

7,407  EFFECT                    7,407  REACTION
7,407  INDOLES                   7,407  RING
7,407  MASS                      7,407  SPECTROMETRY
7,407  NEW                       7,407  TYPE
7,407  NOVEL                     3,703  AB
   >50%        >40%    2 >30%       >20%      4 >10%>    89


 134  DESCRIPTORS RELATED TO     3652  DESCRIPTOR ADDRESS

9,090  RAT                       6,060  CHANGE
9,090  RESPONSE                  6,060  CORTEX
9,090  TERMINAL                  6,060  CURVES
6,060  BRAIN                     6,060  DATA
6,060  CAT                       6,060  ELECTRICAL
   >50%        >40%    2 >30%       >20%      4 >10%>   128


 208  DESCRIPTORS RELATED TO     1159  DESCRIPTOR ADDRESS

6,779  CAO                       6,779  POLYCRYSTALLINE
6,779  CATALYTIC                 6,779  SOLUTION
6,779  GRAIN                     6,779  STABILITY
6,779  NA2O                      5,084  ACTIVITY
6,779  NIO                       5,084  BEHAVIOR
   >50%        >40%    2 >30%       >20%      4 >10%>   202
```

Figure 5   (*Continued*)

47

```
    I.S.I.THESAURUS ANALYSIS   22.8.1975

    SUDDEN                               14   DOCUMENTS ASSIGNED TO
*    % 21,42   APPROXIMATION            14,28   IMPULSE
*    % 14,28   BOUNDARY                 14,28   LAYER
*    % 14,28   CROSS                    14,28   TOTAL
*    % 14,28   ELECTRON                  7,142  ABSORPTION
*    % 14,28   FIELD                     7,142  ANALYSIS
******                     >90%    >80%         >70%          >60%

    FIGURE                               18   DOCUMENTS ASSIGNED TO
*    % 11,11   APPROXIMATION            11,11   IDEAL
*    % 11,11   COMPARISON               11,11   INSTALLATION
*    % 11,11   DETERMINED               11,11   LIGHTING
*    % 11,11   DIGITAL                  11,11   LIQUID
*    % 11,11   EQUILIBRIUM              11,11   MEASURE
******                     >90%    >80%         >70%          >60%

    SUCCESSIVE                           18   DOCUMENTS ASSIGNED TO
*    % 22,22   APPROXIMATION             5,555  ABSORPTION
*    % 11,11   CONSTANTS                 5,555  ACID
*    % 11,11   DERIVATIVE                5,555  ACIDS
*    % 11,11   GROUP                     5,555  ALGORITHM
*    % 11,11   TYPE                      5,555  ANALYSIS
******                     >90%    >80%         >70%          >60%

    LP                                   12   DOCUMENTS ASSIGNED TO
*    % 25,00   APPROXIMATION             8,333  ALGEBRAS
*    % 16,66   DIMENSIONAL               8,333  BEST
*    % 16,66   FILTERS                   8,333  C
*    % 16,66   LIMIT                     8,333  CLASS
*    % 16,66   MULTIPLIER                8,333  CO
******                     >90%    >80%         >70%          >60%

    BORN                                 18   DOCUMENTS ASSIGNED TO
*    % 38,88   APPROXIMATION            16,66   THEORY
*    % 22,22   EXCITATION               11,11   CROSS
*    % 16,66   COULOMB                  11,11   DISTORTED
*    % 16,66   ELECTRON                 11,11   IMPACT
*    % 16,66   MOLECULE                 11,11   IONS
******                     >90%    >80%         >70%          >60%

    CHEBYSHEV                            12   DOCUMENTS ASSIGNED TO
*    % 33,33   APPROXIMATION             8,333  CHARACTERISTIC
*    % 25,00   FILTERS                   8,333  DELAY
*    % 16,66   EXPANSION                 8,333  DIGITAL
*    % 16,66   MODIFIED                  8,333  EFFICIENCY
*    % 8,333   ATTENUATION               8,333  FILTER
******                     >90%    >80%         >70%          >60%

    VALIDITY                             20   DOCUMENTS ASSIGNED TO
*    % 20,00   APPROXIMATION            10,00   EXTINCTION
*    % 15,00   MODEL                    10,00   FIELD
*    % 15,00   TRANSFER                 10,00   IONS
*    % 10,00   CRYSTALS                 10,00   LIMIT
*    % 10,00   EQUATIONS                10,00   MOLECULE
******                     >90%    >80%         >70%          >60%
```

Figure 6

48

```
 75  DESCRIPTORS RELATED TO    4918  DESCRIPTOR ADDRESS

7,142  ANGULAR              7,142  CHANGE
7,142  ASSOCIATED           7,142  COLLISION
7,142  AXISYMMETRIC         7,142  CONTENT
7,142  BEARING              7,142  CONTEXT
7,142  BEHAVIOR             7,142  CORE
 >50%        >40%      >30%    1 >20%     7 >10%>    67


 67  DESCRIPTORS RELATED TO    2535  DESCRIPTOR ADDRESS

11,11  NEWTONIAN            11,11  STREET
11,11  NOISE                11,11  SURFACE
11,11  POST                 5,555  ABSORPTION
11,11  RELATIVITY           5,555  ACOUSTOOPTIC
11,11  ROTATING             5,555  ASSOCIATED
 >50%        >40%      >30%       >20%     17 >10%>    50


 85  DESCRIPTORS RELATED TO    4916  DESCRIPTOR ADDRESS

5,555  ANISOTROPY           5,555  BORON
5,555  ATMOSPHERIC          5,555  BOUNDARY
5,555  BASALT               5,555  CALCULATION
5,555  BASE                 5,555  CELL
5,555  BEAM                 5,555  CELLS
 >50%        >40%      >30%    1 >20%     4 >10%>    80


 46  DESCRIPTORS RELATED TO    3312  DESCRIPTOR ADDRESS

8,333  COMPACTNESS          8,333  DIGITAL
8,333  COMPUTATIONAL        8,333  DISCRETE
8,333  DELAY                8,333  DUALITY
8,333  DERIVATIVE           8,333  ESTIMATE
8,333  DESIGN               8,333  EXPERIENCE
 >50%        >40%      >30%    1 >20%     4 >10%>    41


 84  DESCRIPTORS RELATED TO    1452  DESCRIPTOR ADDRESS

11,11  MODEL                5,555  BIREFRINGENCE
11,11  TERMS                5,555  BREAKDOWN
11,11  WAVE                 5,555  CALCULATIONS
5,555  AMPLITUDE            5,555  CHANNEL
5,555  ANGULAR              5,555  CHARGED
 >50%        >40%    1 >30%    1 >20%     11 >10%>    71


 28  DESCRIPTORS RELATED TO    1638  DESCRIPTOR ADDRESS

8,333  FINITE               8,333  PASS
8,333  GROUP                8,333  POLYNOMIALS
8,333  LOW                  8,333  QUADRATURE
8,333  MINIMAX              8,333  RADAR
8,333  ORDER                8,333  RATIONAL
 >50%        >40%    1 >30%    1 >20%     2 >10%>    24


104  DESCRIPTORS RELATED TO    5277  DESCRIPTOR ADDRESS

10,00  RANGE                5,000  ANISOTROPIC
10,00  SPHERICAL            5,000  ANTIFERROMAGNETISM
5,000  ACID                 5,000  APPROXIMATE
5,000  AIRCRAFT             5,000  BLOOD
5,000  ALLOYS               5,000  BOUND
 >50%        >40%      >30%    1 >20%     11 >10%>    92
```

Figure 6   (*Continued*)

49

```
      I.S.I.THESAURUS ANALYSIS   22.8.1975

      TURBULENCE                            98    DOCUMENTS ASSIGNED TO

*     % 11,22   BOUNDARY                  8,163    MEASUREMENTS
*     % 11,22   LAYER                     8,163    THEORY
*     % 9,183   ATMOSPHERIC               7,142    PLASMA
*     % 9,183   LASER                     6,122    ACOUSTIC
*     % 8,163   EFFECT                    6,122    MODEL
******              >90%          >80%              >70%          >60%

      PLANETARY                            42    DOCUMENTS ASSIGNED TO

*     % 28,57   BOUNDARY                  7,142    EMISSION
*     % 23,80   LAYER                     7,142    INFRARED
*     % 19,04   NEBULAE                   7,142    MODEL
*     % 14,28   ATMOSPHERE                7,142    MULTIPLE
*     % 9,523   STRUCTURE                 7,142    NUCLEI
******              >90%          >80%              >70%          >60%

      SIMILARITY                           19    DOCUMENTS ASSIGNED TO

*     % 15,78   BOUNDARY                  5,263    ACCELERATOR
*     % 15,78   LAYER                     5,263    ACID
*     % 15,78   SOLUTION                  5,263    ACOUSTIC
*     % 10,52   PROFILE                   5,263    ANALYSIS
*     % 10,52   STRUCTURES                5,263    ANOMALY
******              >90%          >80%              >70%          >60%

      VALUE                               108    DOCUMENTS ASSIGNED TO

*     % 46,29   BOUNDARY                  9,259    DIFFERENTIAL
*     % 12,96   SOLUTION                  7,407    POINT
*     % 11,11   EQUATIONS                 4,629    EQUATION
*     % 11,11   INITIAL                   4,629    MEAN
*     % 10,18   NONLINEAR                 4,629    ORDER
******              >90%          >80%              >70%          >60%

      LAYERS                              143    DOCUMENTS ASSIGNED TO

*     % 21,67   BOUNDARY                  6,293    INVERSION
*     % 13,98   SURFACE                   5,594    ANALYSIS
*     % 13,98   TURBULENT                 4,895    ION
*     % 11,88   THIN                      4,895    SILICON
*     % 6,993   PROPERTIES                4,895    STRUCTURE
******              >90%          >80%              >70%          >60%

      LAYER                               286    DOCUMENTS ASSIGNED TO

*     % 31,81   BOUNDARY                  5,944    FLOW
*     % 18,18   THIN                      5,594    DOUBLE
*     % 8,391   TURBULENT                 5,594    MODEL
*     % 8,041   CHROMATOGRAPHY            4,895    SOLUTION
*     % 7,342   SURFACE                   4,545    STRUCTURE
******              >90%          >80%              >70%          >60%

      AXISYMMETRIC                         32    DOCUMENTS ASSIGNED TO

*     % 18,75   BOUNDARY                  9,375    CYLINDRICAL
*     % 18,75   TURBULENT                 9,375    PREDICTION
*     % 15,62   SHELLS                    9,375    STABILITY
*     % 12,50   FLOW                      9,375    VIBRATIONS
*     % 12,50   LAYER                     6,250    BEHAVIOR
******              >90%          >80%              >70%          >60%
```

Figure 7

```
 282  DESCRIPTORS RELATED TO    5213  DESCRIPTOR ADDRESS

6,122  SCATTERING              4,081  SEA
5,102  ENERGY                  4,081  SIMULATION
5,102  SPECTRUM                4,081  TEMPERATURE
5,102  TURBULENT               4,081  TIME
4,081  DIMENSIONAL             4,081  WAVE
  >50%       >40%      >30%          >20%     2 >10%>   280


 134  DESCRIPTORS RELATED TO    4023  DESCRIPTOR ADDRESS

7,142  REGION                  4,761  ANALYSIS
7,142  STARS                   4,761  COUPLED
7,142  SURFACES                4,761  DIFFUSION
7,142  WAVES                   4,761  DIURNAL
7,142  WIND                    4,761  DYNAMIC
  >50%       >40%      >30%        2 >20%     2 >10%>   130


 102  DESCRIPTORS RELATED TO    4663  DESCRIPTOR ADDRESS

5,263  ASSAY                   5,263  CARBON
5,263  ATMOSPHERE              5,263  CHILDREN
5,263  ATOMS                   5,263  CHROMATOGRAPHIC
5,263  BEAM                    5,263  CLOSED
5,263  CALCULATION             5,263  CROSS
  >50%       >40%      >30%          >20%     5 >10%>    97


 314  DESCRIPTORS RELATED TO    5280  DESCRIPTOR ADDRESS

3,703  APPROXIMATION           3,703  PARAMETER
3,703  ENERGY                  3,703  SECOND
3,703  HEAT                    3,703  THEOREM
3,703  INTEGRAL                3,703  THEORY
3,703  OPERATORS               2,777  APPROXIMATE
  >50%     1 >40%      >30%          >20%     4 >10%>   309


 506  DESCRIPTORS RELATED TO    3224  DESCRIPTOR ADDRESS

4,195  CALCULATION             3,496  GAAS
4,195  EPITAXIAL               3,496  INFLUENCE
3,496  DETERMINATION           3,496  SOLUTION
3,496  EFFECT                  3,496  STABILITY
3,496  EXCHANGE                3,496  SURFACES
  >50%       >40%      >30%        1 >20%     3 >10%>   502


 790  DESCRIPTORS RELATED TO    3222  DESCRIPTOR ADDRESS

3,846  CHROMATOGRAPHIC         3,496  LIQUID
3,846  COMPOUNDS               3,496  PLANETARY
3,846  TURBULENCE              3,496  SEPARATION
3,846  TYPE                    3,146  ATMOSPHERIC
3,496  DIFFUSION               3,146  INFLUENCE
  >50%       >40%    1 >30%          >20%     1 >10%>   788


 121  DESCRIPTORS RELATED TO    1327  DESCRIPTOR ADDRESS

6,250  CIRCULAR                6,250  SHELL
6,250  FLOWS                   6,250  SOLUTION
6,250  LAYERS                  6,250  STRAIN
6,250  MEASUREMENTS            6,250  THICK
6,250  MODEL                   6,250  WAVES
  >50%       >40%      >30%          >20%     5 >10%>   116
```

Figure 7   (*Continued*)

51

```
        I.S.I.THESAURUS ANALYSIS  22.8.1975

        CYCLOHEXANONE                         11   DOCUMENTS ASSIGNED TO

  *     %  18,18   CATALYSIS              9,090   ACIDIC
  *     %  18,18   CATALYST               9,090   ALCOHOLS
  *     %  18,18   METAL                  9,090   ALPHA
  *     %  9,090   ACETALS                9,090   BENZENE
  *     %  9,090   ACETATE                9,090   CATALYZED
  ******                  >90%      >80%      >70%         >60%

        HOMOGENEOUS                           79   DOCUMENTS ASSIGNED TO

  *     %  8,860   CATALYST               6,329   THEORY
  *     %  6,329   CATALYZED              5,063   CATALYSIS
  *     %  6,329   PRECIPITATION          5,063   CATALYTIC
  *     %  6,329   SOLUTION               5,063   COMPLEXES
  *     %  6,329   SPACES                 5,063   DETERMINATION
  ******                  >90%      >80%      >70%         >60%

        HYDROGENATION                         61   DOCUMENTS ASSIGNED TO

  *     %  22,95   CATALYST              11,47   PALLADIUM
  *     %  13,11   COMPLEXES              9,836   COMPLEX
  *     %  13,11   NICKEL                 9,836   RHODIUM
  *     %  11,47   CATALYTIC              8,196   HYDROGEN
  *     %  11,47   CATALYZED              6,557   ACTIVITY
  ******                  >90%      >80%      >70%         >60%

        DEHYDROGENATION                       17   DOCUMENTS ASSIGNED TO

  *     %  35,29   CATALYST              11,76   PALLADIUM
  *     %  11,76   COMPOUNDS             11,76   PEROXIDE
  *     %  11,76   METAL                 11,76   RADICAL
  *     %  11,76   OXIDATIVE             11,76   REACTION
  *     %  11,76   OXIDE                 11,76   1
  ******                  >90%      >80%      >70%         >60%

        ZNO                                   19   DOCUMENTS ASSIGNED TO

  *     %  31,57   CATALYST              10,52   FE2O3
  *     %  26,31   EFFECT                10,52   FORMATION
  *     %  21,05   STRUCTURE             10,52   PREPARATION
  *     %  10,52   AL2O3                 10,52   PROPERTIES
  *     %  10,52   BAND                  10,52   TEMPERATURE
  ******                  >90%      >80%      >70%         >60%

        EXHAUST                               21   DOCUMENTS ASSIGNED TO

  *     %  23,80   CATALYST               9,523   ANALYSIS
  *     %  23,80   ENGINE                 9,523   AUTO
  *     %  19,04   GASES                  9,523   AUTOMOBILE
  *     %  14,28   GAS                    9,523   CHARACTERISTIC
  *     %  14,28   NOISE                  9,523   EMISSION
  ******                  >90%      >80%      >70%         >60%

        SUPPORTED                             38   DOCUMENTS ASSIGNED TO

  *     %  42,10   CATALYST              10,52   VIBRATION
  *     %  13,15   NICKEL                 7,894   ACTIVITY
  *     %  10,52   HYDROGENATION          7,894   BEAMS
  *     %  10,52   OXIDE                  7,894   CYLINDRICAL
  *     %  10,52   SURFACE                7,894   PLATES
  ******                  >90%      >80%      >70%         >60%
```

Figure 8

52

```
    62  DESCRIPTORS RELATED TO    1991  DESCRIPTOR ADDRESS

 9,090  CHLORIDE                  9,090  DEHYDROGENATION
 9,090  COMPLEX                   9,090  DERIVATIVE
 9,090  CONDENSATION              9,090  DERIVED
 9,090  CONFORMATIONAL            9,090  DIFLUORIDE
 9,090  COPOLYMER                 9,090  DISSOLUTION
   >50%        >40%        >30%          >20%      3 >10%>      59

   345  DESCRIPTORS RELATED TO    2876  DESCRIPTOR ADDRESS

 5,063  HETEROGENEOUS             3,797  FIELD
 5,063  HYDROGENATION             3,797  FORMATION
 5,063  ISOTROPIC                 3,797  MEDIUM
 5,063  REACTIONS                 3,797  MODELS
 3,797  ANALYSIS                  3,797  PLATINUM
   >50%        >40%        >30%          >20%        >10%>     345

   196  DESCRIPTORS RELATED TO    2907  DESCRIPTOR ADDRESS

 6,557  HOMOGENEOUS               6,557  SUPPORTED
 6,557  IONIC                     4,918  ACID
 6,557  MECHANISM                 4,918  ASYMMETRIC
 6,557  OLEFINS                   4,918  CARBON
 6,557  PHASE                     4,918  CATALYSIS
   >50%        >40%        >30%        1 >20%      5 >10%>     190

    74  DESCRIPTORS RELATED TO    2046  DESCRIPTOR ADDRESS

 5,882  ACTIVE                    5,882  AROMATIC
 5,882  ALPHA                     5,882  ARYL
 5,882  AL2O3                     5,882  AZO
 5,882  AMINES                    5,882  BENZOYL
 5,882  ARENE                     5,882  BETA
   >50%        >40%      1 >30%          >20%      9 >10%>      64

    96  DESCRIPTORS RELATED TO    5449  DESCRIPTOR ADDRESS

10,52   ZINC                      5,263  ADSORBED
10,52   1                         5,263  ANALYSIS
 5,263  ABSORPTION                5,263  AQUEOUS
 5,263  ABSTRACT                  5,263  CARBON
 5,263  ACTIVITY                  5,263  CATALYTIC
   >50%        >40%      1 >30%        2 >20%      9 >10%>      84

    86  DESCRIPTORS RELATED TO    2445  DESCRIPTOR ADDRESS

 9,523  OXIDE                     4,761  ATMOSPHERE
 9,523  THERMAL                   4,761  AUTOMATIC
 4,761  ACOUSTIC                  4,761  AUTOMOTIVE
 4,761  AIR                       4,761  BASE
 4,761  ART                       4,761  CATALYTIC
   >50%        >40%        >30%        2 >20%      3 >10%>      81

   159  DESCRIPTORS RELATED TO    4950  DESCRIPTOR ADDRESS

 7,894  REACTION                  5,263  ALUMINA
 7,894  SILICA                    5,263  BUCKLING
 7,894  THIN                      5,263  EFFECT
 7,894  WAVES                     5,263  ELASTIC
 5,263  ACID                      5,263  ELECTROMAGNETIC
   >50%      1 >40%        >30%          >20%      5 >10%>     153
```

Figure 8 (*Continued*)

53

se. This information is vital for those building thesauri. Relevant paths through the thousands of descriptors establishing search and/ or indexing relationships are suggested throughout these early printouts. Merely having access to the most highly related terms (Figures 4 and 5) with a clear picture of their relational extensions in the files offers an excellent starting point for thesauri revision. Of the thousands of descriptors, these few hundred can lead us to the key interrelationships extant in files.

But as we have also seen such patterns, based on relational strength or groupings around the same highly related term, are not the sole source of search or indexing aids. Our examples in Figures 1, 2, and 3 showed how even the so-called "weaker" extensionally related terms can lead to far more precision in search question formulation than otherwise possible. Thus even with the essentially unedited term lists and the further restriction to terms in titles only for these first runs, we have a clear indication of some of the value of the extensional relationship tables. However, much more analysis of these and later runs is required to permit a full appreciation of the impact of this methodology and technique. Radical improvement of search formulation precision and search results thereby obtained, nonetheless, seem well within our reach for existing files.

Our discussion of technological matters has taken us far enough, however, to offer some insight into the kinds of current problems and solutions, either actual or potential, that might be available. Yet we hope that the preceding discussion has indicated how critically important it is to comprehend such technological issues. And equally important, that it has illustrated the fact that such modifications to existing automated retrieval systems, no matter how worthwhile and necessary to permit meaningful public utilization, do not come often. It is in our interest to see to it that the coming generation of automated information retrieval systems have the appropriate software and file structures. The features of such systems should include those now becoming available [(*f*) and (*g*)] in forms that will facilitate rather than discourage public access. In the following Chapters we describe the required technological features and their characteristics (Chapter 6). But this is better accomplished in the context of a clearer picture of what we might want such technology to offer. We turn now to a broader discussion of the concept of public access to automated information systems and to confront the questions and problems directly involved.

NOTES

1. David Kahn's review of F. W. Winterbottom, *The Ultra Secret,* Harper and Row, New York, 1974, in: *The New York Times Book Review,* December 29, 1974, p. 5
2. "INSPEC—International Information Services for the Physics and Engineering Communities—Catalogue 1973," IEE, The Institution of Electrical Engineers, Savoy Place, London WC2R OBL, England, 1973. D. I. Raitt, *Space Documentation Service: Operations Handbook,* European Space Research Organization, Neuilly-sur-Seine, May 1971. *Computerized Retrieval Service in the Public Library,* brochure about the Lockheed DIALOG retrieval system installed in the Santa Clara County Library, Cupertino, Cal., the San Meteo County Headquarters Library, Belmont, Cal., the Redwood City Library, Redwood City, Cal., and the San Jose Public Library, San Jose, Cal.
3. For a more detailed discussion of these capabilities see CAIR, Chapter 9.
4. See CAIR, p. 51.
5. This concept was demonstrated to the author at AGFA Research Laboratories, Munich, 1970.
6. Plato's "Timaeus" offers a still relevant discussion of this problem.
7. CAIR, Chapter 9.
8. L. S. Onyshkevych and R. Shahbender (RCA Laboratories, Princeton, N.J. 08540), S. Tomkiel and F. Putzrath (Government and Commercial Systems, Camden, N.J.), "Design, Construction, and Testing of a Magnetic Bubble Memory Chip," *RCA Review,* Vol. 35, No. 2, June 1974, pp. 216–233. Nicholas Enticknap, "Memories Are Made of Bubbles," *Data Processing,* Vol. 6, No. 6, November–December 1974, pp. 357–368, 370, 372. "Bubbles Break Into Applications at NASA" (no author given–rubic: Electronics Review), *Electronics,* Vol. 47, No. 10, May 16, 1974, pp. 30–31. Philippe Coeré, Hubert Jouve, Daniel Mauduit, Denis Randet, "Technologie et Utilisation des Mémoires à Bulles Magnétiques," *MEMOIRES L'onde électrique,* Vol. 54, No. 4, 1974, pp. 165–174.
9. For further discussion of this topic see CAIR, Chapter 9

10. W. A. Martin, "A Comparative Study of Terminal User Techniques in Four European Countries on a Large Common On-Line Interactive Information Retrieval System," 1st European Congress of Documentation Systems and Networks, Luxemburg, 16–18 May, 1973; European Space Research Organization (now European Space Agency), Neuilly-sur-Seine, 1973.

11. Zentralstelle für Luft- und Raumfahrtdokumentation und -information (Aviation and Space Documentation and Information Center), Munich.

12. O. Firschein and R. K. Summit, "Computerized Retrieval in a Public Library Setting," paper given at the 10th IEEE Computer Society International Conference (COMP CON Spring 75) February 25–27, San Francisco, Calif.

13. John C. Beresford, "The Formation and Operation of an Open Data Bank—A Case History," United Nations Industrial Development Organization, Vienna, Bulletin No. 21, United Nations, New York, 1974, pp. 25–26.

14. U. Grosse, "PRIMAS—Programm zum Rückgewinn und Indexieren mit Maschinenhilfe; Ein rechnerunterstütztes Erschliessungs-und Recherchesystem mit strukturiertem Thesaurus" (PRIMAS—Program for Machine-Aided Retrieval and Indexing; a Computer-Aided Indexing and Search System for Structured Thesauri), paper given at the First European Conference on Documentation Systems and Networks under the auspices of the Commission of the European Communities, Luxemburg, 16–18 May 1973; Stiftung Wissenschaft und Politik, Ebenhausen, 1973). H. Hering, "Ein Dialogsystem für Analyse und Recherche; Untersuchung auf seine Anwendbarkeit im Deutschen Patentamt" (A Dialogue System for Indexing and Search; Feasibility Study for the German Patent Office), Berichte der 16. Jahrestagung des Ausschusses für Patentdokumentation, DGD-Schrift (APD-3)4/74. See also CAIR for a more detailed discussion of these topics.

15. See CAIR.

16. Grosse, "PRIMAS." Hering, "Ein Dialogsystem für Analyse und Recherche."

17. CAIR, Chapter 9.

18. Contract No. 7/75/SDS to the author from the European Space Agency (ESA)—Space Documentation Service (SDS), 8 July 1975

19. This was made possible through the kindness of Noel Isotta, Head, Space Documentation Service, and W. A. Martin, Technical Director of this effort at Space Documentation Service. The cooperation of Gerhard Mühlhauser, in charge of the computer programming operations at SDS, Frascati, is also gratefully acknowledged.

20. See CAIR for a thorough discussion of why no methods are likely to achieve fully automated indexing.

21. CAIR, p. 160.

Chapter Three

Everyone's Data for Whom

3.1 DEVELOPMENT FUNDING AND DEVELOPING BENEFITS

The development and implementation of computer technology has been, to date, rather a casual affair. It has generally been focused on where the money was at any given time. In our contemporary world, significant development money for the most part comes from you and me through taxation and is allocated predominantly through government channels.* This decision process, the alloca-

---

* Ratios of development funds from the private sectors to those from the government or public sectors are not only difficult to obtain, they are also suspect. Various kinds of indirect arrangements, such as subsidies and tax allowances, are so complicated and "hidden" that it is almost impossible to achieve more than educated guesses. Even so, private funding of development still comes "from you and me" via the prices we pay for goods and services. At least the drug industry has always claimed that high costs of medicines and prescription drugs are required in order that research in the public's interest can take place. For our purposes it should be sufficient to note that computer development, at least during its critical phases in the 1950s, as atomic energy and space research and development, was funded predominantly from government sources.

tion of resources to development through government channels, is not notably better nor worse than our individual choices in expending funds left over after necessities have been obtained. Popular fashion and myth are well mixed with realism, rationality, and greed, whoever allocates "free" or "excess" funds. The trick for both government or private sources is to establish that the "luxury" of development is neither more nor less than a vital national, social, human necessity. Those who have learned to "work that trick" get the development funds allocated.

There is one other, often obscured, factor involved in technological development and implementation. The "pay off" or benefit, often a function of the amount of expenditures, is not necessarily related to the purpose of the expenditures. This means that however "democratic" or otherwise the decision processes were in determining the allocation of development funds, and from wherever such funds came, the distribution of resultant goods or benefits is seldom if ever a direct result of the research and development allocation decision. Now here is a matter for deep meditation for those concerned with the distribution of societies' goods, benefits, or services. For a much more mysterious art than the one useful in obtaining development funds is mastery of the techniques of achieving the ownership of and access to the benefits from the development.

Computer technology provides us with an apt illustration of both kinds of magic. After World War II, the computer scientists found themselves with a computer, rather primitive by today's standards, but most useful in the analyses of data associated with war gaming and war planning. But the war had been won and no one felt like starting another. Computer development was threatened. It might be seen as involving just another postwar luxury when the perceived necessity in the United States and elsewhere involved the production of automobiles and other such goods neglected during war time. Now one could postulate that so many automobiles would be produced and put on the highways and streets that the necessity for computerized traffic control would be perceived. And a good argument could have been made to continue computer development for reasons such as these. But a luxury can be defined as anything we do not require now and the highways and streets were rather empty in Europe certainly and even in the United States in 1947. The reason that we have computers available for traffic control and all the other meaningful services today (process control, banking and accounting systems, data banks of every kind, retrieval and documentation systems) is due to the massive expenditure of development funds beginning in 1947 for quite other purposes. The "trick" was to perceive the vital necessity of air defense. Not one airplane must be permitted to bomb one city with one atomic bomb or all those automobiles being produced. . . . Everyone had a stake in this; computer development became a felt necessity. The manual air defense system was to be improved by automation; all over the country computers were built and nice researchable problems, man/machine interfaces, network communications, on-line interaction, computerized training systems became part of our way of life. Thus we could all follow our peacetime pursuits feeling better about the bomb.

It did not matter too much that the other fellow who got the bomb did not cooperate too well thereafter. The Russians didn't build very many long-range bombers in the first place. But as the new, semiautomated air defense system never worked so well as to be able to shoot down very many long-range bombers, that was not a significant drawback. Someday the Russians might build all those bombers and someday the air defense system might work that well. Instead, the Russians built a lot of long-range missiles, none of which could be shot down by the new air defense systems. The lack of Russian cooperation did not faze us at all. Billions were still poured into air defense. As one result, throughout the 1950s computer development took off at a rapid pace that continues to this day.

However, although the "public" in some sense wound up with the "ownership" of an automated and essentially useless national air defense system created in its interest, computers so developed wound up in the hands of other parties who used them, more or less successfully, to solve more profitable tasks than shooting down war planes or missiles. This result is a function of that second most mysterious trick involving the distribution of side benefits, in this case, the most valuable benefits of the massive public expenditure for air defense.

3.2   A QUESTION OF PUBLIC INTEREST

We are concerned here with one of these many side benefits: the development of computer technology to provide useful information retrieval services to those with established ownership of or access to such services. Only recently has the question of ownership of and access to such automated information retrieval systems and services been raised from the point of view of "the public interest." This, however, is a rather murky notion which some of us have just begun to think about. At the recent 37th Annual Meeting of The American Society for Information Science, Tefko Saracevic observed:

... we combine our intuitive notions of information as a commodity or service ... and of utility as a public service ... in the public interest. However, beyond this intuitive understanding we know precious little ... (1).

Saracevic and others addressed themselves to the question of regarding information retrieval systems as some form of "public utility" providing their services to the broader public (2). Setting up some form of a public utility to provide for and to protect the public's rights and interests with regard to ownership of and access to retrieval systems and services is one option to be considered. However, the record of government regulatory agencies and public utilities in the United States does not inspire too much confidence as to whom and what will be protected and served. In fact we shall argue that although the discussion of this topic is not premature, a specific decision to establish a regulated public utility is probably unwise at this time. A great deal of preliminary analysis, and far more clarity as to what we may be attempting to achieve, are required. A good starting point is to consider what may be involved in the notion of the public's right to information.

3.2.1   Basic Public Rights—Assumptions and Problems

Two assumptions listed in the recently proposed National Program for Library and Information Services offer the most succinct statement of the broad public right to information (3). These are:

1. The total library and information resource . . . is a national resource which should be . . . made available to the maximum degree possible in the public interest.
2. All people have the right, according to their individual needs, to realistic and convenient access to this national resource . . . (4)

Three other assumptions are spelled out in this report. They have to do with the technical feasibility of establishing a national network, the protection of authors, publishers, et al., and required legislation pertinent to the above. These latter three assumptions stipulate that the technological, economic, and legislative means, are all available to accomplish the broad ends stipulated by the first two assumptions quoted above (5).

Given our lack of knowledge and confused value structures, all these assumptions are more than optimistic. In fact, proposals for anything like such a national service (and the report aims higher than the nation reaching out to embrace the world) (6), ought not to beg all the hard issues by postulation of values and facts that are much in dispute. Countervailing notions about access to information are rooted far back in recorded history and are much alive today. Information, power, and wealth are inextricably linked. The wise, the powerful, and the wealthy have not always taken kindly to the idea of letting the public freely browse about in their domains. It has been argued that such "licentious" freedom is not in the public interest. Information too widely dispersed has long been felt to be dangerous; to whom is not often clearly stated, but certainly dangerous. Access to information even today remains surrounded by some rite of admission to the sacred source. One must incant a "need-to-know," fulfill certain criteria involving "in-group" acceptance, or demonstrate an ability to pay. Men of power or wealth have always had recourse to the wise with recourse to the gods, and there found quite eloquent arguments that some such arrangement was precisely in the public interest. And as Zeus demonstrated in his dealings with Prometheus, eloquence passes quickly over into brute force when the need arises.

There is no point in attempting a serious evaluation of either what may be called the "Jeffersonian" or the "Platonic" viewpoints as to the public rights to information. We need simply assert that, once published, information is thereby made publically available. Whatever laws, regulations, and social arrangements may exist to protect the publication and those producers of the information published, sooner or later all such published information "belongs to the public domain." During the periods of copyright protection, the only reasonable position that can be taken as to public access is that it be restricted by no other constraints than those imposed by copyright itself. No other constraints need be taken seriously. Whatever merit or lack thereof may apply to political, philosophical, religious, moral, or national, arguments as to the public interest or the protection of the public, such arguments properly have application only to the decision to publish. If anyone then wishes to preserve information for himself or his group, rightly or wrongly, let him not publish his information. As to others' information, presumably persuasion not to publish is only as legitimate as the means used to persuade. But once material is published, restrictive arguments as to access fall flat when confronted by the very fact of publication. However, computers and computerized information raise more difficult problems.

3.2.2   Computerized Information—Some New Questions

The computer, automated libraries, and data banks with whatever information may be contained therein raise some rather novel problems. If not otherwise published, what public right can be asserted with regard to information stored in computers? And of more relevance to our inquiry, what public right can be claimed pertaining to information abstracted, culled, edited, combined, and otherwise processed and transformed into computer files, even should the source be published material? To focus our attention on automated libraries alone, where information in the public domain can be made available to the public, is as much an error as to be solely concerned with the "privacy issue." The importance and power of computers lie not merely in increased capabilities to handle vast amounts of information. Of more concern is the potential computers offer to process and transform such information masses more in accordance with our various needs. Automated libraries will not, in themselves, offer sufficient countervailing capabilities to the public when confronted by the computerized information retrieval systems of government, particularly the executive arms, industry, and other major societal institutions. It is precisely these existent and near future capabilities to process, manipulate, combine, and arrange information offered by computerized information retrieval systems, to make information far more useful by its transformation into forms and arrangements that better match needs, to which the questions of public access must be addressed. And to the extent that ownership of such systems implies the control of access to these capabilities, then it is the ownership of information retrieval systems that is of far more concern than the ownership of information per se. Suppose information were as freely available to all as sunlight. Asserting a public right to sunlight would have little bearing on the question of the distribution of the benefits of solar energy harvested by those who own or control the harvesting machines.

The comparison of information to energy is not farfetched (7).

To emphasize the importance of access to the computer systems by which information is converted into more powerful and useful forms is to point to the need to establish a new dimension to the notion of our public rights "to know," "to information," and to the control of our several social destinies. For as things now stand the ownership of, control of, and access to these computerized means of information conversion is being left to the eager hands of those with power enough already in all societies. Communist governments are no more, perhaps less, interested in giving their publics meaningful access to such systems than non-Communist governments; nor are the various military establishments, the duPonts or Krupps, the many "revolutionary councils," or the Indira Gandhis. Each may differ as to which parts of their publics may have access to sunlight or libraries, but all agree on the need to preserve their own control of the means of converting information to power. We must further delineate this new dimension of the public right of access; access to the means by which information is converted into more powerful and useful forms.

3.2.3   The Public Right to Computer-Aided Information Retrieval

Any meaningful discussion of the new dimension of the right to information is intrinsically interwoven with technological considerations. In fact, the course that technological developments take in the next few years will determine for quite some time what rights the public and their representatives may have with regard to computer-aided information retrieval. We cannot, and had better not, assume that the technology is now or will be available for satisfying any rights that we may wish to assert. Rather we must clarify what we believe such public rights are and then see to it that the technology is indeed available to satisfy them. This means that we must also know what technology is required and press for its development. There is no valid reason to suppose that decisions concerning the allocation of development funding, private or governmental, will otherwise result in systems that provide meaningful access for the public and the public's representatives to computer-aided information retrieval. We offer a detailed description of the required technology (Chapter 6) and a plan for its implementation and its initial operational test phase, including the public's participation (Chapter 7). We also indicate the costs for such a developmental and experimental operational phase. Our present discussion of what should be involved in the public rights to computer-aided information retrieval should be understood in the context of its technological and economic feasibility.

3.2.3.1 Apparent Versus Real Access   A rather common idea concerning automated information retrieval, shared by many professionals as well as "laymen," is that one need merely formulate one's informational needs in more or less ordinary language. These then are furnished to the computer, which responds with all pertinent citations available. Most users of automated information retrieval have found this to be far from the case (see Chapter 2). Nonetheless, such overoptimistic expectations lie behind the belief that the public right to information can be satisfied by automated public libraries.

We have no quarrel with the public's right to libraries, automated or not; nevertheless, it is best to be quite clear as to what the public can expect from automated public libraries. Michael D. Cooper has observed that funds expended for libraries in the United States have remained at roughly the same level over the years. Approximately 1% of total municipal expenditures, according to Cooper, are allocated to support public libraries (8). Those attempting the application of conventional automation to public libraries doubt that libraries will receive additional funds for this purpose (9). Yet only by a radical increase in library staff and staff services can even an apparent satisfaction of many of the public's real needs be obtained through conventional means of access to automated information retrieval systems. We suggest that the apparent satisfaction will become increasingly dubious as we become more familiar with what we are being offered. Next we look into what is best termed "supplemented automated library services," where access to conventional data banks are offered in the context of public libraries. We see that this too falls far short of satisfying our legitimate needs for useful information. This chapter then closes with a section describing what technology should offer towards the satisfaction of the public needs for information and stipulates the public rights to the full capabilities offered by computer-aided information retrieval systems.

3.2.3.2 Public Library Automation We are not concerned here with the benefits, cost savings, efficiencies, and so forth that may arise from the automation of the administrative data flow within and involving libraries. Better inventory control, accounting, ordering, and other administrative processes can improve services to the public. To the extent that improvements in administration help provide better public services, this form of automation is significant; it can, for example, free librarians from drudgery, permitting them to offer more time to public library users. But aside from this kind of potential impact, automation of administrative data flow has little if anything to do with directly providing the public with enhanced capabilities to satisfy their informational requirements.

The sort of automation that does concern us applies to the informational resources within the library. These informational resources vary widely from library to library and the publics to which libraries offer their services.* We do not pretend here to

---

* The fact that there are quite different "publics" with perhaps incompatible needs is becoming more and more recognized by librarians. Consider as an example the "typical" modern branch library in more affluent sections of the United States or in Germany. Almost always there is a children's section with brightly colored tables and chairs, appropriately sized, surrounded by attractive looking books and posters. Now imagine just how "attractive" all this might be to the elderly patrons who find no chairs or tables "sized" for them, nor any particular environmental atmosphere or consideration for their special needs. With the numbers of "senior" citizens increasing, librarians are also paying increasing attention to "geriatrics." But while the youth culture has been catered to, little has been done to make libraries more· comfortable or attractive for the elderly or even to provide for their basic physical, let alone their special informational, needs.

describe the many specialized services offered by central or main libraries and certain branch libraries. Books, limited source material, a few journals and newspapers selected for entertainment, current fads or fashions, materials for self or "adult education," hobbies and "how-to-do-it" instruction, "popular" science and "journalistic" interests, and so forth constitute the core of informational materials available at those libraries to which the public has easiest and simplest access. Such libraries are not set up, funded, staffed, or supplied in a manner that could permit them to provide their publics with access to informational resources even remotely equivalent to those available with the automated information retrieval systems owned by private industry, institutions, or government. Automation within the context and applied to just those existing resources of such libraries simply will not do very much in transforming this wide discrepancy into a more equitable distribution of a societies' information retrieval capabilities.

Suppose one wants to know something relevant about the effects of marijuana on mental and physical functions, county land use or zoning regulations, solar energy conversion methods applied to home construction, the voting record of a congressman, the amount and quality of police or fire protection for a given area, the distribution of state funds produced from sales taxes over the last 5 years, the requirements for introducing a proposal to a city council, the comparative costs of operating two different schools for 1 year in two specified different neighborhoods or perhaps the same neighborhood, the actual funds provided to a mayor for travel expenses last year, the distribution of a given labor union's funds from membership dues for a selected time period, the expenditure by management of a given corporation for advertising or perhaps the ratio of the expenditures for advertising versus research and product development, or the actual costs of city, county, or state provided services to a local institution, industry, firm, organization, or inhabitant group. Equally important, suppose one wants to know enough about any such topics in time to take what one considers appropriate personal, social, or civic action. "Timing" is often vital and the relevant opportunities for effecting decisions on any of these matters are seldom under our personal control. Under these quite typical conditions automated public libraries per se will not provide us with significantly more help than they already provide. How much help such libraries now provide is best left for the determination of anyone who might wish to try out the local library by attempting to obtain information useful in dealing with the real problems or topics just listed or similar concerns affecting everyday life. And for those cases where appropriate information has been so obtained, one should consider the time and effort involved in obtaining it, whether the information obtained was sufficient to enable knowledgeable action, and whether the ordinary interested and concerned individual can afford to expend the time and effort on all the occasions when this might be required. And even then, should some form of qualified positive answer be obtained, one must consider how often and how many concerned individuals or groups can take the time and effort to balance the massive resources and pressures of government, industry, or other powerful institutions seeking to persuade us to think their way about any of these and similar issues; or seeking to so persuade our local legislative bodies. Clearly if public libraries are to provide us with even a partial balance with regard to the question of access to the informational resources available, their current capabilities and files must be supplemented. We now consider attempts in this direction.

3.2.3.3 Supplemented Automatic Library Services During the last few years a new kind of "industry" or "service" has developed; the source supplier for automated information retrieval systems. INSPEC, which started as a selective dissemination service in England, collected, indexed, and computerized documents from several informational fields pertinent to engineering and industry (10). For some time INSPEC has offered batch processing computer search services to external clients. More recently, INSPEC has provided magnetic tapes constituting INSPEC's own files to other search centers to be processed by software and systems other than INSPEC's. For example, the Space Documentation Service (SDS) of the European Space Agency (ESA, formerly European Space Research Organization, ESRO) now receives regularly updated INSPEC tapes covering Physics, Electronics, Computers and Control (at present approximately 600,000 citations) to add to their previous collections (11). SDS clients may now request SDS to search INSPEC files instead of going directly to INSPEC.

The problems involved in entering data, structuring and building files for documents, and other informational carriers for automated search systems have been touched on and are further discussed (12). Such source suppliers as INSPEC help to fill the demand for already indexed (however satisfactorily) documents and citations prepared for machine entry and available on magnetic tapes. Such machine readable, direct entry tapes help to fill the everpresent gaps in our system files. In the United States the Lockheed DIALOG system is an example of retrieval services available to clients similar to those offered by INSPEC in England (13). DIALOG's coverage includes INSPEC data bases but is far broader (14). For example, as supplements to certain public libraries in California, the following data bases are available:

Scientific and Technical Data Bases

NTIS—The complete Government Reports/Announcements file from the National Technical Information Service. More than 400,000 abstracts of government research from over 240 agencies including NASA, DDC, AEC, HEW, HUD, DOT, Commerce, and many others. File dates back to 1964, is updated every 2 weeks, and is growing at a rate of 60,000 abstracts per year.

INSPEC (SCIENCE ABSTRACTS)—Abstracts from the Institution of Electrical Engineers. Covers from 1969 to present. INSPEC data bases include:

Physics Abstracts—Over 400,000 abstracts from 2000 journals covering worldwide literature.

Electrical and Electronics Abstracts—Over 200,000 abstracts covering 300 subject areas encompassing electrical and electronics engineering.

Computers and Control Abstracts—Over 110,000 abstracts embracing all areas of computers and control engineering.

CHEMICAL ABSTRACTS CONDENSATES—Some 600,000 records from the Chemical Abstracts Service. Covers 1972 to present.

CHEMICAL AND ELECTRONIC MARKET ABSTRACTS (CMA/ EMA)—Over 45,000 abstracts of domestic and foreign information on all chemical process and electronics and data processing equipment industries. Covers 1972 to present. (Produced by Predicasts, Inc.)

COMPENDEX (ENGINEERING INDEX)—Over 200,000 citations and abstracts from 3500 journals, publications of engineering organizations, and selected government reports and books; published worldwide. File growth is at a rate of 84,000 citations and abstracts per year. Covers 1972 to present.

PANDEX—The Macmillan Information Company's Current Index to Scientific and Technical Literature, including extensive biomedical coverage. Over 900,000 titles and bibliographic citations from 2400 journals. Covers 1971 to present.

TRANSDEX—Some 150,000 citations to document translations from U.S. Joint Publications Research Service (Macmillan Information Company).

SOCIAL SCIENCES CITATION INDEX (SSCI)(R)—Over 300,000 citations of social and behavioral science journal literature from the Institute for Scientific Information(R). Covers 1972 to present.

EDUCATIONAL, PSYCHOLOGICAL, AGRICULTURAL, AND BUSINESS DATA BASES

ERIC—The complete file of educational materials from the Educational Resources Information Center of the National Institute of Education and other sources. Covers 1966 to present with subfiles:

Research in Education (*RIE*)—Includes 70,000 abstracts of Educational Research in the areas of curriculum development, learning disabilities, educational technology, and others.
Current Index to Journals (*CIJE*)—Includes 68,000 abstracts of journal articles in education.

EXCEPTIONAL CHILDREN ABSTRACTS—Contains 12,000 abstracts of material of particular interest in this field. This file is produced by the Council for Exceptional Children. Dates from 1966 to present.

ABSTRACTS OF INSTRUCTIONAL AND RESEARCH MATERIALS (AIM/ARM)—Includes 7000 abstracts of instructional and research materials, indexed by the Center for Vocational and Technical Education, Ohio State University. Covers 1966 to present.

PSYCHOLOGICAL ABSTRACTS—Over 150,000 abstracts to journal articles in psychology. Dates from 1967. Issued by the American Psychological Association.

ABSTRACTED BUSINESS INFORMATION (ABI/INFORM)—Over 14,000 abstracts from business and financial journals in the areas of management, administration, finance, and so forth. Covers 1971 to present.

NAL/CAIN—The complete Bibliography of Agriculture file from the National Agricultural Library, including the contents of the NAL catalog as well. Over 475,000 citations of agriculture-related material. File growth is at a rate of 140,000 citations per year. File coverage is from 1970 to present and included the recently added Food and Nutrition File (15).

Furthermore, new data bases are being considered for continuing expansion of DIALOG coverage.

Supported by a National Science Foundation Grant, DIALOG terminals have been made available to the public at four California branch libraries (16). Strictly access to the computer and the DIALOG data bases for on-line search is through the reference librarian, although it appears that in some of the branches "lay" individuals are instructed in console operation and may conduct their own searches (17). Here then is a sufficiently rich computerized supplement to "typical" public branch libraries. Will this form of access to automated information retrieval satisfy or fulfill the public's rights to their national informational resources? It might well seem so:

Are you writing a paper on microbiology, linguistics or cat leukemia? Do you administer an air conditioning business? Teaching a class of hyperkinetic children? Interested in community services? Perhaps you are writing a book . . . need background data. How about bee culture or plant nutrients? Do you need to know more about management . . . , affirmative action programs, the four-day, 40 hour work week? Are you interested in your community's environmental impact studies?

We can find the current technical and scientific information you need, as well as data from the fields of education, psychology, agriculture, and the social sciences (18).

Nothing in what follows should be taken as in any way undervaluing what access through DIALOG terminals to the data files listed above might mean for the patrons of these California libraries. It is to be hoped that this National Science Foundation experiment finds favor with the California public, at least to the extent that this public would pay for the search charges after the NSF funds allocated for this purpose are expended. One wishes that other California counties, and other states would extend this service to their public library users. Yet there are some grounds for expecting this experiment to have mixed results and perhaps dissolve in confusion as to both costs, problems, drawbacks, and benefits.

For example, in a preliminary analysis of the NSF/DIALOG experiment (DIALIB), Alice E. Ahlgren found that average search costs may range anywhere from $15 to $25, "and this figure does not include staff time or fixed expenses" (19). For the 6-month time period studied "the average search time is approximately 30 minutes" (20). Although Ahlgren finds that search time has been dropping slightly (21), most of the library patrons requesting DIALOG searches to date have been requesting highly technical searches (22). Experience with automated information retrieval systems indicates that 1 half-hour average search time per search request is by no means unusual, and furthermore, that when one introduces nontechnical queries, search times are more than likely to increase radically (23). In any event such expenditures of time and associated costs do not include the large amounts of staff support and services involved in helping patrons to formulate search questions and to analyze the obtained results (filtering out irrelevant citations, obtaining reference or source materials and the citations themselves, and extracting the relevant information). In Chapter 2 we noted that manual filtering alone in search centers using conventional automated information retrieval systems can involve center staff for as much as $3\frac{1}{2}$ hours per search request.

In DIALIB, given the highly technical search questions covering such topics "as 'Ion Beam Processing,' 'Aerated Concrete,' 'Semiconductors,' 'Extruded Polyvinyl Chloride,' and 'Auger Spectroscopy'" (24), and patrons who for the most part are technical professionals or graduate students, college students, education specialists or librarians (from over 50% to over 70% of the DIALIB patrons, depending on the particular branch library) (25), Ahlgren finds "that almost 70% of the patrons felt that the results of their DIALOG search were of considerable or major value" (26). At the same time, only "48.1% of the DIALOG patrons indicated that the results . . . provided sufficient references to answer their question adequately" (27). When one considers the nature of the DIALOG patrons and their technical skills and information requests, we can once again see the lack of high-quality recall and relevance ratios discussed in Chapter 2 confirmed by DIALOG. DIALIB patrons tend to be highly educated: "Over 60% of DIALOG patrons have some graduate work and over 40% have advanced degrees" (28). DIALIB patrons are not a significant segment of the population of traditional library users. In fact, Ahlgren observes that DIALIB to date has been providing services for the most part to groups that do "not traditionally use . . . (library) reference service" (29).

For the more general public, when overly high expectations are combined with the conventional approach to automated information retrieval, an unhappy result can be expected.

In an early discussion of this experiment, Firschein and Summit state: "News media tend to describe computerized services in a somewhat exaggerated manner . . . The public then expects the system to be able to perform at a much higher level than is actually possible" (30). It is not, however, the news media alone who may attempt to interest the public by exaggeration. The San Mateo County Headquarters' bulletins and releases contained, as we have noted, some rather optimistic claims, "We can find the current technical and scientific information you need, as well as data from the fields of education, psychology, agriculture, and the social sciences" (31).

DIALOG does not achieve significantly worse nor better results than other similar systems. About half of the information one "needs," often much more than half, is simply not retrieved. This refers only to the "typical" retrieval of 50% of the relevant citations within the data files. Naturally, even if all relevant citations within the data files were obtained this would not mean that all relevant information was obtained. Much is often not within the computerized files. And more than half, for the typical case, of the information one does obtain is not relevant to the expressed need. Furthermore, DIALOG does not retrieve "the information you need" at all; it offers a list of citations or references to documents stored elsewhere with very little if any information beyond the titles concerning those references. It is left to the requestor to somehow or other decide whether any of the citations listed by the computer contain information of any use in satisfying the need. This means that the requestor has to obtain the documents cited, with the help of the research or reference librarian, and read or check through them before it can be determined whether any of the documents cited are relevant.

In the present experiment, the public often has the impression that the system retrieves information (sic) rather than *references* to information. Thus, someone . . . may be disappointed to be given references to documents that *might* contain the answer (32).

And to return to the librarians and their burdens, this entire process imposes quite an arduous, if not unacceptable load. The librarian must help obtain not only cited documents but also "source document materials indicated by the computer printout (must be located even) when the sources are esoteric in nature" (33). In addition, the librarians "often find themselves deluged by reference questions" (34). Furthermore:

. . . this onslaught of work can be quite unexpected and overburden the reference librarian. Another problem that arises is that of locating source document materials . . . (35)

The reference librarians are even supposed to do their part in helping the system perform at the 50% or better level by:

1. *Screening requests*—It is important to forward only those requests that are probably suitable for DIALOG. . . .
2. *Obtaining information* (search question formulation)—(For likely DIALOG requests) it is important that the . . . librarian do a thorough reference interview to get from the patron a detailed statement of the question, and to get as many as possible search terms and synonyms. (36)

Again as with conventional automated retrieval systems, DIALOG offers little guided help to the librarian or anyone else in formulating and reformulating search questions.

It is also helpful for the CIN (Cooperative Information Network of public, school, and corporate libraries that share information and resources in the San Francisco Bay area) librarian to do additional research at the CIN library . . . to provide the DIALOG librarian with other synonyms, relevant references, and names of people publishing on the topic, and other information that will help focus the search. (37)

Finally, given data bases prestructured by source suppliers to serve major clients in government, industry, or other powerful institutions, no computer help is available to restructure the files more appropriately for any other individual or group. Thus search results, however mediocre from the point of view of those for whom the files were principally created, are simply not going to prove very satisfying for the varieties of public users.

A major corporation, for example, can afford a skilled staff to do the initial screening, the formulation of search questions and their refinement, the study of term lists and thesauri, the location of cited documents and indicated source materials, however esoteric or hard to find, the tedious read through and postscreening, the analyses of what may survive the relevancy checks, and the summarization of significant facts or data. Or it can hire a search center to do all these laborious and time-consuming manual tasks. Paying for the search time on the computer is the least of the prob-

lems. But neither the public nor the public libraries, even supplemented within reasonable bounds, can be expected to afford any of
these essential elements beyond paying, perhaps, for the actual
computerized search time. Much of the public, including most of
us, will not be well-served even though the burdens we may impose
on our supplemented public libraries and their already overburdened librarians prove to be immense. And certainly we shall not
have the countervailing access to the national informational
resources that the major corporations, government agencies, or
other institutions possess. We won't even come close.

This will not be the fault of the public libraries nor of attempts
such as the NSF/DIALOG experiment. It will be due to the use of
the wrong kinds of computer software, which may lead to a disillu-
sionment so profound that not even supplemented public libraries,
however inadequate, will be made available to the public. Here we
may have a case where "something is better than nothing" being
not good enough, leads to nothing at all. Technology can do better
than that, and the public deserves better than what it is likely to be
offered. It is time to delineate just what this could be.

3.2.3.4 *Minimal Requirements for Meaningful Public Access* Meaningful access to automated information retrieval
cannot be achieved second hand by offering the public access to
systems and files developed for other institutions or purposes. We
must acknowledge the relative paucity of resources available to the
public for file construction, analysis and description, search question formulation, filtering, and all the many tasks involved in
obtaining and putting together information relevant to given
concerns or topics. Mere automated search through pre- and
poorly structured files is not going to satisfy very many of the
public's needs. Given the lack of supporting staffs available to
government and major organizations, the public and the
representatives of the public will require an even better package of
automated retrieval capabilities than is now being offered generally

to anyone anywhere.* Nonetheless, the requirements for public access that follow are reasonable in the sense that technology is capable of satisfying them and the costs are feasible. However, these requirements are also minimal in the sense that technology will not be expected to provide complete satisfaction of all the public's needs for relevant information. Rather technology should offer the public a reasonable chance to satisfy their informational requirements by providing computer-aided access to the national informational resources.

First of all, the public needs to know what constitutes the available informational resources, how these informational resources are described and structured, and how to formulate informational needs in terms descriptive of the informational resources and acceptable to the computer. Usually the information available for computerized search is characterized as belonging to differing informational fields or "pools" similar to the description of the DIALOG data bases in Section 3.2.3.3. Within such informational fields, citations to documents are often further grouped according to subject heading categories. However, at this point the search question formulator is left to seek through conventional thesauri, which are little more than attempts to provide controlled lists of computer acceptable expressions. Or, for certain systems and applications, the search question may be formulated in "natural language" terms or expressions that the computer then "looks for" by scanning the stored textual material and/or special files. In both cases, and in those cases where a combination of thesauri/natural language search is possible, little if any computer guidance is available to help the searcher. Worse yet, no help at all is offered to reformulate such term lists or natural language possibilities in terms conducive to the public's understanding of them (38).

Imagine being confronted with conventional controlled term lists,

---

* It is not only the "public" that is deserving of better automated information retrieval systems than those generally available. See CAIR for more detail on this subject.

often containing twenty, thirty, forty, fifty thousand and more of terms or expressions, with little structural grouping other than hierarchical and that often illogical or inconsistent, and informed that such a thesaurus constitutes the entry point into the computerized files. Or equally worthy of meditation, imagine being informed that one has to find within one's own "natural" language the vocabulary to match the terms and expressions of the textual material from thousands if not millions of sources, producers, and authors, textual material with esoteric, unfamiliar, specialized, and professional languages! And then imagine yourself as that underpaid, overburdened reference librarian dealing with the public, that undescribably varied public with its wide range of expressional capabilities and informational needs. The conclusion is inescapable that a clear, convenient, friendly, and transparent access mode to the files, to the description of the information there contained, and to the means for expressing the wide variety of informational needs, is essential for achieving meaningful public usage of such automated information retrieval systems.

A second fundamental requirement has to do with restructuring files in accordance with the public's varying and changing informational needs. Although it may not be feasible to thoroughly revamp existing indexing and document description for the general public, there is no reason why specific public groups and their representatives should not have this capability. As a given public group begins to clarify its interests and needs through use of automated information retrieval, its informational retrieval requirements will be better served by structuring or restructuring the available files accordingly. In this manner the many data bases offered by source suppliers, obtained "from the public domain," or created by legislation for public use can be reindexed or described by the specific public groups themselves, providing computer-aids for this purpose are available. The results of such group specific indexing in accordance with equally group specific interests and needs should be included in thesauri available to the members of such public groups. Such thesauri structured according to principles described elsewhere (39) should be incorporated within the computer; the automated information retrieval system thus provides its own guided paths through the available files through the transparent windows of the computer-stored thesauri.

Last, the full range of computer-aids for search question formulation and reformulation based on such thesauri and the direct feedback from interactive searches will be required. The computer can be programmed to suggest descriptors to both searchers and indexers to permit the refinement and/or expansion of search questions or indexing choices. There is no need for librarians or laymen to be expected to perform this task in full when the computer can do it faster, better, and more conveniently for both librarians and the public.

These basic requirements for meaningful public access to automated information retrieval call for more than the conventional search only systems. A certain amount of computer software development will be required to fulfill such requirements. The costs of such developments are, however, also "minimal." Something on the order of $800,000 or DM 2.000.000 would be involved, a rather small fraction of the funds expended on conventional software for private systems; or expended on planning studies about national information networks and resources! Chapters 6 and 7 describe such computer software and further delineate the methods to achieve meaningful information retrieval for more of us.

NOTES

1. Tefko Saracevic, "Questions about the Notion of Information Utilities," Proceedings of the 37th ASIS Annual Meeting, Vol. 11, American Society for Information Science, Washington, D.C., 1974, p. 1.
2. Ibid. pp. 1-7; see also T. D. Wilson, "Factors Affecting the Coordination of Information Agencies to Form Public Information Utilities," pp. 8-12; Marc U. Porat, "Structure of the Specialized Common Carrier: Implications for the Information Utility Industry," pp. 13-17; John M. Carroll, "The Computer 'Discredit Bureau'—An Extension of a Community Information Utility," pp. 18-23. Carroll's article offers a particularly illuminating example of the utility

of public access to automated information retrieval systems. All of the articles are valuable, both in themselves and as an indication of the gradually dawning awareness of the importance of these topics.

3. The National Commission on Libraries and Information Science, "A National Proposal for Library and Information Services: A Synopsis of the Second Draft Program," Information Storage and Retrieval, Vol. 10, Nos. 9/10, Sept./Oct., 1974, Pergamon Press, New York, pp. 343–348.

4. Ibid., p. 343.

5. Ibid., p. 343.

6. Ibid., p. 348.

7. C. E. Shannon, "Mathematical Theory of Communication," Bell Systems Technical Journal, 1948, pp. 379–424, 623–656.

8. Michael D. Cooper, "The Economics of Information," *Annual Review of Information Science and Technology* edited by Carlos A. Cuadra, **8** (1973), pp. 6–40.

9. Alice E. Ahlgren, "Factors Affecting the Adoption of On-Line Search Services by the Public Library," paper presented at the 1975 Midyear Conference, American Society for Information Science, Portland, Oregon, June 1975.

10. IEE INSPEC, Literature Search Service, London (England), 1975; INSPEC Science Abstracts List of Journals, "Journals Abstracted Completely," London, June 1972.

11. Telephone conversation with Zentralstelle für Luft- und Raumfahrtdokumentation u.-information (Aviation and Space Documentation and Information Center), Munich, November 1975.

12. See also CAIR.

13. "Data Bases of Dialog (TM), computerized retrieval service in the public libraries of Santa Clara and San Mateo Counties," San Mateo County Library Headquarters, Belmont, California, 1974.

14. Ibid.

15. Ibid., slightly edited.

16. O. Firschein and R. K. Summit (Lockheed Palo Alto Research Laboratory), "Computerized Retrieval in a Public Library Setting," Compcon 75, Tenth Computer Society International Conference, San Francisco, Calif., February 25–27, 1975.

17. Ibid.

18. "Would a Computer Help?", brochure issued by San Mateo County Library Headquarters, Belmont, California, 1974.

19. Ahlgren, "Adoption of On-Line Search Services by the Public Library," p. 4.

20. Ibid., p. 3.

21. Ibid., p. 3.

22. Ibid., p. 4.

23. INSPEC and DIALOG search charges are much higher than those given for DIALIB, £20 (ca. $50 or DM 120) per search for INSPEC and $25 to $150 (DM 63–DM 375) per contract hour for DIALOG; see Chapter 4, p. 96.

24. Ibid., p. 4.

25. Ibid., p. 7.

26. Ibid., p. 4.

27. Ibid., p. 5.

28. Ibid., p. 8.

29. Ibid., p. 8.

30. Firschein and Summit, "Computerized Retrieval."

31. "Can a Computer Help?" (San Mateo County Library Headquarters).

32. Firschein and Summit, "Computerized Retrieval," (emphasis in original).

33. Ibid.

34. Ibid.

35. Ibid.

36. "Helping the DIALOG Reference Librarian," from "Computerized Retrieval Service in the Public Library," San Mateo County Library Headquarters, Belmont, Calif., 1974.

37. Ibid.

38. For an excellent and quite detailed comparison of what the major or well-known information retrieval systems offer, RECON, STAIRS, GOLEM, TELDOK, see Ivo Steinacker, "Dokumentationssysteme—Dialogfunktion und Systementwurf," de Gruyter, Berlin/New York, 1975, pp. 221-244, unfortunately available only in German. Other systems are also described in this book. In the main, some systems offer searchers the ability to "browse" through the thesauri or computer-acceptable term lists. When thesauri possess hierarchical structures, the "browser" can be led to lower-level terms covered by more general terms or expressions in the thesaurus. Occasionally preferred spellings are offered and "see also" references. But none of this is made easy or comprehensible to the novice nor are the dialog functions very impressive. In short, expert search question formulators are more or less necessary to obtain even mediocre results in all conventional systems.

39. CAIR, Chapters 7 and 8.

Figure 1   Original drawing by Marie Marcks, Heidelberg, 1976.

Figure 2   Original drawing by Marie Marcks, Heidelberg, 1976.

Figure 3   Original drawing by Marie Marcks, Heidelberg, 1976.

Chapter Four

The Need for Access

4.1 MODELS, MINDS, AND COMPUTERS

What ought to be the price of a barrel of oil? No computer in this world can definitely answer such a request for information. Any answer at which we are capable of arriving depends at least as much on the ways "ought" is defined as on the factual information stored within computers. As there is no ultimate or absolute definition of the many "oughts" that might interest us, no ultimate or absolutely correct decision model can be programmed for our computers.

People who have access to computers and are interested in convincing others, changing minds, and influencing the influential often try to hide their "ought" models behind a lot of complicated "is" models. People without access to computers have attempted the same trick of course, but such "manual" attempts are easier to see through. A computer can juggle complicated models in many differing ways and fill the arena with masses of data more blinding than all the old-fashioned ticker-tape parades ever held in New York. One of the ways by which we are misled more often than not is by obscuring a most important fact. All "is" models themselves contain significant "oughts." Any model is a human attempt to pick out certain features of the world as being for certain purposes descriptive of the world. There is no way to pick out certain features of the world as being descriptive of the world, even for specified purposes, without some degree of error and some amount of "ought" (1). The purposes for which our description of the world is to serve contain quite a few "oughts" and so do any resultant descriptions; in other words, that is the way the world ought to be if our descriptions are to be valid for those purposes.

In the days of only hand-wrought models, we all, more or less, had the same kind of hands with which to model and to poke holes in each other's models. We had a roughly equivalent means to point out the differing "oughts" maskerading as "is" models and used in the many on-going battles for "the minds of men and women." Things have changed with the advent of computers.

Not everyone has heard of the Club of Rome but almost everyone is talking about the problems of too much growth. The Club of Rome, that group limited to 100 of the world's self-declared top minds, has shown with its computers and models that growth inevitably now leads to disaster. The "world computer models contrived by Jay Forrester, Dennis Meadows, and their colleagues for the Club of Rome . . . (establish the) claims that the modern era of population and economic growth is about to be halted . . ." (2). These models come out with the results "that continued population and economic growth will lead to mass starvation, resource exhaustion . . . pollution to lethal levels . . . billions will die" (3).

When these "conclusions from the computer" were announced a few short years ago, it was claimed that the Forrester-Meadows models were run backward and forward, that every possible assumption was tried, every input attempted, and the result came out about the same: ecological and social disaster (4). And indeed, the notion that "growth must be limited" if not reversed has rather well captured the public's fancy. Even though "the computer models used by Forrester and Meadows have been run forward, backward, and sideways, *and each variant has revealed a new error*" (5).

To sense the "oughts" behind the computerized "is" models of the Club of Rome, to check the errors, and to raise alternate perspectives above the din, equivalent staff and access to equivalent computers becomes, today, a minimum requirement. It is possible though to make the attempt: "Recently a team of scholars at the University of Sussex demolished the world (Forrester-Meadows) model . . ." (6). In time, perhaps in time to prevent only a one-sided view from grossly affecting pertinent decisions concerning the questions related to economic and population growth, issues certainly of importance to each and all of us, the Club of Rome's computers can be balanced by those at the University of Sussex.* But not everyone today has access to computers equivalent in power to the Club of Rome's, or the University of Sussex', or General Motors', or the Central Intelligence Agency's, or the KGB's. Not everyone has access to a computer to help pierce through the "is"-models to sense the "oughts," the errors of fact, and the fictions. What opinions do you have today? What beliefs, what expectations and fears? Where did you get them? How can you test or check them against your own "oughts" and "is"-models relevant to your own concerns and your own world descriptions?

These are large questions—and we shall try to address them, at least in part, by describing the means and the methods by which access to computers can be broadened in a plausible fashion. But

---

* About the only thing that can be taken for granted with any of these so-called "world models," is that "billions will die." When you come to think of it, everyone alive now, and there appear to be billions of such folk, will die sooner or later. Such trivial conclusions too often are given most grave attention when issuing from the mouth of computers. Sadly, whether attended to or not, such trivia also often are the only valid conclusions to be found when toying with "world models."

first let us return to a supposedly simpler question: What ought to be the price of that barrel of oil?

4.2 A BARREL OF OIL

Given our thesis concerning models, we may never be able to obtain a final answer as to what a barrel of oil ought to cost. Yet we have observed that computers provide those who have access to them with some quite profound advantages. These advantages are not only those involved in being able to convince someone else that you know how much they ought to pay for a barrel of oil. Access to computers also can have the advantage of permitting us to see through any such claims as to what we should pay for that barrel of oil, to assess such claims, and to determine our own realistic estimates of such costs. We may obtain a better idea of what we ought to pay or, at least, what we are willing to pay. To provide us with such capabilities we shall need more than manual means to handle data and information. For the manipulations required will be many, and the data to be manipulated are often extensive and varied.

Once the appropriate data and factual information are in computer storage, we can have the computer process that data in many varied and pertinent ways. (We call attention to the assumption just made; it is not trivial, although sometimes so treated by computer salesmen. We are willing to assume that the required information is in computer storage in this case; the comparisons implied are to the situation where the same information is stored manually and is available only on a manual basis. The problems of data entry and the prior information analyses and descriptions required for meaningful later search have been raised in Chapters 2 and 3 and are treated at some length in later chapters.) To begin, we can have the computer inform us as to the cost of our barrel of oil at a wellhead, say, in Algeria. We could also look up the same information in manual fashion. However, with the computer we can formulate our question so as to furnish us with the cost of a barrel of oil at a wellhead at some location X, where X ranges over a stipulated or program defined list of places with oil wells. We can further limit or transform any such list of places to suit our interests: Middle East, North America, Southern Hemisphere, and so forth. Now the similarity between the capabilities of the computer and the best manual information center begins to vanish. Manually we would have to start, more or less, with one question at a time. For each X, say California, Texas, North Sea, Saudi Arabia, Iran, or Abu Dhabi the cost information would have to be both retrieved and collated manually. Such collation or grouping is only the beginning. We would want to put together such information about costs according to cost ranges, political factors, and sulphur content, to name just a few, other than simple geographic groupings. For example, we might wish to group our wellhead costs according to shipping distances from some place Y, where Y can range over many places too! And again this may be only the beginning of possibilities where access to computers makes the greatest difference. There is a whole series of questions concerning the costs of that barrel of oil delivered to some refinery Z (with Z varying if we wish) and then refined into products A, B, C . . . and so on. And so on in fact, until grouped and structured in comprehensible formats, the available answers to these questions begin to offer us a meaningful picture. The costs of that specified barrel of oil lying in the ground, at wellheads, on sea, in refineries, in distribution pipes, on delivery trucks, as certain products in stores or stations, begin to become meaningful to us and pertinent. Pertinent to what? To our specified and often special interests. And pertinent to our arriving, using also whatever are our powers of reason and imagination, at what we think the price of that barrel of oil has any right to be!

The needs for reason and imagination do not mute the point concerning computer capabilities. Reason and imagination remain necessary supplements to any computer process. However, without access to the computer, we would not have very much to which to apply our powers of reason and imagination. Without information

on which to ponder, reason and imagination are notorious for spin-
ning quite vociferously as in a vacuum and getting nowhere at all
except overexcited.

The cost of that barrel of oil only concerns us when the costs of
the products derived begin to bother us. There is a very long list of
such questions that do not trouble us until we begin to be bothered
by their effects. There is hardly any way of preparing purely
manual systems to accommodate our sudden and specialized
concerns.

4.3   A QUESTION ABOUT A LIGHTBULB

Consider the clever, but small manufacturer of some ordinary
household object such as a light bulb. Until just a few minutes ago
this manufacturer was quite content with his share of the light bulb
market. He had an efficient production plant and a good marketing
staff. But now the manufacturer has just been confronted by one of
his better and brighter employees. A new way of making better
light bulbs has been proposed. Because this manufacturer is clever,
his employee's novel suggestion does not make the manufacturer as
happy as one might have supposed. Up to this point his factory had
been doing fine supplying light bulbs for its share of the market.
Our manufacturer would have liked things to remain that way; now
changes are threatened as suddenly everything is different. The
manufacturer is in serious trouble. He has to make an extremely
complicated decision. The new way of making better light bulbs
could turn the small manufacturer into a big one. It could just as
easily put him right out of business. A simple negative decision will
not do because better and brighter employees have the disturbing
habit of going elsewhere to peddle their too quickly rejected ideas.
And it could turn out that the customers for light bulbs might like
the better light bulb so much that only the new light bulbs would be
on the market in a few years. A simple positive decision will not do
either, as that better light bulb might just not suit the public's fancy

or pocketbook, and the factory that produces them may find itself smothered in unsold products.

Our small manufacturer may pride himself on his imagination and reason, on his ability to make tough decisions "by the seat of his pants." But the fact is that our small manufacturer has had to make tough decisions by guess and gamble because he has never been able to afford the supporting staff and computer systems used daily be General Electric or Allgemeine Elektricitäts-Gesellschaft (AEG)! The varied production change simulations, product analyses, cost estimates for new ways of fabrication, costs of new alloys required, and increased energy costs as a function of the new processes per 20,000, 50,000, 200,000, or 2,000,000 units are beyond his reach. Not to mention the market surveys and analyses of customer preference data as related to costs, light bulb changing requirements, or electricity used per available wattage. His ability to evaluate marketing plans and sales campaigns and to develop such plans in the first place are meager. The small manufacturer can have recourse to the purchase of computerized search services generally available. For more or less standard informational needs, such services supply more or less adequate information. However, an intensive batch of informational searches plus the processing involved in complicated model building and simulations for planning purposes will prove extremely expensive if obtainable at all. On occasion, and depending on luck and simplicity of problem, the small manufacturer of light bulbs can seek such outside computer and staff services. But he does have to be lucky because he may not know how far off his case may be from the "normal," and the outside centers may not be able or willing to tell him. Following such "guidance" based on "normal" cases could be and has been disastrous. Such "disasters" have happened to the giants, even with the staffs and computers they could afford. A sad but well-known case in point was the Ford "Edsel" of shortlived fame. But the giants occasionally can afford a few such disasters. They have enough staff and computers to avoid disasters enough of the time. That is why no matter how good such "seat of the pants" small manufacturers may be, over time they stay small and smaller. And the GE's and AEG's stay larger and larger and larger.*

4.4 INDUSTRY'S COMPUTERS

Many of the giants are reluctant to say very much about their usage of computers. Xerox Corporation is not a small manufacturer. On being queried as to their use of computers for market or product planning, the answer turned out to be that such matters were highly sensitive and company confidential. Xerox Corporation is going to stay larger. So are 107 major American corporations in 10 industry groups plus 11 state and local governmental bodies from which data has been obtained.

Diebold Europe S.A. with their Management Implication Series has gathered a great deal of useful information on major industrial usage of automated data processing systems. Over a period of 3 years, data from the 107 largest American industrial and manufacturing corporations and 11 city and state governmental entities has been put together in a comprehensive report, "Expenditure Patterns for Management Information Systems—II" (7). These corporate organizations were grouped according to ten industrial kinds: Aerospace and Electronics, Utilities, Automotive Products and Industrial Equipment, Leisure and Education, Petrochemicals, Consumer Products, Metals, Building Materials and Forest Products, Transportation, and Information Processing (8).

The typical corporation among the ten industries spent an average on data processing of

1973—$11.8 million
1971—$10.6 million (9)

. . . the average budget for 1974 (was) $14.2 million (10).

---

* For this example, we have not opened Pandora's Box of patent problems, another worry for small manufacturers with bright employees (see CAIR, Chapter 4.2).

We saw an increase in such expenditures between 1971 and 1973, discounting an assumed 8% inflation rate, of about 3½%. The percentage increase is itself increasing. If the 1974 expenditures were realized, "data processing costs will have increased by an average of 20 percent over 1973 . . ." (11). Again discounting for inflation, we have about an 11% increase between 1973 and 1974. Economic conditions during the current "downturn" may have slowed this increase; however, it is safe to expect an overall upward trend to continue even if the growth rate fluctuates from time to time. The Diebold report actually suggests a recent leveling off of expenditures for data processing with recent increases just about keeping up with the rate of inflation as determined by " . . . the percent of ADP allocations in relation to corporate revenues . . ." (12). In any event, we note that the average major corporation is spending over $10,000,000 annually for data processing and that the dollar amount is rising each year. Despite short term downturns, starting around 1970, each major corporation could well have spent over $200,000,000 on internal data processing applications by 1990. Some conglomerates have probably exceeded that 1990 total expenditure already.

A direct spot check in Germany confirmed these Diebold average figures. For the major German corporations in the electronics/power industry group, Allgemeine Elektricitäts-Gesellschaft (AEG)-Telefunken, Brown, Bovery & Co. (BBC), and Siemens AG, private sources indicated that approximately .3% of research and development expenditures are allocated per year to scientific and technical documentation systems. In 1974, for example, Siemens AG spent approximately 1500 million DM on research and development (13). This corresponds to the industry average research and development expenditures, which run about 10% of sales per year. In any event, using .3% of research and development expenditures, 1974 expenditures for scientific and technical documentation systems would have been approximately 4.5 million DM ($1.8 million). Considering the fact that ADP applications to scientific and technological documentation systems per se constitute a relatively small part of the entire corporate ADP budget, the Diebold $10 million average per year spent on ADP would seem conservative. As a rough guess, combining documentation applications with management information and decision-making applications, one could assume that roughly 50% of the $10 million Diebold average ADP expenditure figure currently is allocated to the kinds of information retrieval systems with which we are concerned. This would give us approximately $5 million per year expended on information retrieval applications by major corporations as a *conservative* estimate. We shall return to the Diebold Report and the big industry groups in Section 4.7, pp. 100–103.

4.5 COMPUTER POLITICS—INFORMING THE CANDIDATES

Incumbents and candidates for public office have increasingly turned to computers for the production of various voter and issue analyses during election campaigns. In his first campaign against Mayor Samuel Yorty of Los Angeles, Thomas Bradley had the support of some capable computer programmers with access to computer time. In 1969 with memories of the Watts riots still alive and with a predominantly white population, Mr. Bradley, a black, came close to defeating the incumbent. Mayor Yorty had proven himself to be a skilled campaigner at least within the Los Angeles City limits. He had been capable of manipulating such issues as the regulations for garbage collection into continued popularity and incumbency. In many senses Mayor Yorty was a good, old-fashioned campaigner and did not much concern himself with modern techniques. Mr. Bradley on the other hand, continued to turn to computers and those skilled programmers who supported him. In 1973 Los Angeles had a new mayor, Thomas Bradley.

Some of the skilled programmers who had supported Mayor Bradley were inclined to lend their talents and computers to the Democratic candidate for governor in California in 1974.

California now has a new Democratic governor, Governor Edmund G. Brown, Jr., a young man with talent, drive, and computer support. Governor Brown might well become a Presidential candidate in the near future.

These two California examples represent only a small number of the candidates and incumbents, Democratic, Republican, Independent, or "Third Party," who found computers to be essential apparatus for election campaigns. Californian examples are particularly apt as California is a microcosm of the United States and often now presents a picture of the way the rest of the country is going to "look" within a few years. California's population mix, even while changing, does in fact represent the United States as a whole, if not the world. There are Buddhists, Catholics, Jews, Protestants of every variety, Mormons, Moslems, Seventh Day Adventists mixed with non- and unbelievers, and representations of every sect or "persuasion," including Scientologists, Astrologists, sun worshippers, desert mystics, and the major psychiatric tongs. Such people do not all live, think, or vote alike. Neither do the "colonies" of blacks, browns, Southerners, Northerners, Midwesterners, Russians, Swedes, Italians, Hungarians, Frenchmen, Japanese, Chinese, and so forth, found living quite actively and voting in California. There also are all economic classes, from the very very rich to the transient poor.

There is no claim here that election victories are obtained solely by those who have access to computers. It does seem, however, to be working out that way. Not all candidates have supporters with access to computers. Nor do all candidates have the funds to buy the expensive staff needed and the computer time necessary to plan and conduct effective campaigns for today's and tomorrow's elections. Complex population mixes, complex issues, complex fears and wishes about complex worlds have to be confronted and understood. The news media have the power to distort, magnify, or perhaps worse for politicians, ignore. Candidates have to know how to handle such attention-getting prisms in order to be "seen" and make news. Issues and positions have to be carefully selected or

manufactured often merely to be displayed. Just to obtain meaning-
fully clear pictures of the temporal slices of fluctuating realities
during an election campaign necessitates the collection of masses
and masses of data. Demographic data, economic data, past voting
records of important neighborhoods or voter groups, preference
ratings, opinion samples on the relevant issues (or those thought to
be relevant), indicators of concerns, worries, fears, wishes, and all
the rest have to be processed and determined—often at frequent
intervals. Effective presentations of candidates' views, responses,
stance, and reactions have to be manufactured and pretested via
feedback of responses from "sample" voter groups—again often at
frequent intervals. Computers and the associated supporting staffs
have become increasingly vital elements of contemporary election
campaigns. Getting and staying elected inevitably are becoming
much more difficult for politicians without access to computers
and a staff who can use the computers well and wisely. A candidate
may not always win with such access and support, but it is a new
fact of political life that candidates usually lose without such
access.

4.6 COMPUTER POLITICS—INFORMING
THE ELECTORATES

Election campaigns may be getting increasingly difficult for candidates but these same campaigns are becoming ridiculously impossible for the voters. Fewer voters than candidates have access to
computers and expensive supporting staffs; certainly the average
voter does not, and he is most of us. Most of us simply are being
increasingly manipulated by those who can control our access to
information and can shape the information to which we have
access.

We have seen how some with access to computers can shape our
thinking and opinions on such all-embracing matters as economic
and population growth. Our current economic situation pinches

some and hurts many; it may even kill or starve more. That is one way to cut population growth. When we accept such strangulation as necessary and accept living with it ourselves, we may think we are better off than those who will starve. But do we really have any reasonably solid knowledge as to why we accept as fact that any such limits to economic or population growth are necessary? Do we have reliable information as to the consequences to ourselves and others of so accepting such notions as facts?

Economic and population growth limits are not the only matters of concern and broad impact for which our opinions are received at best. Every voter, everyone in fact has something at stake concerning decisions about pollution and the ecology, energy, buying barrels of oil and even, as we have seen, making better light bulbs. Consider, for example, the issues of war and peace, international tranquillity, and foreign policy. According to Walter Laqueur: "At a moment when the American (mass) media are more powerful than ever . . . , news coverage and . . . comment . . . are worse than in past decades" (14).

Walter Laqueur is referring to our currently accepted shibboleths and disorientation concerning foreign policy, defense policy, and world affairs: "As suddenly as a 'major story' breaks, it disappears. . . . (Readers or viewers are not permitted) to understand why an important event occurred and what happened once the shooting was over. The American media, even the best among them, are insufficient as a source of information on world affairs" (15).

Laqueur then offers a list of items that have occurred while the mass media were focusing the "informed public's" minds on other matters. For example, "Swinging London" was featured at the time when the current economic crisis in Great Britain could have been clearly depicted, the general rejoicing accompanying the Portuguese 1974 revolution was emphasized but its subsequent dangers not noticed, the veneer of West European prosperity and stability, particularly in West Germany and France, were well-touted but the malaise beneath ignored, the moods and idiosyncrasies of Secretary of State Kissinger have been documented while substantive matters of American foreign policy were ignored (16).

For our purposes it is of little concern whether we agree or disagree with the opinions or analyses of Walter Laqueur as to foreign policy and international affairs. What is important is that the point we made earlier concerning the necessity for solid information on which to exercise our powers of imagination and reason is reemphasized by Laqueur: "... the analysis and interpretation of events cannot rely on intuition but have to be grounded in a solid factual basis, debates over foreign policy and defense are frequently exercises in ignorance" (17).

And, we would add, so are debates on the price of barrels of oil, the desirability of better light bulbs, economic and population growth, and debates during election campaigns. We would further agree with Walter Laqueur that the fault is not to be laid entirely at the doors of the mass media. Nor have we any right to place the blame on the uninformed, poorly informed, or misinformed public. When becoming better informed simply is too time-consuming, too expensive, too laborious, and practically impossible given our current means and methods of obtaining access to information, we need not look elsewhere to find the real sources of the problem.

4.7   THE COSTS OF ASKING QUESTIONS AND GETTING ANSWERS

We have found that a single average search through automated files for information costs about $30, for the computer search alone. For example, rates per contract hour of computer search range from about $25 for the Exceptional Children's Abstract File, $50 for Psychological Abstracts, $90 for Chemical and Electronics Market Abstracts, to $150 for search through American Chemical Patents using the Lockheed DIALOG system, which is discussed in more detail in Chapter 3 (18). Such costs are typical for what we have called conventional automated information retrieval systems. For example, the INSPEC (Institute of Electrical Engineers' system, London, England) computer search costs are £20 (about $45) per search with additional costs for printouts that go beyond 30 items and with the right reserved to negotiate higher prices for exceptional cases (19). The time for an average computer search per search request typically runs about one-half hour. Yet the cost of the computer search time per se usually is only the beginning. The search result output consists of document citations and sometimes document abstracts. The documents cited somehow have to be obtained. Once obtained these documents have to be checked for relevancy, that is, filtered to determine whether the information desired is likely to be contained within the document. At this point one may have to reformulate the search request if too little relevance is found, a frequent occurrence. Then the information one is looking for has to be found wherever it may be located within the relevant documents. Here again search request reformulation may be required. The information obtained from the various documents then has to be arranged into a coherent "answer" to the search request. Very often a far from complete "answer" results. There usually are documents in the files, but not cited in the previous search results, that could have provided the missing information. Often this missing information is as vital as that found. In such cases, a new search request must again be formulated. Even if we have not added up the costs of the additional computer search found necessary to satisfy the reformulations of our basic search request (about $30 minimum per search question reformulation run), somebody has to do and be paid for all the manual work. The computer output itself will not help matters much without the staff, and very expensive staff, to accomplish the follow-up manual tasks just delineated.

There seems to be a partial counter-argument to the above analysis. It has been called the Cleverdon argument and states that a 25% document recall ratio (the percentage of documents cited as a ratio of all the *relevant* documents in the files that should have been cited ideally) is often equivalent to 100% recall of the information needed (20).

This argument has a certain delicious plausibility. It is based on the observation that given the poorly structured status of conventional automated information retrieval files, and possibly under any conditions, much redundant information exists in the files. We shall set aside the problem of defining redundancy in meaningful pragmatic terms. We simply note that there are all kinds of redundancy, some highly useful, some not, and that information redundant to one person may be necessary to another. And we shall agree that there may be several or even many cases where recall of 25% of the relevant documents in the files satisfying a given search request may be sufficient to satisfy the search request. Which of the many possible 25%'s? Nobody knows in advance, nor often afterward! For each computer run in satisfaction of a search request, do we always or even predictably get the right 25%? We certainly do not! Search question formulation notoriously is far from a standardized affair. It should be obvious that for almost any search request there are many document sets representing 25% recall that certainly will not satisfy the search request; some indeed can be extremely misleading and result in utterly outrageous decisions based on partial information. Do we know how to avoid obtaining these bad 25%'s? We do not. The argument attributed to Cleverdon turns out to be a "backhanded" admission that conventional automated information retrieval systems have poor recall ratios with regard to their search results. Such systems also have poor relevancy ratios. One of the nastier filtering tasks is to get rid of the irrelevant citations that can often outnumber the relevant ones. We shall see that there is no need to live with either conventional systems or any sophisticated apology for them.

There are other costs involved as well. The costs already cited assume that the indexing and analysis of documents in preparation for their input into computerized files, and the input itself, are covered. This is true only in part. It is valid for searches conducted by outside centers through documents such centers have previously prepared for computer entry. Such analysis and preparation costs are also covered by the costs of searches through computerized files constructed from computer tapes supplied by such external centers wherever such searches may occur. However, should anyone, for many good reasons, not wish to be dependent on such external source indexed, prepared, and computer entered documents as the sole source of automated information, other serious costs are involved. The computer files have to be developed and built, the documents indexed, analyzed, and entered. Conventional systems, as we have previously observed, provide no significant computer support for these processes. As a result, the manual effort is incredibly expensive and time-consuming and at times beyond the reach of even well-funded governmental or private institutions.

Yet we have pointed out that meaningful access to information cannot solely depend on information structured for us by others. Even with source supplied preindexed documents, we shall need to restructure the information there contained by reindexing these documents to suit our own informational requirements. We intend to show that this can be done, both well and feasibly, and that we can at the same time build up our own user-unique files. However, we shall not find the means and methods to accomplish these tasks among the offerings of the conventional automated information retrieval systems. Public access to such conventional automated information retrieval systems or offering access to that part of the public that can afford the costs of computer search per se is not going to do very much good. The number of search requests is large. Some may be able to afford the costs of the computer searches. Fewer will be able to afford the costs of staff or time to analyze, filter, compare, and put together in meaningful terms the information we need—however much we need it.

We have emphasized the needs for supporting staff to accomplish all the many analytic, filtering, and indexing tasks. We have indicated that such staff work is costly, far more costly than the costs of computer search alone. For data processing systems in general, such supporting staff personnel costs appear to equal or slightly exceed the costs of hardware and basic software combined. For the major corporations covered by the Diebold Report, expenditures for the required supporting staff exceed and continue to exceed the expenditures for hardware. For all the 10 industry groups expenditures for data processing in 1973 were as follows:

Hardware	34.7%	
Computer operating personnel	27.7%	
Systems personnel	24.5%	
Supplies	7.9%	
External services	5.2%	(21)

These figures present little change from a similar breakdown for 1971. They mean that for every dollar spent on computer hardware, the industry group on the average spent more than one dollar on supporting staff.

These supporting staff costs are particularly enlightening when one considers that the great bulk of data processing applications to date have been intended to reduce personnel and staff requirements. The major allocation of corporate data processing funds have been applied to administrative data flow operations. These generally involve batch processing operations and handle relatively well-defined data in standard ways. The requirements for the kinds of staff support needed with conventional information retrieval systems are far less when payroll, accounting, and other administrative functions are handled via batch processing systems. Yet rather high staff support costs relative to hardware costs were found even when the data processing applications were mostly for such administrative data flow functions. Broken down according to corporate functions, data processing applications were as follows:

	1973	1971
Financial and administrative	34.8%	30.7%
Personnel	4.2%	4.4%
Total essentially administrative:	39%	35.1%

Corporate planning	2.9%	2.8%
Marketing	15.1%	12.4%
Research, development and engineering	6.6%	9.2%

Total of mostly information retrieval or management information functions	24.6%	24.4%	(22)

As "marketing" constitutes the largest ingredient in this second group, one should note that a significant portion of marketing application could well be inventory control and ordering systems with characteristics similar to batch processing/administrative data flow applications (23). The same holds true for two further functions, where much of what is going on is likely to be process control and/or inventory control, both data processing operations typically intended to reduce staff:

	1973	1971
Distribution	8.2%	10.1%
Manufacturing	24.1%	26.6%

Likely inventory or process control operations total:	32.3%	36.7%	(24)

(We have restructured the data given in the tables above from the Diebold Report according to our own grouping concept. Our subtotals do not add up to 100% as "Other," 4.1% for 1973 and 3.8% for 1971, was omitted.)

Yet even with the emphasis on administrative data flow and process or inventory control systems, supporting staff requirements and costs are surprisingly high. Much larger staff support requirements and costs can be expected for information retrieval systems based on conventional information retrieval software.

We shall select two of the ten industry groups studied by Diebold for further enlightenment concerning the staff support requirements. For the Automotive and Industrial Equipment Group, as well as for the very different Building Materials and Forest Products Group, computer operators and programmers constitute less than 50% of the supporting staffs. Systems analysts and programmers are 29.3%, computer operators are 18.1% for the Automotive and Industrial Equipment Industry Group. Other personnel are classified as 36.4% noncomputer operators, 15.4% management, and .8% other (25). For the Building Materials and Forest Products Group there are only 12.7% computer operators and 21.7% system analysts and programmers, whereas noncomputer operators are put at 50.2%, management at 10.4%, with other at 5% (26). It is precisely this part of the supporting staff, the noncomputer operators and personnel, that will be required to accomplish the tasks we have previously described as necessary for information retrieval applications. And it is precisely to these tasks that the newer software discussed in later chapters must be addressed if we are ever going to provide meaningful access to information retrieval systems, and more equitable, broader access to automated information retrieval systems within our societies.

The Diebold Report offers us some information as to governmental expenditures on data processing. Though less per year than the industrial groups, the 11 state and local governments covered spent an average of about $8.5 million in 1973 or a total of a little over $94 million (27). Although this might imply that there is a rough equivalence in data processing power between some governmental bodies and some corporations, it doesn't help the public per se very much. If we could assume that such state and local governments were spending that data processing money for us as citizens, each of us would come out with about $3.70 worth of data processing per year. (28) This assumption is no more laughable than the presumed benefit to the citizenry. At this rate each citizen would have the funds for the computer search only for one search request every eight years ($3.70 × 8 = $29.60, or approximately the cost of computer search time per average search request).

How much the citizen might profit from such largesse is obvious enough; but according to the Diebold Report, there seems to be a relationship between profits and allocation of industrial resources on data processing: ". . . the more profitable companies seem to have allocated a larger portion of their available resources to ADP than the less profitable ones" (29). This relationship while "tenuous," has an even more interesting corollary: "A similar pattern is evident with respect to ADP staff. The higher the rate of profitability, the greater the percent of total work force devoted to ADP . . ." (30).

We have tried to indicate by recourse to various "this world" examples the relative status of individual citizens with regard to having access to data processing support. Our $3.70 per year compared to over $10,000,000 and more per year for big industry and big government is not an understatement of the actual relationship. The legitimate needs for most of us to have meaningful access to information have not and are not being equitably satisfied. The next chapter may indicate that we have only a limited amount of time left to begin to meet the general public's requirements for information through providing enough of us with access to appropriate automated systems. Later chapters provide a definitive description of what are the essential characteristics of such appropriate automated information retrieval systems. The description includes a detailed presentation and discussion of the required second generation software—what it is, how to achieve it and how to use it to achieve more equitable public access to the resultant systems. We intend to show as clearly as we can that the satisfaction of the public's needs for access can be accomplished. Accomplished within the time span, the technical, organizational, and human capabilities, and the funds that we do have available.

NOTES

1. See "Science and the Citizen," *Scientific American,* Vol. 233, No. 3, September 1975, p. 54. In discussing a report of a study group appointed by the American Physical Society concerning the safety of nuclear reactors, Scientific American under their "Science and the Citizen" Section observes this same feature of

models even when applied to purely physical phenomena: "Recognizing the impossibility of accurately modeling all the physical variables in three dimensions (which says the report, "would instantly exhaust the potential of the largest computer"), the code devisors have sought to err on the side of conservatism in their drastic simplifications." However complicated nuclear reactors and their mechanical safety devices may be, they are simplicity itself compared to what such "world models" as we are discussing are supposed to represent.

2. B. Bruce-Briggs, "Against the Neo-Malthusians," *Commentary,* Vol. 58, No. 1, July 1974, pp. 25–29.

3. Ibid., p. 25.

4. D. H. Meadows, *Limits to Growth: A Report for the Club of Rome's Project on the Predicament of Mankind,* Universe, New York, 1972.

5. Bruce-Briggs, "Neo-Malthusians," p. 25, italics added.

6. Ibid.

7. "Expenditure Patterns for Management Information Systems—II," Document No. E131S, Management Implications Series, The Diebold Research Program—Europe, Diebold Europe S.A., Frankfurt/Main, West Germany, 1974, pp. 1 and 2 of Abstract. Much useful information is also contained in "Investment in Management Information Systems—Research Survey," Document No. E117S, Management Implications Series, The Diebold Research Program—Europe, Diebold Europe S.A., Frankfurt/Main, West Germany, October 1973; but we choose to cite from the more recent report indicated.

8. Ibid., p. 7.

9. Ibid., p. 5.

10. Ibid., p. 5.

11. Ibid., p. 6.

12. Ibid., p. 8.

13. Siemens AG, "Siemens aktuell '75."

14. Walter Laqueur, "The West in Retreat," *Commentary,* Vol. 60, No. 2, August 1975, p. 49.

15. Ibid., p. 50.

16. Ibid., p. 50.

17. Ibid., p. 50.

18. Rainer Kuhlen, "On-Line Retrieval. Konsolidierung oder Stagnation," report about the Fifth Cranfield Conference Mechanised Information Storage and Retrieval Systems; 22–25 July 1975, Cranfield Institute of Technology, U.K.; Lehrinstitut für Dokumentation, 6 Frankfurt/Main, Westendstr. 19.

19. IEE INSPEC Literature Search Service, London, England, 1975.

20. Kuhlen, "On-Line Retrieval," p. 2.

21. Diebold Research Program Europe, "Expenditure Patterns . . . ," p. 13.

22. Ibid., p. 15.

23. For further discussion of the distinctions among administrative data flow, control, command, or management, and decision-making support systems, see Andrew E. Wessel, "Data Automation Development and Systems Implementation—Some Problems and Conclusions," P-3648, The RAND Corporation, Santa Monica, California, August 1967, pp. 2–7.

24. Diebold, "Expenditure Patterns . . . ," p. 15.

25. Ibid., p. 37.

26. Ibid., p. 47.

27. Ibid., p. 135.

28. Ibid., p. 136.

29. Ibid., p. 19.

30. Ibid., p. 19.

Figure 1   Original drawing by Marie Marcks, Heidelberg, 1976.

Figure 2   Original drawing by Marie Marcks, Heidelberg, 1976.

Chapter Five

Some Binary Digits Were Missing— A Contemporary Tale

If you can't make clear what you are trying to say to an intelligent child, then you'll have difficulty with me, and I would imagine, with yourself.

A sentiment I attribute to my father.

In a time and a place becoming all too familiar to most of us in our times and places, there was once a young man who wanted to become a knight of the realm. By this time and in this place, however, knights, dukes, princes, and even kings were no longer

---

Any persons finding any resemblances to other persons or recent events in the Federal Republic of Germany, the United States, France, the Soviet Union, the People's Republic of China, and many other places, should be thankful that Art only feebly imitates Life and vice versa.

born but rather made; such noble members of the realm were made, in fact, by such as you and I, as suited our fancies, desires, and fears.

The young man who wanted to be made a knight was not particularly tall nor short, thin nor fat, wise nor foolish. He was rather much like the rest of us with nothing, from the point of view of the heavens, particular at all to recommend him or to differentiate him from the knight already available where he lived; or any of the people thereabouts. Except ambition! And cleverness!

He was clever enough to think up a rather useful idea to get himself made a knight. As he had nothing very special to offer the people, he would make up and invent some very special things about the already made knight. These special things would be of just the sort to make the people thereabouts very uneasy and quite suspicious about the knight they had already made. And as the young man was rather good at sharing and spreading fears and prejudices, he was made a knight of the realm and the older knight was sent out to pasture by the people thereabouts.

In the beginning the young man made up and invented special things about his enemies all by himself. But now that he was made a knight of the realm, he attracted some friends who also liked to make up and invent things about the same enemies. And they worked together long hours and many days doing just that. The young man and his friends became so good at making up and inventing special things about their enemies and sharing their fears and prejudices with the people thereabouts that the young man was soon made a duke of the realm. As there were many fewer dukes than knights, being made a duke was a better and much more important thing to be made than a knight. So the young man was almost content, and his friends were almost content with him.

But the young man was particularly ambitious and clever. He now wanted to be made the prince-apparent, next in line to the king himself in that realm. When some of the young man's enemies found out about this, they began to say a few special things about the young man. But the young man and his friends were much better at doing that than his enemies, and they were better sharers and spreaders of fears and prejudices. So the young man, after some difficulties true enough, was made prince-apparent next in line to the king himself. He was the prince-apparent for so long a time that now the young man wanted to be made the king. He wanted this for a very long time. And finally, with the help of his growing number of friends and despite his growing number of enemies, he was made the king of the realm.

The young man wanted to stay king for quite a long time. So he and his friends continued to make up and invent special things about their enemies and to become even better in sharing and spreading fears and prejudices. He remained king in that time and place for quite a while. And he might well have stayed as king in that realm for ever and ever. Except that the young man was particularly ambitious and clever and not so young any more. So now he wanted to be made emperor.

There was a problem. In that time and place there weren't any emperors. The people just didn't think they needed an emperor so they had never made one.* The now not so young man and his friends thought about this problem for quite some time. For one thing the people every so often got restless and considered getting rid of their king by making a new one. Certainly if the now not so young man ever wanted to be made an emperor, he had to stay made a king. Even though just staying made as king wasn't good enough any longer for either his friends or himself. They all actually and easily could have kept this king made as king, for the alternative available at this time, although rather fanciful, produced a lot of fears, prejudices, and even despairs all by himself. All the king and his friends would have needed to do was to help a little perhaps. But the king and his friends were particularly ambi-

---

* There is a legend concerning a time in that place when troubles were many and fears and prejudices were so widespread that no one had to make up or invent any. And it is said that the king at that time was so good at sharing and spreading fancies and desires that the people almost made him an emperor. But this clearly did not happen, so the legend is obviously ridiculous.

tious and clever. They wanted what had never been done before; they wanted the king to be made the emperor. So they needed a new idea, a new way to convince the people thereabouts to make the king himself an emperor.

The king and his friends were the most powerful people in that time and place. They could get all sorts of help from all sorts of helpers. So they got themselves the most powerful computer then available. And as computers need information to work with, the king and his friends filled the computer with all the special things they could make up or invent about their enemies. As by this time they had gotten very good at making up and inventing things and had even more enemies than ever before; they certainly thought that they had put quite enough information in the powerful computer.

So they asked the computer: "How can the king be made emperor of this realm?"

"Insufficient data," answered the powerful computer.

So they all got together and made up or invented lots more special things and placed them all in the computer.

And again they asked the computer: "How can the king be made emperor of this realm?"

But unhappily for the king and his friends, this was an exceedingly difficult question, even for their powerful computer. The computer knew that never had there been an emperor in that realm, so it merely repeated: "Insufficient data."

And because the powerful computer was so very large and could store so much data, there were too many empty storage places for even the king and his friends to make up or invent special things to fill. For even though new lists of enemies were made and new special things to make up or invent about them, and even though all this was entered into the computer, the computer kept answering:

"Insufficient data, Insufficient data, Insufficient data, Insufficient data, Insufficient data, Insufficient data, Insufficient data, Insufficient data."

Clearly a new way of filling up the computer's banks was needed, rather than making up or inventing special things about the king's enemies. And as the king and his friends were ambitious and clever, one day they thought they found the answer.

Someone, whether it was the king himself or one of his closest friends may never be known, said: "If we can't make up or invent enough data about our enemies for that EXPLETIVE DELETED computer, let's steal it!"

And then someone else said: "Yeah, and let's steal it everyway we can, even electronically for we have to fill up an electronic computer."

And they all said: "Yeah."

And they tried.

Now the king and his friends were both ambitious and clever, but they were lousy thieves. They had been so used to making up or inventing things that they had little know-how about stealing real things in the real world. So they made quite a mess out of what became known as "Operation Missing Binary Digits." Even worse, they got caught.

The people thereabouts were quite used to their knights, dukes, prince-apparent, and their king making things up. They didn't really mind that sort of thing much at all. But although a certain amount of stealing went on in that time and place, one was not supposed to steal things after being made a knight, duke, prince-apparent, or the king himself. Such folk were thought by the people thereabouts to be well enough off as knights, dukes, prince-apparent, or the king himself, not to have to steal any more, no matter what they may have done before. So the people thereabouts got very angry, even those who were not the king's and his friends' enemies. And the people thereabouts got rid of that king and his friends and made themselves a new king.

It would be nice to think that after this everyone was happy again in that time and place. The new king didn't make too many things up and he didn't have too many enemies. He certainly didn't steal. But there remained a small uneasiness in the realm that was never fully understood. The people thereabouts had done nothing about that powerful computer. In fact, even more powerful computers were being built in that time and place. And somebody, someday, somehow might find out a way to fill up a powerful computer with enough data to get a correct answer from the computer about how to be made the emperor. Should that ever happen in that time and place, the people thereabouts might never again be able to make their knights, their dukes, their prince-apparent, and their king himself. For the emperor they might make certainly would never let them.

It would be a good idea for the people thereabouts to get computers for themselves so that some of the knights and dukes, and certainly the king himself, would not be the only ones to get such questions about making emperors answered. It might be a lot easier for the people thereabouts to get their own computers to tell them how not to make an emperor instead of trying to prevent the king and his friends from asking their computer how to accomplish things the people would not like. That is, this might be a good idea if the people thereabouts and everywhere else want to keep on making their own kings.

If this totally imaginary tale can be said to have significance, perhaps its meaning is:

Sometimes the only way to protect yourself from someone with a computer is to get one yourself.

The remainder of this book is intended to show those who may be interested just how to go about getting computers to help all of us keep on making our own kings behave.

Chapter Six

Second-Generation Computer Software for a Public Information Retrieval System

6.1 EXISTING SOFTWARE SYSTEMS

Although operational software and hardware have undergone rapid development toward real-time processing recently, functional software for dialogue information retrieval has remained within an essentially first-generation framework. IBM's STAIRS, Lockheed's RECON/DIALOG, Siemens' GOLEM, and the less well known-AEG/Telefunken's TELDOK are search only systems. They provide interactive dialogue functions permitting the formulation of search questions, and conduct the computerized search through their files. On-line, dialogue input, file changes, document indexing, and the interactive functions required for thesauri construction, test, and maintenance are not available.

Such first-generation, conventional, systems do handle extremely large numbers of documents. Furthermore, these systems have the capability to store very large numbers of documents in accordance with a much larger variety of user interests and viewpoints than is the case manually. But the capability to store documents according to multidimensional retrieval interests does not, in itself, provide anyone with the means to so describe the stored documents in the first place. Conventional systems can store documents for later retrieval only as well and to the extent that the documents have already been described. First-generation systems offer no help with these preliminary descriptive tasks.

User viewpoints and interests from the perspective of automated information retrieval must be organized to some extent. Even "free text or term" search involves the construction of partially controlled term or phrase lists. The methods by which the stored documents are described seriously affect the capabilities offered to formulate search and retrieval requests, and equally, determine the quality of the search results. Methods of document and content description cannot be chosen at random. They must reflect user interests and needs and function in a manner compatible with the users' actual capabilities in formulating search requests. The "translation" of user retrieval interests into the language of document and content description is the key problem confronting automated documentation and information retrieval systems (1).

Many steps toward the development of second-generation information retrieval and documentation software have already occurred. The Siemens PRIMAS system represents one, perhaps the first, such partial break through. On-line, dialogue indexing, document entry, and search have been successfully implemented within PRIMAS as a coherent software package (2). However, Siemens AG has, for reasons partly best known to itself, not offered PRIMAS to the general market. Quite the reverse, PRIMAS has been restricted to only a knowledgeable few external customers who have had to demand it. For one thing PRIMAS competes, and rather successfully, with another Siemens system, GOLEM. Far more resources, money, and manpower have been expended on GOLEM. And although major efforts to improve GOLEM have occurred over the years, and still go on, it remains a first-generation software system. As with the other conventional systems, the basic concepts and framework were developed at least 10 years ago. Improvements to such systems are attempted by attaching new functions as a "back-pack" to the existing framework. As indicated in CAIR, the result of such retrospective improvements has been increased system complexity (3). The conventional systems, GOLEM included, become more error-prone and no longer optimal. Many quite necessary, and now established as required, functions can no longer be added simply to such systems and often cannot be added at all.

The designers of such first-generation systems need not be faulted. To a significant degree the earlier system designers had to anticipate the needs and the potential behavior of their future users. At the same time the thrust of development was based on the rather general expectation that computers soon would be taught how to handle the problem of content description via fully automated textual analysis. Now acknowledged arguments that such expectations were indeed erroneous were then not much in fashion (4). More importantly perhaps, the newer thesauri structuring principles developed in conjunction with computer software were not yet available (5). The quite powerful aids to thesaurus development, to document content description and document indexing, and to search request formulation based on the combination of automated retrieval software and thesauri were only in their early experimental stages (6).

We are, however, in a far better position today than were the designers of the first-generation systems. Such systems have provided their users with data banks covering many informational fields and millions of documents. Analyses of such systems and the experiences of their users are available (7). Furthermore, the typical working processes and procedures (and those not so typical) occurring in libraries, documentation centers, archives, and industrial and governmental data collection centers are better understood now having been better studied. From both semiautomated and manual information retrieval experiences of the last decade, certain standard features and equally standard problems could be identified and the important unique aspects determined. The key problems involving those tasks of document and document content description became more and more universally understood and acknowledged.

The consequences of the failure of the first-generation systems to resolve these problems could be seen quite clearly in terms of the generally mediocre quality of the obtained search results:

... the yet unresolved problems preventing widespread use of automated retrieval systems involve just those tasks requiring extensive amounts and critical degrees of human endeavor ... the information available for retrieval must be well described. The accurate formulation of search requests depends upon the accurate and consistent description of the material to be searched. (8)

Yet it is not merely the experience of the past 10 years that permits a set of coherent, integrated functional requirements to be developed and understood. Better operational software permitting both multiuser, multidata base operations and on-line file changes, better hardware represented by the minicomputer developments offering contemporary computer capabilities at less cost, better thesauri structuring methods, all combined with our current understanding of information retrieval requirements to make possible the quantum jump from first- to second-generation software. We now know what the meaningful requirements are and what the interactive system functions should offer users. And we know how to satisfy these requirements and to implement the system functions. Second-generation software became feasible.

6.2 SECOND GENERATION GENERAL SYSTEM FUNCTIONS

We shall list and briefly describe five basic or general system functions that constitute the essential ingredients of second-generation information retrieval and documentation systems. These general functions are detailed and clarified in Section 6.3.

a. Search

The first such general function is search, both batch processing and on-line interactive, a function also provided by first-generation systems. This involves what is called retrospective search as well as selective dissemination according to established user profiles. The differences between first- and second-generation systems here are not so much in the basic search functions but in the far more powerful aids to search question formulation and reformulation to be expected with second-generation systems.

b. Document Entry

On-line document entry and acceptance of changes in and during such entry constitute the second general function supplementing the essentially batch processing modes found in first-generation systems for this function. All of the techniques offered by the newer thesauri structuring principles should abet this process. In particular, format fill-in possibilities and/or requirements should be suggested to users during document entry occurring on-line at input consoles.

c. Indexing

Computer-aided indexing combines the newer thesauri structuring principles with computer software to lead users, experienced or novice, through and to the varied means to describe documents and their contents available with second-generation information retrieval systems. By suggesting descriptors or descriptive phrases additional to those initially chosen by the indexer, offering fill-in formats and optional and/or mandatory indexing rules, indicating the indexing patterns of previous, highly skilled indexers or indexing committees, profound improvements in indexing quality, consistency, and completeness can be attained by "ordinary" indexers. Indexing speed is enhanced as well with indexing costs for comparable quality of indexing significantly reduced.

At the same time, second-generation systems accept documents previously or otherwise indexed by manual or automatic means. Computer-aided indexing is then available for improving the quality of such preindexed descriptions. It is available also to restructure and redescribe such preindexed material in accordance with new or differing interests and informational requirements.

d. Thesaurus Construction, Development, and Maintenance

The on-line, interactive capabilities available with the preceding general functions provide the methods to make changes to files, to suggest the appropriate inputs or changes, and to accept such changes in an on-line mode. These capabilities permit the direct development of thesauri: changing, qualifying, expanding, and refining their controlled term or phrase lists and thesauri rules, and thus supporting on-going thesauri maintenance. Furthermore, by providing almost immediate feedback from search and indexing tests, also conducted via on-line modes of interaction, thesauri development and construction can be tested at each and any of the user-determined check points for these processes (9).

e. Computer-Aided Self Instruction

Console instruction on request represents the last general function provided by second-generation systems. All of the specific system functions to be discussed—console operations and means to enter files, to explore thesauri, to determine document categories, to index, and to search—must be made accessible and "transparent" to users however inexperienced or knowledgeable. Such training programs are to be available to the lay individual as well as the experienced librarian or documentalist. At the same time, there should be no necessarily predetermined or preferred set of operations or sequence of specific systems functions. Each user group will work out such operational sequences as a function of their own needs, skills, and inclinations.

6.2.1   General System Characteristics

This last point brings us to three most desirable second-generation general system characteristics. We term these "Independency Requirements." They are:

a. Independence from specific documentation methodology,
b. Independence from specific user operations,
c. Independence from particular hardware constellations.

The second-generation software should consist of a coherent group of individual program functions. From these specific users or user groups and organizations should be able to choose their own perhaps unique integrated "packages" of individual functions. In this manner all (or at least most) of the varying "standard" documentation methodologies and operational procedures can be accommodated. The second-generation system features include and emphasize the newer thesauri structuring principles and the related computer-aids to indexing, search, and thesauri development. However, specific users can start with what they have. They then can proceed to incorporate any and all of the newer computer aids and thesauri principles to the extent that their own indexing and search and thesauri building needs indicate. Or to put this same point somewhat differently, such newer features can be incorporated within a given user's "operations" and documentation methodology as such users discover the great benefits deriving from such second-generation features. On-line search and indexing tests feasible with the second-generation systems will offer such users readily available and comprehensible data on which their choices can be based. User "intuitions," preferences, and existing practices can and should be accepted; they need not, however, remain as permanent limits to the obtainment of more meaningful information retrieval. Finally, there should be no software dependency on special hardware configurations. This is not to claim that hardware does not matter. Some kinds of hardware appear to offer greater advantages for information retrieval systems that can better serve the public than other kinds. But such advantages lie in other directions, however important, than the ability of standard hardware to accommodate second-generation software. In fact by choosing to go the minicomputer route, a fourth general system characteristic could be achieved. This would be: d. Independence from computer center maintenance and operating personnel.

The second-generation software having had the advantage of previous software developments, is based on a broader but simpler programming concept than the first-generation software, where each "improvement" added to the initial program complexity. When combined with minicomputers, second-generation software could come rather close to the achievement of a trouble-free "automat," offering its services on demand. Costs would likely be lower as well. The Defense Scientific Information Service of the Canadian Army reported in 1973 that computer costs were reduced by a factor of 5, using their own minicomputer documentation system instead of renting time on a large computer (IBM 360/65), as had previously been the case (10).

Present costs of a minicomputer amount to approximately $20,000 (DM 50,000.-). However, the overall hardware price essentially is determined by the cost of peripheral equipment, consoles, and disk stacks. It should be noted that the prices for minicomputers have gone down radically in the past 2 years. We can expect that prices for the costly large external disk storage will also decrease in the near future. To offer some idea of current costs, a basic hardware configuration module consisting of four consoles and storage space for 100,000 documents could now be purchased at less than $200,000 (DM 500,000.-) or rented for approximately

$7000 (DM 15,000.-) per month. However, second-generation software itself imposes no upper limit as to the total number of documents or consoles.

A private minicomputer documentation system offers the following advantages:

- Availability of the dialogue system around the clock,
- Gradual expansion of hardware and services as required,
- Minimum space requirements and no air conditioning facilities,
- No EDP operating personnel if second-generation software is used,
- Better data protection,
- And, obviously, no long-range communications costs.

Whether this fourth general system characteristic is achievable through the use of minicomputers will be partially determined in the next year or two by developments in the effective core storage capabilities of the minicomputers. This is not so much a matter of the ability to store millions and millions of documents and their associated descriptors as disk storage is available for this purpose. It is rather a question of whether the effective core within the minicomputer will be sufficiently large to permit the required loading of the interactive programs necessary to carry out second-generation system functions. The newly developed semiconductor memory may well resolve this problem of achieving effective core storage within the minicomputer. For example, Kevin Smith has indicated that the semiconductor memory has already penetrated the computer main-frame market (11). It is interesting to note that Smith believes "it is probably fair to say that 1975 will be remembered as the year . . . (that) the semiconductor devices will make their first entry at the high-performance end of the rotating memory market" (12).

In any event our second-generation information retrieval software is not dependent on the use of minicomputers, or indeed any specific hardware manufacturer's equipment. However the advantages just described warrant serious consideration of minicomputers. We return to this topic in Chapters 7 and 8, where an implementation plan is described.

6.3 SECOND GENERATION SPECIFIC SYSTEM FUNCTIONS

The specific system functions (see Table A following) described herein have not as yet been fully implemented in any one software package. The feasibility of such a software package has been determined recently by Kayser Threde & Co, Munich, West Germany (13). Certain of the key elements underlying these system functions have been programmed under a subcontract from the author under a contract from the Space Documentation Service (SDS-ESRIN), The European Space Agency (ESA, formerly ESRO) (14). These programmed elements constitute a special implementation of the concept of extensional relationships,

Table A   Specific System Functions

The system functions are listed here with the chapter subsection numbers for reference to their specific discussions.

6.3.1   DESCRIPTOR SELECTION
6.3.2   SEARCH REQUEST FORMULATION
6.3.2.1 DISPLAY OF SEARCH RESULT OUTPUT AND FEEDBACK
6.3.2.2 REFORMULATION OF SEARCH QUESTIONS
6.3.2.3 EXTENDED SEARCH
6.3.3   DOCUMENT INPUT
6.3.3.1 ASSIGNMENT OF DESCRIPTOR TERMS
6.3.3.2 DESCRIPTOR QUALIFIERS AND QUANTIFIERS
6.3.3.3 DESCRIPTOR CHANGES
6.3.4   THESAURUS CONSTRUCTION AND MAINTENANCE
6.3.5   DOCUMENT MAINTENANCE
6.3.6   FURTHER UTILIZATION OF ENTRIES

described in Chapter 2. As of the Summer of 1975, these programs have been checked for internal consistency and errors on an IBM 370/158-OS. By the end of 1976 operational tests will have been completed at ESRIN (Frascati) on their IBM 360/50 using recent NASA Abstract Tapes. A version of the full software package, "IDS—Dialogue Data Bank System" could be completed in about 2 years, given appropriate funding (15). The reality of our concept of second-generation software and the feasibility of its implementation in the short-term future independently have been established.

6.3.1 Descriptor Selection (Indexing and Search)

Descriptor selection may begin in quite a primitive fashion. When selecting a descriptor for indexing or for search, users normally approach documentation systems with certain concepts in mind. At the same time, specific expressions or verbal forms reflecting these mental concepts are part of the natural vocabularies of users. With second-generation software, users simply can enter these natural verbal forms or expressions, whatever they may be, by keyboard entry at the console. If the natural form or expression corresponds with a system-accepted descriptor, this would be indicated by the computer display. However, as may happen often, when no system-accepted descriptor corresponds to the natural expression, descriptors and descriptor synonyms from the immediate alphabatical neighborhood of the initially entered expression or verbal form are displayed on the computer console. In this manner the computer attempts to guide users toward the system-acceptable descriptors. The same kind of system guidance occurs in response to only the first few letters of the natural language term or phrase (truncation).* This technique has two objectives. One is to reduce the amount of keyboard entry necessary. The second is to offer guidance toward system accepted descriptors, even if the natural

---

* See Section 6.4 for more detail concerning the technical characteristics identified within parentheses here and throughout this discussion.

expression is uncertain, or if only the initial letters of the spelling are correctly known.

In addition to the display of system-accepted descriptors, the number of their current document assignments throughout the files are given. If lower-level terms associated with these descriptors exist, their number is also given in association with each system-accepted descriptor displayed. Singular and plural forms, derivations, and compounds with the same beginning as the initially-entered expression are indicated, as well as the number of documents available as potential search results.

If users are interested in a lower-level term or any other displayed associated descriptor, all that need be done is to mark that term using the console cursor. The next visual display indicates the marked descriptor and all the associated references to its lower-level terms or other related descriptors. If more than one descriptor is marked, the computer stores the commands and processes them successively.

The user can be offered further guidance by the computer in descriptor selection if a systematic thesaurus is available. A visual display of the higher-level thesaurus descriptors can be requested. The user decides which of the descriptors comes closest to his interests and, on marking the descriptor desired, obtains the more detailed descriptors covered by the higher-level term chosen. In this manner the computer can lead users to the most relevant term available in the particular thesaurus.

The thesaurus may be monohierarchically or polyhierarchically structured. Second-generation software is capable of displaying any thesaurus including graphical structures, such as term fields, multi-lingual thesauri, classifications, faceting, and mixed structures. Other pertinent thesauri structuring information is made available to users in simplified forms. With each descriptor, relevant thesauri rules and associations can be listed, including related descriptors, descriptor qualifiers, and fill-in formats. On request the user may have additional thesauri information relevant to a descriptor displayed. This may include thesauri definitions, interpretive or applicative rules, explications or explanations, and so forth. Here, too, users need merely enter such requests by marking the descriptor with the cursor and entering the appropriate command. These various forms of explanatory information associated with descriptors, storable in the descriptor textual fields, may also include negative relations rejecting the assignment of descriptors under certain conditions. For example, the assignment of a descriptor may be dependent on whether or not the user has requested the applicative or interpretive rules relevant to that descriptor.

The availability and utility of such functions just described involves thesauri, and second-generation software is also capable of handling several differing thesauri in parallel. For example, search terms of the same category, such as authors, product names, patent numbers, document producers, or publishers found in differing thesauri can be treated collectively.

Independent of thesauri per se, all the aids for obtaining more useful and relevant descriptors based on the concept of extensional relationships (see Chapter 2) are available on-line with second-generation software. Furthermore, the existence of a thesaurus is not a prerequisite to the initial use of second-generation software. Those users without thesauri can begin to use second-generation software for indexing and search immediately. Additionally, second-generation software can aid such users in the development of their own unique thesauri as users see fit and wish to take advantage of better descriptor structuring principles and techniques.

6.3.2 Search Request Formulation

We assume a descriptor has been selected by one of the procedures described in Section 6.3.1. To use the descriptor for search, it must be entered with the appropriate command, marking the descriptor using the console cursor or by keyboard entry. A group of several descriptors can be accepted in a search question by one such entry.

Such descriptors are normally linked by the logical "OR" if the group can be described by appropriate criteria. For example, a descriptor with all its lower level descriptors, or all terms beginning with the same sequence of letters, can be accepted using one command (automatic grouping).

A display of the search question can be requested. All the accepted descriptors and descriptor groups in the search question are thereby displayed with their specified logical connections. Their connecting logic is determined by an equation using the Boolean operators and parenthetical bracketing. Moreover, conditions such as "larger," "smaller," "equal," and "from-to," referring to descriptor qualifiers or quantifiers, can be entered.

Search questions can be stored. Such stored search questions can be used for selective dissemination services or, more uniquely, to better satisfy at some later date an incompletely satisfied search request. Second-generation software provides the capability of retrieving such stored search questions by treating them as documents satisfying normal search questions. Thus, in effect, a previous search question can be treated as a single quasi-descriptor in a new search question. This is a powerful new technique that can offer current searchers the results obtained by previous searchers.

6.3.2.1 Display of Search Result Output and Feedback

After entering a search command, the number of documents retrieved is displayed. Then a list of the individual documents (or document citations) or sections can be requested. Depending on the size of the search result, limits can be imposed on the output. For example, only specified document sections (titles, abstracts, etc.) can be indicated for display on console for later paging through a sequence of visual displays. The output display can be halted at one document and a look at its contents be requested before further paging of the previously specified sections. Documents considered irrelevant in this process may be excluded from the search result.

The documents found as the search result are usually displayed in the reverse order of their entry. Thus the most recent document, having been entered last, will be displayed first. However, the order of the documents can be changed by alphanumeric sorting; the user taking the option to indicate by which document parts (author, document identification, etc.) the sorting is to be done.

Search question and search result can be preserved as hard copy by requesting a printout.

6.3.2.2 *Reformulation of Search Questions*   If a search question does not produce the desired result, it can be modified by reformulating individual parts rather than reformulating the entire search question. The associated lower-level or upper-level terms of a descriptor can be added. Descriptor qualifiers can be suggested for consideration. Furthermore, descriptors can be deleted or introduced in the search question based on textual elements of documents displayed. As the other descriptors associated with the retrieved documents (those not part of the original search question) can be displayed, selection from among these can further refine or expand the search question.

Significant aids to the user are offered by suggesting descriptors to further narrow down the result (see TELDOK and PRIMAS). Descriptors occurring in the retrieved documents and not contained in the search question are suggested to the user according to their associative frequency, their extensional relationships, or according to thesauri rules, if existent.

When a search question has to be expanded it is often inconvenient to obtain documents in the new search result that have already been included in the previous search result. Users have the option to exclude such repeated documents from the result of a new search question. However, all relevant documents will be preserved during the later searches and printed out or presented at the console on request.

6.3.2.3 *Extended Search*   The possibilities previously described apply only to system-accepted descriptors. In terms of the data files such descriptors are inverted (16). To permit search also for elements that have not been inverted, extended search is possible via sequential screening of documents or document parts for any given sequence of characters.

6.3.3   Document Input

With second-generation software, all inputs made simultaneously from several terminals, even for differing data banks, can be accepted (data collection system). All on-line inputs are directly processed in real-time operation and are immediately available to other users, or can be made available in accordance with organizational regulations. A surprising amount of flexibility is offered with the Document Input function. For example, anything defined as a document by the user can be accepted; size and forms of documents may vary as well.

Each document can be subdivided into any number of desired sections. The individual sections may vary in length and can incorporate any kind of data, including graphical representations, tables, and so forth. A document is defined simply as the sum of its sections.

Fill-in formats designed for keyboard entry of bibliographic data, such as journal title, volume, year, page, document title, language, and author can be displayed on the console. The formats are determined by the user; they can be expanded or changed at any time. If format entry is not desired, each document part that is to be treated as a section may be entered using a stipulated code.

Each document part is checked formally according to user specifications. In addition, the user may stipulate any other input categorization procedures and checks according to user requirements.

The user may determine how much text per document is to be included and stored in the data bank. Second-generation software permits the storing of any amount of text in capital and small letters for each document section. A reference to an external textual file can be included to handle as much additional textual material as desired.

The user may request a console display of a document that has been entered or is being entered and, if needed, thereupon make desired corrections by inserting or deleting (textual processing system). This second-generation software capability of interactive correction of documents and change or deletion of document data offers major advantages even where document input is not accomplished interactively, that is, by batch processing. This may occur when tapes from external source suppliers are purchased or leased to supplement user specific files. However the documents are entered, it is inevitable—as existing data banks indicate—that erroneous data are stored in the process. The on-line change routine is the organizationally simplest and most work-saving way to correct such errors. To avoid abuse, the application of the change routine is protected by special code words and protocols.

6.3.3.1   Assignment of Descriptor Terms (Indexing)   The user may stipulate with which kinds of descriptors the documents covered by the data bank should be searchable. In addition to content description by descriptors (discussed immediately following) these may include the following formal data:

Document descriptors for document identification—such as international book number, patent number, library reference, journal title, year, volume, page, author or authors, place of publication, date of publication, publisher, institute, language, and price.

In general, by "formal" data we mean data that can be unambiguously extracted from any given document by specific rules. Instructions must be given as to which data are to be searchable from each respective document section. For example, the document title could easily be regarded as a document section, where all nouns or names there contained could be searchable. By this means the document is searchable by individual words occurring in the title. The difference between formal data and descriptors is not in the differing treatment of the search terms but in the mode of their entry.

In terms of computer files, all these data later used for search are inverted during input and, at the same time, automatically included in the appropriate list of search terms.

During the content description of the document the console offers users the possibility of scanning through the thesaurus for the most appropriate descriptors. Similarly, the user may scan on the console the authors file or any other file to determine whether a term to be entered is already available. The descriptors so obtained can be assigned to the document by marking. This procedure helps to reduce the problem of differing spellings of the same term, which often leads to multiple entry in first generation systems.

Should it be necessary to introduce a new term, this may be accomplished in real-time operation as well. However a variety of organizational limitations and rules can be established for the introduction of specific groups of new terms.

Intellectual indexing of documents is further aided by a procedure where second-generation software suggests relevant descriptors. The computer obtains the relevant descriptors by picking descriptors from similarly indexed documents by means of internal algorithms. This procedure has been first introduced by M. J. Strumwasser and the author at the RAND Corporation in the United States (17) and has been further implemented in the Siemens AG PRIMAS System (18). With second-generation software, this procedure is made even more selective and powerful using new combinations of associative frequencies, extensional relationships, and incorporating expert or consensus indexing. For example, one such aid to intellectual indexing is offered by having other documents similarly indexed identified by the computer in the dialogue indexing process. Such features offer the indexer important self-checking possibilities, insuring the consistency and completeness of indexing.

Conventional automatic indexing methods normally handle the document files by means of special batch processing programs.

Such preindexed documents can be accepted by second-generation software per se. More importantly, their typically poor indexing quality can be improved, very significantly, by second-generation software, which accepts such documents as a normal input. They are then made available for the second-generation software indexing modes just described.

6.3.3.2 Descriptor Qualifiers and Quantifiers   Along with each descriptor, numerical data, that is, quantifiers, can be stored and used for search. Quantifiers may be physical data (measures, weights), performance data (amplification factors, number of rotations), economic data (prices, turnover), or dates. Quantifiers, moreover, permit a weighting of the descriptors. Additional informative power can be added to descriptors by associated verbal statements, that is, qualifiers (19). Second-generation software handles such qualifiers and quantifiers by inverting these data according to a new method. Such detailed, descriptive information can thus be included in search questions without causing any mentionable time delays. In general, first-generation software lacks this capability or has recourse to time-consuming sequential search.

6.3.3.3 Descriptor Changes   As distinct from first-generation, second-generation software is capable of handling new assignments, renaming, regrouping, and deleting descriptors in on-line dialogue modes. The change of a descriptor can involve changes

a. Of references to or from the descriptor within the term list,
b. Of documents associated with the descriptor,
c. Of descriptors associated with documents.

The appropriate change functions are provided by second-generation software. It is impractical, if not impossible, to add them to conventional first-generation systems. Where references from one descriptor to another are entered or changed, the references associated with the second descriptor are automatically checked, deleted, changed, or supplemented as needed. If, for example, a new descriptor is associated now to an existing one as a lower-level term, the already existing descriptor is automatically established as an upper-level term to the new descriptor (thesaurus maintenance system). If existing descriptors are changed, the descriptors assigned to documents are changed accordingly. For example, if a descriptor is transformed from its plural form into its singular for a given term list, the singular will then appear with all documents that have this descriptor assigned.

All or parts of the documents associated with a given descriptor can be transferred to another descriptor. The group of documents for which the descriptor is to be changed can be determined by a search question. This permits a very specific selection. For example, all documents that had been assigned the terms "vessel" or "means of transportation" and "sea" can receive the new assignment "boat," and the previous assignments can be deleted.

All these capabilities are relevant to the processes of thesauri construction and maintenance to be discussed next.

6.3.4   Thesaurus Construction and Maintenance

Documentation systems based on an a priori constructed thesaurus often demonstrate in their practical applications that some descriptors are superfluous, whereas others are missing, and that parts of the thesaurus should be differently structured. On the other hand, documentation systems that are not based on a thesaurus often have the drawback that the term lists become increasingly large, impenetrable, and inconsistently applied.

In both cases the quality and utility of such documentation systems are severely limited. To improve matters, the term lists, the thesauri, the name files, and so forth, must be changed significantly. Second-generation software is based on the concept that such changes must be accomplished in dialogue modes. Otherwise, and without the dialogue computer-aids, the process is so time-consuming and costly that most users are forced to live with the severe limitations imposed by conventional indexing and thesauri methods. Search-only software is simply insufficient. Equally relevant, on-line dialogue modes for these thesauri and term-changing processes permit immediate testing of the effects of changes. Not only do such dialogue functions make the required work easier and plausible for users, the other functions of the system, such as search, are immediately available to provide immediate feedback, permitting users to evaluate any such changes. Before deciding to merge new with old descriptors or to otherwise transform descriptors, for example, the number of assignments and the time when the specific descriptors were first assigned can be requested on-line. Other information offered on-line can indicate whether the same subject matter is covered by other descriptors. A further technique is the tentative introduction of descriptors. Should such descriptors be used poorly or seldom in practice, such on-line dialogue modes permit the transformation of their *tentative* document assignment to other more useful descriptors.

Second generation software makes possible thesaurus development for essentially completed as well as for newly started document files by means of these flexible and efficient change routines (20).

6.3.5   Document Maintenance

The on-line functions previously described also permit obsolete documents to be deleted. Obsolete parts of documents can be specifically updated, including their indexing. Documents can be supplemented by comments and by references to other documents (document concatenation) and to secondary or additional document pools or files. Second-generation change routines also permit the selective correction of document indexing errors. Computer guidance during these processes is available.

Automatic inclusion of such changes in later entries, whether entered via dialogue or batch processing (preventive maintenance), reduces the amount of managerial and manual file maintenance to the minimum. To illustrate, these change routines permit a differing spelling of a proper name or a new synonym for a descriptor, for example, to be traced back to a preferred term. If such differing expressions are to be used later they can be "established" as computer-accepted references to the specified preferred terms. Such references can be also declared "mute;" that is, not displayed on the console during the normal dialogue, but activated only by special dialogue or batch requests (mute synonym). If, on the other hand, such synonyms or differing expressions associated with a preferred term later should be treated as unique computer accepted descriptors (preferred terms on their own), decisions to this effect can be retroactively implemented (quasi-synonym).

Second-generation software offers the partial automation of many such file maintenance processes. Managerial analysis of the result, and the "history" of these automated maintenance functions, is supported by the computer display of all such "change" entries in the chronological order of their occurrence.

6.3.6   Further Utilization of Entries

If desired, index cards for a conventional or "classical" subject catalog can be produced in conjunction with the document input functions. Such subject catalogs can be produced during the initial operational phase and maintained as an on-going process with minimal manpower required. For thesauri more complicated than subject catalogs, subject headings associated with each entered descriptor must be established. Several descriptors are associated, usually, with the same subject heading.

Subject catalogs, thesauri, the lists of all authors, publishers, documents, and the like, can be printed out on request. In addition, references to literature covering a certain topic can be listed. A search question is used to establish the appropriate subset of documents pertinent to the specific topic. The computer printout can be limited to just document sections that contain the source, the author, and possibly, the title. Such document part selection is a profound step toward "fact retrieval" within the context of documentation systems.

All such printouts can be offered on tape for use by external printers. By combining the use of second-generation descriptor selection functions with these selective printout capabilities, significant computer aids now can support directly such "library" processes as ordering, accounting, and dissemination.

6.4   SECOND GENERATION SOFTWARE TECHNICAL CHARACTERISTICS

This section is not addressed only to those interested in the technical problems of providing a programming solution to achieve second-generation software. Administrators, elected officials, and representatives of the public should find this discussion worth study. So should "decision makers" concerned with the allocation of resources and potential system users. It does not pretend to be exhaustive. Functional reasons for the technical characteristics are emphasized; then the purely programming or internal system grounds are given cursory treatment. Nor is one best solution path offered. Computer programming experts will seek and discover other alternative methods and solutions to the varied and complicated problems. However, the software characteristics suggested here represent perhaps the first coherent description of a technically and economically feasible second-generation software package that supports all the functions discussed in previous sections.

In fact, these system characteristics stem from the IDS System Description produced by Kayser Threde & Co in association with the author (21). The software characteristics of the IDS System represent far more than any one individual's views. IDS is a second-generation software package implementable in operational form within a 2-year time period. Therefore, we discuss a realistic basis that can be used for informed comparison by both programmers and users alike. No one need settle for less in their quest for meaningful and comprehensive information retrieval systems.

6.4.1   Construction of the Dialogue Language (User-Machine Communication)

Experience with many user organizations indicates that differing applications of the same information retrieval system would achieve a better "fit" with user needs if the dialogue language could vary accordingly. Even within one given application, it is useful to have the dialogue language available in various levels of sophistication, serving the expert as well as the beginner. To provide for such communication flexibility in the dialogue mode, the internal program includes a translator between the syntax used on the console and the actual system functions. These system functions are constructed and treated by the program as complete working steps. Using the translator, several such functions can be called up by one dialogue step. However, additional dialogue steps can be inserted for easier comprehension and system utilization for the beginner. In its broadest sense these additional guiding steps can form various learning programs adapted to specific users, their capabilities and needs. Second-generation software functions are thus made self-explanatory to users.

The use of such a translator between the syntax of the console and the system functions permits the dialogue language to be adapted by appliers without affecting any system function.

6.4.2   Priority and Legitimation

There is no preferential treatment of individual users according to preset priorities. Instead, various system functions that require only short processing times are preferred to those that require longer processing times. For example, paging through a descriptor list gets preferred treatment over search, and search over change of descriptors. For functions requiring differing amounts of processing times (e.g., sequential search), a "time-sharing" procedure ensures equal consideration of all participants.

The use of the various dialogue functions, such as search, input, change of documents, change of descriptors, is subject to a hierarchically structured legitimation control that is "opened" by passwords. Individual document sections and terms can be similarly secured. For example, certain terminals may permit search of the data banks only. The results displayed could be additionally limited to certain document parts in accordance with organizational regulations.

6.4.3 Data Protection and File Security

Access to a data bank via a terminal is secured by means of several passwords. The passwords can be changed by the user at any specified intervals. Within the system, the documents and the term lists are stored on disks in coded form. Simply "unloading" the files via an unauthorized disk copy printout would leave such data in undeciphered forms. In general, file copies can be read by another system user only if the program has been given the appropriate password.

File protection is accomplished by producing file copies on security tapes at regular intervals. Tape protocols of all changes and new entries are produced simultaneously during the dialogue. Should disk failures occur—physical destruction of the disk or parts thereof—the file can thus be reproduced.

All programs are capable of resumption. This becomes useful when a system interrupt occurs during a processing step due to a computer failure. This capability ensures that operations can readily be resumed on reentering the program. Only what has been actually processed is receipted to the user. Inputs that have not been receipted have to be repeated by the user. In terms of program technology, this means that even half-completed inputs are completed by renewed entry (22).

Last, a protocol printout can serve as a management control for various changes produced in the data bank by individual users.

6.4.4   Search Term or Descriptor Structures

Search term descriptors are structured to permit the full range of software capabilities to be offered as available options to all users. As such, differing users may make use of the search term descriptor structures in organizationally unique ways. The abstract structures, however, persist in all applications.

For each descriptor (or search term) the following structural fields exist:

a. An indicator or aspect characterizing field. The field is used to identify the type or group appropriate to the given descriptor, for example, "author," "content descriptor," or "bibliographic entity."

b. One or more key fields. These fields are used for storing the descriptor's alphanumeric identification or textual form. Any given descriptor (or search term) may have several system acceptable equivalent key field forms functioning as synonyms, spelling variations, abbreviations, or coded forms. Such alternate key field forms function as different available entry points for the desired search term or descriptor.

c. Console display form field. This field stores the alphanumeric and coded forms of the descriptor. These alphanumeric and coded forms may be user-stipulated and represent the preferred user expressions. Furthermore, these descriptors are to be presented on the console as the given descriptor. As such, the display form field will contain the "preferred" descriptor or search term forms. It may include selected elements from the key field, indicators of hierarchical place, thesauri status, whether it is a quantifier of qualifier, and so on. It also gives the number of lower-level descriptors covered and the number of document assignments.

d. Descriptor textual field. Definitions, explanations, references, fill-in formats for qualifiers or quantifiers, usage rules, and other associational information can be stored in the textual field for each descriptor. The textual field is unformated. Unlike the console display form field, it is offered to the user only on special request.

e. Descriptor reference field. Whereas the textual field is unformated, the descriptor reference field functions as a basic format where descriptor associations, "see also" references, and other descriptor relationships are stored in system specified forms. Such references are automatically maintained and updated as changes occur in the users' thesauri or term lists. The reference field formats contain a code for reference type and the console display field.

f. Internal descriptor field. Used for internal organization only and not normally available to the user. The Kayser Threde IDS System concept, for example, has its own unique internal descriptor fields. Other software manufacturers will find their own specific solutions.

6.4.5 Document Structures

Almost no constraints as to document structure (see Section 6.3.3) need be imposed on users. As previously noted, a document may consist of any number of user-defined textual fields.

6.5 SYSTEM INTEGRATION CAPABILITIES

We have previously stated that second-generation software can accept outputs produced by the various source suppliers. Such material is immediately available for dialogue search. In addition, all the other system features are applicable to such externally supplied tapes. We have indicated that these tapes may be screened and documents selected in a dialogue mode. The documents can be supplemented and transformed by indexing or translation, and otherwise changed according to user requirements.

As a direct corollary of such capabilities, second-generation software can also provide magnetic tape services—compiled according to profiles—to external as well as internal users. These corollary capabilities provide an extremely simplified means for systems based on second-generation software to be "linked" via exchange of tapes to other information or documentation centers.

A further level of integration is provided by a literal incorporation of second-generation software systems in an integrated network of other information and documentation centers. Second-generation software provides interfaces that can link into almost any network of systems or form a network of their own.

6.6 THE KAYSER THREDE IDS SYSTEM PROGRAM CHARACTERISTICS

Many of the features, functions, and system characteristics of second-generation information retrieval and documentation software described in this chapter are novel and presented here for perhaps the first time as a coherent system. Those familiar with the actualities, not just the promises, of conventional first-generation systems, may have some doubts concerning how "fantastic" or "realistic" our discussion has been. For this reason we conclude this chapter with a lengthy quotation from the Kayser Threde IDS System Description cited earlier (23).

The IDS program concept is based upon the new, better understood, advanced file structuring technology. This technology has been applied both to achieving extremely flexible file changing functions combined with high-speed, user oriented, real-time interaction. IDS is the first of a newer generation of software packages making available the full range of data processing functions for information and documentation applications. It provides not only for search through voluminous files according to a wide variety of user interests and prospective needs, but also for file development, construction, transformation, protection, and maintenance.

This is accomplished by

- establishing a novel data block file structure
- establishing focused access to the structured files through a hierarchical superstructure
- establishing symbolic as well as literal file access addresses
- establishing integrated and generalized functions resulting in great program simplification
- utilizing advanced techniques of data compression
- incorporating the experiences of earlier system utilizations to provide a user-oriented and self-guiding dialogue
- all of which is incorporated in a software package which minimizes access time, internal organization, management and operational costs, and maximizes trouble-free user access.

We turn now to some serious questions concerning the implementation of this technology. How do we go about using, adapting, and further developing second-generation software to provide us with access to information? How do we use such software to initiate the meaningful participation of the public in the processes of evaluating and understanding contemporary societal alternatives and the making of decisions affecting everyone?

NOTES

1. See CAIR.
2. Ibid., Chapter 10.
3. Ibid., Chapter 9.
4. A. E. Wessel, "Some Thoughts on Machine Indexing," P-3869, The RAND Corporation, Santa Monica, California, June 1968; see also T. D. C. Kuch and Robert Magnuson, "A Network-Oriented System for Computer-Supported Indexing," *Proceedings of the ASIS Annual Meeting,* Vol. 11, 1974, pp. 63, 68;

and H. Fangmeyer, "Semi-Automated Indexing State of the Art," North Atlantic Treaty Organization, Advisory Group for Aerospace Research and Development, AGARD-AG-179, C.C.R.-EURATOM/CETIS, Ispra, Italy, 1974, p. 2, for an indication that fashions have changed somewhat.

5. CAIR, Chapters 7 and 8.

6. Ibid., pp. 43–44.

7. For example, see Steinacker, "Dokumentationssysteme;" W. A. Martin, "A Comparative Study of Terminal User Techniques . . ."

8. CAIR, p. 1.

9. For further detail concerning these topics, consult CAIR, Chapters 5–8.

10. R. A. McIvor, "A Mini-Computer Based Information System," North Atlantic Treaty Organization, Advisory Group for Aerospace Research and Development (AGARD), AGARD Conference Proceedings No. 136, London, December 1973.

11. Kevin Smith, "Evolution of the Semiconductor Memory," Electron, No. 77, 19 June 1975, IPC Electrical-Electronic Press Ltd., Dorset House, Stamford Street, London SE1 9LU, pp. 20–24.

12. Ibid., p. 24.

13. H. E. Seelbach, "IDS—Dialogue Data Bank System," Dr. Erwin Kayser Threde & Co, Munich, May 1975.

14. Contract No. 7/75/SDS, 8 July 1975.

15. Seelbach, "IDS."

16. CAIR, Chapter 9.

17. M. J. Strumwasser and A. E. Wessel, "Progress Report: RAND/United States Patent Office Data Automation Studies," RM-5812-PAT, The RAND Corporation, Santa Monica, California, November 1968.

18. CAIR, Chapter 10.

19. CAIR, Chapters 7 and 8.

20. "Entwicklung eines EDV-Verfahrens zum dynamischen Aufbau einer Fachdokumentation bei gleichzeitiger Erstellung eines Thesaurus," (Development of an EDP-Procedure for the Dynamic Construction of an Informational File with the Associated Construction of its Thesaurus), Dr. Erwin Kayser Threde & Co., Munich, March 1975 (available in German only).

21. Seelbach, "IDS," and "Entwicklung eines EDV-Verfahrens" (Kayser Threde).

22. See CAIR, Chapter 9, for further discussion of the problems avoided by this approach.

23. Seelbach, "IDS."

Chapter Seven

An Implementation Program

Complex systems behave in many ways similarly to organic structures. A market plan and an advertizing campaign, however good and necessary, are not sufficient to bring such systems to "life." They must be nurtured, "grown" in the context of their expected operational environment. Through adaptation and other forms of "learning," such systems evolve (hopefully) into active partnerships with their makers and users. This process is a two-way street. The word "Interactive" as applied to information retrieval systems has become a catchword. Often we forget that interaction involves at least two parties: in this case, machines and people. Adaptation and learning, within the context of an environment containing automated information retrieval systems and people, apply to both the systems and the system users.

User participation during the implementation phases is an absolute requirement. It is absolute because without such user participation during the implementation phases, interactive learning and adaptation will be forced on us during the subsequent operational stages. When this occurs so late in the evolution of the system, both system and user prove much more recalcitrant to the required transformation and adaptation. Costs and tempers soar, magnifying all the "normal" implementation problems (1).

We have described second-generation software, which can provide the much needed flexibility and responsiveness to user requirements and to the users developing perceptions of what their requirements are. The discussion that follows, of an implementation program for this system software, includes the equally needed and responsive participation of potential users.

7.1 A SHORT REVIEW AND SOME BASIC QUESTIONS

A review of the major themes so far discussed can serve as an introduction to our implementation program. We begin by observing that existing, conventional computer software and hardware systems are relatively inefficient and costly when applied to the more generalized tasks of information storage and retrieval. To date, computer technology has made it possible to store vast amounts and kinds of information in automated data banks and documentation systems. Within the next several years, we will see further increases in the computer's capacity to accumulate and store information. The problem, to date only partly and often poorly resolved, is to get such information out of the computers again in order to satisfy our search requirements—at a reasonable cost with acceptable utility.

Recent developments in computer software already have increased the efficiency and reduced costs of information retrieval systems. Second-generation software described in previous chapters offers a quantum jump in utility and flexibility for almost all potential users. This means that we now can turn our attention to two most socially relevant questions. First, will the previously described benefits of second-generation software be brought to fruition? Second, who among us will benefit? To spell out these two fundamental questions in a little more detail, we need to know specifically:

a. Can the described technology provide useful public access to information retrieval systems?
b. How useful?
c. What information will be available?
d. How is such information to be made available?
e. Who will use such access?
f. How often?
g. Where?
h. When can public access begin to take place?
i. How much will it all cost?

This chapter can help us to obtain some meaningful answers to these questions. We offer a detailed implementation program, set up to provide the pertinent hard data. We shall find other problems and concerns, not all of which can be resolved by any one program or any one person. Yet at the least, we shall have discovered how to begin in a manner most likely to achieve success.

7.2 GENERAL PROGRAM FEATURES

Our goal is to begin to distribute more equally the existent and coming benefits of automated information retrieval throughout our various societies. The implementation plan that follows includes the actual realization of the first steps toward achieving this goal. An experimental center providing a significant degree of public access to selected automated files, to be built, transformed, and enhanced within the time frame of the implementation program, is established. A 3-year program is envisaged.

The fundamental goal of the implementation program is to

demonstrate the feasibility of providing public access to automated information retrieval systems. The questions of system utility, utilization, and costs are regarded as primary. The 3-year program includes a 6-month planning phase, an 18-month development and implementation phase, and a full year of operations at the resultant center for public access. The 3-year implementation program is intended to effect a change of direction for our implementation policies for automated information retrieval technology. A new implementation policy is to be demonstrated as technically and socially feasible: A specific national policy to provide broader and more equitable access to automated information retrieval capabilities for all interested persons.

The word "international" should be considered as a substitute for the word "national" in the sentence above. In fact, we suggest a version of a two-country, two-language exchange program during the time period of our experimental center operations. No better test of system flexibility and adaptability could be envisaged than in a binational, bilingual setting. Even should the international character of our program be delayed to a later stage, planning for precisely this sort of operation is included at the beginning. This ensures that certain quite important problems concerning communications, hardware and software, peripheral equipment, participating user groups, files, operational procedures, and exchange of information and experiences are highlighted. We return to these topics later in our discussion.

7.3 PHASE 1—PLANNING

Planning phases sometimes effectively become endless. When this occurs we have a rather good indication that the plan is likely to be pointless or worthless. As T. Finley Burke would put it, "To make a project plan means that you must clearly state what the project staff are to do at 8 a.m. on the morning that the project starts. And similarly for the mornings and afternoons throughout the project! After one knows this, some leeway can be established (2).

We apply Burke's advice one step earlier. We are going to state as clearly as we can what the planning staff is to do from the first to the last day of Phase 1. The 6-month planning phase is to accomplish the following:

a. The specification of an overall software package including its scheduled implementation during Phases 2 and 3.
b. The selection of software elements in accordance with (a) (both system operational and functional), and the specification of the required modifications and developments within the time frame of Phase 2.

We have noted previously that existing conventional automated information retrieval software systems do not offer generally well-described or indexed files. Nor do such systems provide us with realistic or economic means to restructure or improve the indexing of existing information in files. Previous chapters, particularly Chapters 2 and 6, have presented a realistic and hopefully clear description of the kinds of software required for our purposes (3). The Kayser IDS System, a coherent second-generation software system concept, is being offered for development (4). The time required for test and implementation of IDS is compatible with the time frame of our project. The planning group thus has a model for comparison and for possible selection.

The functional requirements for the project software have been described in previous chapters as well (5). These requirements place strong emphasis on the necessary interactive file change and construction routines, which in turn permit computer-aided indexing, file description, thesauri development, and the use of previously automated files as well as the construction of new files. Computer-aids also for search have been described as a central required feature. These permit the ready test of user-oriented file structures and thesauri. In combination, the satisfaction of such requirements would provide us with the software capabilities for Phase 3 operations at the experimental center for public access.

Thus far we have provided a good start for Phase 1 planning; but more is required. A hardware configuration must be specified as part of the Phase 1 effort. To continue:

c. The specification of a hardware configuration compatible with the software (a and b).

The hardware must be capable of providing five console, on-line, multiuser operations for the experimental center during Phase 3. Expansion to a 20-console operation must be permitted without significant adaptations. Communications link-up for remote consoles must be possible; however, remote operations initially may be conducted by means of exchange of files using tapes. File storage capacity must be such as to accomodate both files initially containing several thousand well-indexed documents and files containing a few million documents. For well-indexed files, the average number of descriptors per document should be about 25, with each pertinent thesaurus containing about 5000 explicit thesauri descriptors. For conventionally indexed files, a much larger number of descriptors may have to be handled at first. Using some of the simpler thesauri structuring methods now available, such descriptor masses can be reduced and better organized (6). But the storage capacity must, nonetheless, accommodate files made available through source suppliers or otherwise consisting of conventionally indexed documents.

Some possible hardware configurations are described in Chapter 8, pp. 190–191. However, during Phase 1, a good look at the most recent hardware developments and minicomputer penetration of the data processing applications market is required. In fact, the most difficult technical question to be resolved by the Phase 1 effort is to choose between a normal large "main frame" computer or a minicomputer system. Chapter 6 introduced this topic. The Phase 1 Planning Group must carry this discussion forward to a conclusion. We observe here, however, that appropriate hardware is available from many of the principal hardware manufacturers.

The weakest elements in the hardware configuration likely to be selected from available equipment are the interactive consoles. Cursors, light guns, and other display screen "marking" devices should offer far more reliable and flexible entry capabilities than they yet do. There seems to be no valid technical reason for the lack of development here. Rather it would seem to be another example of the concentration on search-only systems and the corresponding neglect of the human functions associated with on-line input, indexing, file structuring, and thesauri development. Hardware manufacturers could stand some prodding. We suggest one means to accomplish this during the discussion of the "nationality" of our project (Chapter 8).

We turn now to some nontechnical specifications:

d. The selection of two or three distinct public groups.

These should stem from already existing associations such as those found formally or informally among legislative bodies, small business or industrial associations, labor unions or organizations, consumer associations, voter, citizen, or community study or action groups, student associations, Rotary or Chamber of Commerce associations, representative religious associations or institutions, to name a few likely candidates. The public groups initially selected must be willing and capable of offering, without cost to the project, at least one full-time participant for Phases 2 and 3. Part-time participation is also required during Phase 1 to aid in the selection of the informational fields to be made available and to help begin the construction of thesauri and descriptors for these fields. Such participants from the user groups must also be acceptable to the project staff.

It may be that an overwhelming public response would make this initial selection difficult. On the other hand, although many are interested in the benefits of access to information, fewer are willing to do the necessary work, and perhaps less have the available time. One further stipulation could reduce the number of those groups willing to participate initially. Such groups must agree to permit other groups at the experimental center to make use of their group specific and structured files. Constraints on such information exchange are desirable; the determination of what such constraints should be is a task to be accomplished during Phase 3. These constraints should be based on experiences and the learning process to take place during Phase 3 rather than on existent fears and prejudices. For these reasons, the Phase 1 Project may find itself in the position of seeking out appropriate participant groups, rather than being sought out. This is probably the most difficult nontechnical problem to be resolved during Phase 1.

e. The selection of the initial informational fields and files.

As just stated, the information and its general descriptive structuring is to be selected with the participation of the specific public groups concerned. In earlier chapters, examples of the kinds and varieties of information were given. Further detail will have to be provided during Phase 1; yet some general considerations are worth noting. It would be well to have a mix of files: some from source suppliers' preexisting data, or from documentation systems with standard or conventional indexing, others to be built during Phase 2 by the project staff in cooperation with the participant user groups.

File size, the number of available documents indexed and stored, will depend on the file mix just suggested. For files starting from ground zero, one could expect to produce files containing several thousand documents during Phases 2 and 3. Such file sizes could be increased at a faster rate as indexing practices are adapted to take full advantage of the computer-aids and the better developed thesauri. With source or preexistent files, the total number of documents can run into the millions. But the subset of reindexed and well-indexed documents from such files will grow less rapidly. With some luck, however, the reindexing practices associated with source supplied or conventionally indexed files could result in file sizes greater than with totally new files by a factor of two, three, or even higher. Well-indexed file subsets structured in accordance with group specific interests of over 100,000 documents each can be expected during Phase 3. The search operations during Phase 3 will, thereby, offer us rather realistic evidence of expected utilities. We may soon after be able to remove the term "experimental" from the name of our center for public access.

The remaining tasks for Phase 1 are:

f. To work out procedures for obtaining a binational character during Phases 2 and 3.
g. To obtain Phase 2 and Phase 3 funding.
h. To select additional project personnel for Phase 2 and estimate Phase 3 staff requirements.
i. To produce a Phase 1 Final Report.

The question of funding for such a project is connected with questions concerning the "nationality(ies)" of the project. Both (f) and (g) take us on quite a detour at this point in our project discussion. We reserve further discussion for Chapter 8. We assume here that funding on the order of $100,000 is obtainable for Phase 1 itself. (The project should be organized on a not-for-profit basis.) Furthermore, we need not envisage vast sums for the entire project.

Manpower requirements for Phase 1 (6-month duration) are as follows:

Phase 1—Project Staff Requirements

Personnel	Man/years
Two senior, full time staff	1
Two senior, half time staff	$\frac{1}{2}$
Consultants	$1\frac{1}{2}$
Supporting technical staff (3)	$1\frac{1}{2}$
Project management	$\frac{1}{2}$
Secretary/typist, full time	$\frac{1}{2}$
Total	$5\frac{1}{2}$ man/years

Assuming a Munich, West Germany, location for Phase 1, computer time, project housing, office equipment, and expenses are included in the estimate previously stated. However, travel costs may add about 15% to this estimate if a binational project is accepted and includes the participation of the United States. This estimate does not include costs for the representatives of the participating public groups in accordance with our stated requirement that the participant groups be willing to provide such representatives at no cost to the project.

In accordance with Burke's maxim previously quoted, larger staff and a longer Phase 1 will not be required to fill in the appropriate details and to arrive at the decisions just outlined.

7.4   PHASE 2—IMPLEMENTATION

The 18-month implementation phase is to provide directly or preferably through subcontract the software and system configuration necessary for the initial operations at the experimental center for public access. Initial center operations are based on the availability of five on-line consoles providing multiuser access to the computerized files. These consoles are used for computer-aided indexing and document entry, file construction by the selected user groups, computer-aided thesauri construction in association with the files, and computer-aided search and indexing tests for undertaking an evaluation program. During Phase 3, the consoles are available to continue these processes and for computer-aided search of selected files under participant user group auspices. The selected user groups would have access to their own files for file development, indexing, and search. Each of the two (or three) "representative" user groups would begin to build one new file for their own use. The other files adapted for specific group usage should be made available, in principle, to all participants. However, the special files created "from vacuo" (the new file per user group), could be established as "private" files with tentatively restricted access during Phase 3. Final decisions as to such limited access files should await the results of Phase 3 operations and analyses.

7.4.1 Specific Phase 2 Tasks

There are 15 specific Phase 2 tasks. To permit a quick review of Phase 2, these are first listed here and then described in Section 7.4.2.

1. File definition and primitive thesauri construction (CAIR, Chapters 6, 7, and 8).*
2. *Software adaptation, development, and test†* (Chapters 2 and 6, this book).
3. Initial intellectual document indexing using primitive thesauri (CAIR, Epilogue).
4. *Completion of prototype functional software for initial computer-aided indexing sessions and search tests* (Chapters 2 and 6, this book; CAIR, Chapter 10).
5. Computer-aided initial indexing and document entry; initial file construction (CAIR, Chapter 6).
6. Thesauri revision in accordance with results of (5) (CAIR, Chapters 6–8).
7. Construction of search samples—search results and search requests (CAIR, Chapter 4.2).
8. Computer-aided search tests (CAIR, Chapters 6 and 10; Chapters 2 and 6, this book).
9. Production of draft versions of operational thesauri for Phase 3 use (CAIR, Chapters 7 and 8).
10. On-line completion of prototype operational files for Phase 3 use and additional development (CAIR, Epilogue).

---

* The discussion in this section should be sufficient for our purposes of exposition and clarification. However, for those interested in more or related detail than is offered here, references to other materials are in parentheses.

† Italicized items indicate tasks that should be preferably accomplished under subcontract during Phase 2.

11. Design and test of user group specific search strategies for Phase 3 (CAIR, Chapter 4.1).
12. Design and test of Phase 3 user group specific and general search tests.
13. Development of standard and user group specific operating procedures for Phase 3.
14. *Completion of tested prototype functional and operational software for Phase 3 operations* (Chapter 6, this book).
15. Production of documentation—system functions, systemsware, and operational procedures.

7.4.2   Discussion of Specific Phase 2 Tasks

Normally the determination and clarification of Phase 2 tasks would be accomplished during Phase 1, and constitute a major part of the Phase 1 Final Report. Our discussion so far has, in effect, already begun Phase 1. We emphasize, however, that Phase 1 cannot be completed by any one person. Therefore, Sections 7.4.1 and 7.4.2 should serve not only as a description of a much needed project, but also as important inputs to the Phase 1 staff for their subsequent analysis and revision.

The tasks in Section 7.4.1 have been listed in the rough order of their intended completion. The italicized items taken together constitute a potential subcontract for the production of the required computer software and programming. Whether accomplished within the project or, as we prefer, externally, one critical requirement needs emphasis. In order that other Phase 2 tasks may proceed within the 18-month time frame suggested, *prototype test indexing and search functions must be programmed and made available quite early during Phase 2*. Thus Item 4 should be started within the time frame of Phase 1. There is no valid technical reason for not doing so; but there is a serious technical decision to be made. Should these prototype indexing and search functions be based on the on-line table look-up programs (Chapter 2, Section

2.3.2.3.1) alone? Or should such prototype functions go beyond "extensional relationships" and be identical in all essential aspects to the computer-aided indexing and search functions to be made available as part of the completed functional and operational software package (Item 14) for Phase 3?

The advantages of limiting the early indexing and search computer support may seem obvious. Similar programs to provide these computer-aids would have been programmed and tested prior to the start of Phase 1 (7). Their necessary adaptations for Phase 2 purposes might not appear to be complex or costly. We might expect that the completion of Item 4 would not delay other Phase 2 tasks.

However, there are some possibly serious drawbacks. Although the table look-up and the computer-aids to search and indexing so derived would provide on-line interaction, the production of the tables themselves is accomplished by batch processing means. This limits the degree and kinds of dialogue interaction available to support the early indexing and search processes necessary for file building, thesauri construction, and the specification of operational procedures. All the nonitalicized Phase 2 items are affected by these limitations. The most probable impact of such limitations would lie in initially restricting the participant user groups to already existent or source supplied files. Such files could be restructured during Phase 2. Whether they could be restructured to a sufficient degree for Phase 3 purposes is difficult to assess. The development of the "new" user specific files, one per participant user group, would be severely impeded during Phase 2. This just might not be so bad a consequence. The participating user groups and the project staff may have quite enough to accomplish and to learn during Phase 2, so that the special development of the "new" files could await Phase 3 operations. We repeat, this is a difficult decision.

Discussions with possible subcontractors should help to resolve this question. If a commitment to provide on-line computer-aided indexing functions comparable to those to be later implemented

(Item 14) is obtainable, we should choose this as the better option. The feasibility of this option is indicated by the PRIMAS system. Many of the on-line computer aids to indexing (and to search) provided by PRIMAS have been illustrated in Chapter 10, CAIR. Should PRIMAS software be applied for this purpose or some PRIMAS-like equivalent, one stipulation is essential. Documents so indexed and entered in files must be directly processable by and thus available for the Item 14 software functions. We return to this topic in Section 7.4.2.1.5.

The costs for undertaking and completing these italicized software production and test items should be within acceptable and feasible ranges. The IDS software system could serve as a model here as well; approximately $800,000 (about DM 2.000.000) is a safe estimate. Program development and production costs could be reduced from the point of view of our implementation project if the software manufacturer would agree to participate by cost sharing. Under such circumstances, licensing rights should be clarified. The Experimental Center should retain specific licensing rights for use of the software package described above. Such "rights," however, could be restricted to not-for-profit applications intended to broaden public access in the public interest. To reduce the cost figures, the software manufacturer could retain control of the programs for applications in industry, or more generally, in the sphere of private enterprise. Any software manufacturer would benefit through the implementation and testing, the feedback from the use of this second-generation software package during the first year of the experimental center's operations. However, only actual negotiations can determine the extent of cost sharing by the manufacturer.

Having stated the costs of software production above, we hereafter exclude such costs from our later discussion of project costs. Additionally, we defer consideration of hardware rental or purchase costs until Chapter 8.

7.4.2.1 *Remaining (Nonprogramming) Phase 2 Tasks* The remaining Phase 2 items cover the categorization of chosen informational fields and the construction of user specific files; the beginnings of thesauri development and document indexing and entry; testing, refinement, and further development of files for search; developing indexing and search strategies and associated operational procedures; and documentation. We have nothing novel to say here concerning the latter other than that documentation is required and should be started early and well. Last minute rushes to document result in project collapse at least as often as project continuation.

7.4.2.1.1 LEARNING AND UNLEARNING   In attempting the remaining tasks, consideration should be given to the learning processes implied. Mistakes are to be expected and corrected; this takes time and patience. It also requires user and change oriented software. The novelty of the latter can have two surprisingly opposite effects. Individuals used to conventional and rigid software and thesauri building techniques may fail to perceive, initially, the potential of second-generation software. Such conventionally experienced individuals will have learned, most appropriately, how difficult it is to accomplish these tasks. As a result, too little will be attempted. On the other hand, individuals with great expectations as to the potential of automated data processing may attempt too much. Although second-generation software will come closer than previously available technology to satisfying such expectations, the propaganda mills have done a lot of grinding on these topics. The conclusion in both cases happily is the same: We must allow for a good bit of unlearning as well as learning before the scope of these tasks can be fully defined.

A significant amount of just plain fear of computers and automated data processing has been generated. The number of persons who have been sent threatening letters produced by computers on matters of credit, debt, and bills is not small. Almost everyone knows someone who has been entangled in such periodic bouts with computer "bureaucracy." A personal example is offered for purposes of comparison and commiseration. It should be noted that this incident is not the sole fault of the corporation involved or the many other corporations inflicting similar incidents on their customers or clients. We have here a particularly apt example also of the severe difficulties associated with introducing changes in files based on conventional software.

Andrew E. Wessel

8000 Munich
25 September 1973

American Express
Credit Card Division
6000 Frankfurt/Main 16

RE: Your invitation to apply for an American Express Card

Gentlemen:

Because of convenience and other normal reasons, I was a holder of an American Express Card for many years. I no longer am nor will I be—here is why.

About two years ago while still recovering from a prolonged and serious illness, I returned an American Express Card "renewal" letter WITH MY OLD CARD stating that I could not use the card for the time being.

Can you guess what happened?

After getting several increasingly insulting and threatening letters informing me that if I did not pay my bill (only for the new card; all previous charges had been paid) for a card I had long since returned I would lose my credit rating. . . . I wrote once more giving the facts. I requested that somebody over there ought to put in the little IBM card needed to pacify the computer.

The insults and threats continued for a few more months. Then silence from American Express. . . .

Very sincerely,
Andrew E. Wessel

This sort of incident combines with our Chaplinesque fantasies, as in his "Modern Times," or with "production line" realities to produce and deepen fears of mechanization. Too often such fears are appropriate. ". . . the conventional approach to automation is . . . machine-oriented rather than centered upon the needs of the human . . . Full automation is aimed at replacement of the human . . . not (aimed at) providing him with machine aids" (8). Those kinds of social engineers or human factors experts enamoured of producing acceptance through clever manipulation might attempt the accomplishment of Phase 2 tasks within a "Skinner's box." The predictable result would be neither too much nor too little. In all likelihood it would be nothing at all. The only guidance we can offer toward overcoming such fears is to emphasize the fact that semiautomation, unlike full automation, leaves much to be done by the user groups and their participant members. This fact should be made clear in the most honest fashion possible. At the same time the natural resentments against full automation may be overcome by such honesty with regard to "the very people *semi*-automation could help (with flexible computer aids)" (9). It also would help to have a clear notion of what human work will have to be done and how to do it. Let us make the descriptive effort.

7.4.2.1.2 INITIAL FILE BUILDING—BEGINNING THE THESAURI Much material covering the topics be to discussed here can be found in the references cited in Section 7.4.1—the list of Phase 2 tasks. We summarize the relevant information and add what may be helpful.

We are concerned with two different kinds of file building tasks. One is to restructure and redescribe the documents available in source supplied or preindexed computerized files. One such file remade in the image of each participant user group has to be produced in Phase 2 for Phase 3 use. The other file building task is the construction of a computerized document file from "normal" informational materials. These two tasks differ not so much as to what has to be done but as to how and how much has to be accomplished during Phase 2. To avoid repetitive phrases, we mark material applying to preindexed files, "PRE," and material pertinent to normal or new files, "NEW." Unmarked passages apply to both kinds of files.

The creation of primitive term or phrase lists begins the process of thesauri construction. Terms or phrases form the initial sets of descriptors for indexing and subsequent search. There are few reliable computer aids available to support this initial selection process. However, with second-generation software, there is no need to produce a complete, accurate, or even initially consistent list of accepted descriptors. The manual or intellectual effort should be limited during this early stage as rather powerful computer aids later can be applied to refine, make more coherent, and expand the descriptors of primitive thesauri. The number of content descriptors should be held below 1000 per file during this early stage. Name classes and other grouping descriptors should be selected to cover document descriptors (Authors, Publishers, Document types such as books or journals, and other bibliographic data). No attempt should be made to produce complete lists of the members of such grouping classes (the list of all authors, publishers, journal names, etc.).

NEW: The only computer aids useful at this stage would be lists of terms or phrases selected from sample textual material from the specific files. Using standard software, various batch processing programs are available to produce such lists. Frequency counts are employed with "stop" functions, which reject unwanted terms or phrases such as articles ("the," "an") or such often high frequency expressions as "etc." After the basic content descriptors have been intellectually selected and the document descriptors used for grouping or class formation have been chosen, such batch-processing produced lists may offer some help in filling out the primitive thesauri. But not before! Such computer-generated lists could be taken too seriously. These lists also differ with programming technique and sample of textual material. The combination of these two likely happenings produces only conflict and confusion. Once an intellectual basis or pattern has been agreed on, however, such computer generated lists can be absorbed within a meaningful perspective; that of the user group building the thesaurus.

PRE: These files may have up to 50,000 (in certain cases more) terms or phrases used for search. Computer programs that produce the on-line tables showing the extensional relationships among such descriptors should be applied to these files. By thoughtful selection of printout formats, quite significant information concerning these descriptors can be made available. When combined with the descriptor basis created by intellectual means, such information helps to reduce the number of descriptors to more meaningful proportions and groupings. The remaining useful descriptors (utility is readily determined via measures based on extensional relations) fit more coherently into such groups. The "fit" is accomplished by use of the extensional relationships connecting the remaining descriptors to the descriptors in the thesaurus basis.

We have arrived at primitive thesauri containing descriptors to be used for the first round of indexing.

7.4.2.1.3   BEGINNING INDEXING   The primitive thesauri constructed by the participant user groups and project staff contain up to 1000 thesauri descriptors. Certain of these descriptors cover large numbers of implicit descriptors, such as lists of proper names and bibliographic terms. Perhaps a few definitions, explanations, and rules for interpretation and usage will accompany the thesauri descriptors. However, at this stage such thesauri apparatus need not be taken too seriously. The very same staff and participant users who have created the primitive thesauri first must attempt to use their thesauri. This means that a few hundred documents should be indexed and entered into the appropriate files; intellectually and manually. One important rule must be followed during this process: Only thesauri descriptors may be used for indexing (or the implicit descriptors thereby covered).

Terms or phrases that are desired as indexing descriptors but not yet within the primitive thesauri should be listed. A "committee of the whole" should be established per selected file and participant group to admit such candidate descriptors into the thesauri.

Each staff or participant indexer should index from 25 to 50 documents without help from others. Documents so indexed should not be entered into the computer files.

From 250 to 500 documents per selected file should be indexed as follows:

a. Jointly by two indexers.
b. Indexing reviewed by the "indexing committee" established within the participant group and containing one project staff member.

After acceptance within the thesauri of any new candidate descriptors resulting from these processes (or any other resultant thesauri changes) such indexed documents should be entered into the computer files. Depending on the status of on-line entry software, such document entry could be batch or via console.

NEW: During the indexing process resulting in documents to be entered, hierarchical groupings and/or general subject heading descriptors should be established. Grouping of the descriptors via descriptor qualifiers or quantifiers should be attempted. Such structural improvements should be added to the Name Class concept already incorporated within the primitive thesauri. Thesauri rules for descriptor interpretation and usage may be suggested as candidate rules but should not be introduced into the primitive thesauri at this point.

Boundaries for the number of descriptors assigned to each document should be established. For content description this should be held to less than 30 and more than 10. Bibliographic categories desired, and the document descriptors required, should be established. A document descriptor format(s) could be attempted during this process.

No further thesauri development need take place at this time.

PRE: Obviously only a small subset of the available computerized file is being set up as a separate special file. Should a later comparison between search results obtained from this special file and those from the full file be desired, selection of the documents to comprise the subset involves sampling. This problem may apply to the NEW files as well, since they are often subsets of noncomputerized files. Phase 1 staff should be alerted to this problem. A plausible solution is made easier to obtain by selecting a random sample from documents recently entered in preexistent files (say up to 2 years back). Note that the sample subset will be much larger than the 250 to 500 documents entered at this point!

Should the indexers be given the index terms or phrases now "attached" to documents? Probably not. For one thing the preexistent indexing assignments per document may be extremely difficult to obtain. This is yet another surprising consequence found with first-generation, search only software. Where only the inverted file exists for computer search, new batch processing programs may be required, plus unbelievably long computer run times involved in producing such lists of document indexing.

Second, the variation among such indexing lists per document, their indexing patterns, consistency, completeness, and so on cannot be experimentally controlled. In fact, without the program runs based on extensional relationships, no one knows, or knows feasibly how to determine what such indexing patterns have been.* This is another interesting characteristic of files produced for and by search only systems.

This, however, does not mean that such lists of the preindexing per document should be hidden from the project indexers. If available, let anyone so interested have them. We simply assert that such lists are not required as part of the indexing process per se.

We have now arrived at the beginnings of quite valuable thesauri and computer-aided indexing.

---

* We are not talking about laboratory samples here or files so small that computerization is silly anyway. We are talking about files containing 1,000,000 preindexed documents, more or less! We hope it is obvious that our small-sized intellectually indexed files (250–500 documents) will become large enough by the end of Phase 2, and much larger still during Phase 3.

7.4.2.1.4 INITIAL THESAURI CONSTRUCTION—STEP ONE
Certain practical directions are given here to supplement a review
of material found in Chapters 7 and 8 of CAIR, where structural
principles for thesauri to be used in conjunction with computer aids
were given and illustrated. The 1000 (or fewer) thesauri content
descriptors, and the fewer explicit document descriptors, should
now be expanded. During this implementation stage, the number of
both content and document descriptors found desirable per selected
file can approach 5000. Mandatory thesauri rules should be held to
the minimum; interpretive rules given more emphasis. Thesauri
explications for those thesauri descriptors serving as hierarchical
grouping or main subject headings, for those descriptors possessing
qualifiers and quantifiers, for Name Class descriptors, and for
those descriptors with group specific meaning should be produced.
(See CAIR, Chapters 7 and 8.)
NEW: Candidate descriptors for which no group agreement
obtains as to their meaning or utility should be listed in a special
category. So should all descriptors where their status as to hierarchical place, qualification or quantification, usage, or association
with other descriptors remains controversial. Through project staff
and further group analysis the number of such controversial
descriptors should be restricted to the number displayable in one
(preferably) or two visual displays. This limitation is significant
during computer-aided indexing. At the same time, should the
number of such controversial descriptors remain very much higher
than the amount listable on one or two visual displays, we would
have our first important warning sign that continued automation
for this selected file and possibly for this user group may not be
warranted.
  Fill-in formats for bibliographic data desired concerning the
documents should be constructed. These specify the document
descriptor groups from which selection during indexing is to be
required. Fill-in formats for content descriptors should be
considered but probably not attempted at this point.
PRE: The previous sentence may not apply here. Given the extensional relationship tables, which will have indicated the existent

association patterns among the preindexing "descriptors," fill-in formats are likely to be do-able at this stage. Where such preindexed terms or phrases have been subsumed under thesauri descriptors as qualifiers or in other ways linked with thesauri descriptors, fill-in formats and their associated thesauri rules can be established. Here potential or actual synonyms, "see also" references, detailing requirements, and cross-hierarchical ties, can be treated within thesauri fill-in formats or with other forms of interpretive or applicative usage rules. Even here, we suggest that no attempt at completeness or exactness be made. "Learning" and "growing," with their resultant transformations, are more relevant and productive than efforts toward perfection.

We may assume that the first 6 months of Phase 2 have elapsed. We now are ready to use the computer directly.

7.4.2.1.5 INITIAL COMPUTER-AIDED INDEXING—ON-LINE Here we are confronted with the consequences of an earlier technical decision as to the kind of computer-aided indexing to be made available at this stage of the project (Section 7.4.2, pp. 154–156). Should we have opted for software limited on-line to extensional relationship tables produced by batch processing:

NEW: Probably only intellectual and committee indexing continue. File size for beginning Phase 3 operations would remain small, perhaps amounting to less than 1000 indexed documents. Even if additional documents could be so indexed and entered, to do so would be a waste of time and effort. Rapid increase of file size would be accomplished early in Phase 3. The effort and time are better applied to continued thesauri refinement and the later incorporation of thesauri descriptor explanatory and associational structuring within the framework of Phase 3 computer aids.

PRE: It is best to admit clearly that we do not know enough. That is to say we do not know how the extensional relationships among the preindexing terms and phrases will be related to the newly created thesauri descriptors. And we shall not know this until the attempt described in Section 7.4.2.1.4 has been made.

Yet here we may sense one value of second-generation software:

its powerful capabilities with regard to supporting the re-indexing of documents. Any documents indexed during Phase 2 readily can be reindexed in accordance with the better developed thesauri descriptors to be available in Phase 3. (This applies to NEW files as well.) Thus if file sizes are kept within Phase 2 bounds, rather little human effort and time will be involved in the probably necessary reindexing during Phase 3.

Assuming that the extensional relationships among preindexing terms and phrases can be connected with thesauri descriptors to any significant degree, computer-aided indexing can begin. The general features of such computer-aided indexing do not differ greatly from those to be described.

Should we have opted for software comparable to that to be provided via Item 14 (see CAIR, Chapter 10, pp. 140–162), the following applies:

Although later computer-aided indexing times should average roughly 5 minutes per document including the document entry into the computer, we are going to start more slowly. Our goals are indeed plural; we wish to accomplish more than document indexing. First, we want to teach indexers how to index with on-line computer aids. In our terms of reference, this means to guide indexers to the point where they teach themselves. Second, we want to learn what dialogue computer-aided indexing procedures and strategies should be for the specific user groups and their files. Once we have learned this, we may be able to teach others how to learn the same strategies and procedures themselves. Third, we want to discover what additional refinements should be added to our thesauri. Later search tests will continue this process. Fourth, we want to increase the size of our indexed files for use in those later search tests and for Phase 3 operations. We can allocate another 6 months of Phase 2 effort for our purposes. This should result in individual file sizes of up to 5000 indexed documents.*

---

* Depending on just how extensional relationships occur within the PRE files and how successfully we thereby can relate such preindexing to our thesauri, PRE files could grow much faster. Files of 100,000 documents or more would be possible with sufficient "luck."

Each participant group, in conjunction with project staff, should work out their own organizational means to provide for indexing consistency and completeness checks. The checks themselves would amount to agreement comparisons between two different indexers for the same document, or agreement with committee spot check indexing of certain documents, or some combination of both. Assuming an average of ½ hour per document so indexed and 4 hours per working day of indexing, we would add about 1000 indexed documents per indexer per file during this 6-month period. In actuality, the file sizes should be larger as indexing times per document should be cut in half after the first 1 or 2 months. When the 250 to 500 indexed documents produced during the purely intellectual phase are added, file sizes of about 2000 indexed and entered documents can be expected. For our purposes such file sizes are large enough. In fact, we do not want our files to be much larger at this stage. Such file sizes, whatever their theoretical limitations, permit the construction of valid "ideal" search results to be used for later search tests. Such theoretical limitations as there may be will soon be rendered irrelevant by rapid file growth during Phase 3.

As the specific indexing strategies and procedures are participant group and file dependent, only some general features are discussed here.

NEW and PRE: Intellectually and committee indexed documents are to be entered into the appropriate computer files. In so doing, it may be of great value for training purposes to add the bibliographic document descriptions via the on-line mode. For this purpose, document input formats should be established per participant group per file. Thus document identification or title and bibliographic fill-in formats with their thesauri descriptors should be displayed on console for indexer selection. During this document input, a small degree of additional content description could expand the indexing already accomplished. Again training purposes would be predominant.

However, there is one more aspect involved in reviewing indexing of documents during input. The descriptors already assigned to the document by intellectual or committee indexing are displayed on the console screen. During document input, the controversial descriptor list can be displayed as well. If such controversial descriptors are felt worthy of being assigned to the documents often enough, this alone should end their controversial status. Such descriptors can be both added to the thesauri and assigned to the document. Those not deemed useful often enough would also lose the controversial status simply by being accordingly dropped. What descriptors may remain on the controversial list would be those for which dispute continues within the participant group as to the expression "often enough" used above. In these ways console operations for computer-aided indexing become familiar to users, and document entry is accomplished.

Although the evidence is far from complete, what we have indicates that the powerful computer suggest functions offer significant help to indexers after only a few hundred indexed documents have been entered in file (10). The general indexing strategies and procedures should take advantage of such help. This would mean that only few thesauri descriptors (2 to 5) should be selected through thesauri browsing, document scanning, or other means of initial descriptor selection. After these few descriptors have been assigned on-console to the document, further content description should occur via selection from computer suggested lists based on the descriptors initially selected. (Of course the computer suggested descriptors also are based on the suggest algorithms.) Here indexers need only mark with the console cursor those descriptors to be assigned to the document from among those displayed on screen via computer suggestion. Computer suggested descriptors also can be used to provide focused thesauri browsing or look-up. A certain amount of this should be included as part of the indexing strategies and procedures. The bibliographic and other document description should occur using mandatory or suggested computer fill-in formats. Closing procedures should include the display of all descriptors assigned to the document. This should be checked by the indexer, other indexers, or the indexing committee for agreement or consistency. One further computer suggested list could be requested. Rejection of all such descriptors from the "final" suggested list would be an acceptable indication that indexing is completed for the document in question. Of course another look at controversial descriptors could take place, but this should not be repeated beyond this point. Decision to reject remaining controversial descriptors can be made by fiat after such a third look. Document entry in file is accomplished automatically by concluding indexing, or a special entry code may be established permitting "approved" entry.

In building files containing about 2000 so-indexed documents the major time expended by the indexers after initial learning will not be in indexing. Rather, time is spent participating in the development of indexing strategies and procedures specific to the user group and file. Once such learning and development of strategies and procedures have stabilized, indexing times per document should decrease quite radically: 15 minutes per document should emerge as the indexing average even during this stage. Indexing times of 5 minutes per document can be expected and certainly set up as approachable norms for Phase 3. Such times include document entry, an important time-consuming factor in many documentation centers. Yet reduction of indexing time per document takes second place to thesauri refinement during Phase 2. We now return to the thesauri and their Phase 2 construction.

7.4.2.1.6   INITIAL THESAURI CONSTRUCTION—STEP TWO   NEW and PRE: We have allocated approximately half the time available (4 hours per day) to computer-aided indexing for initial file development. The remaining allocation of time should go towards the further refinement of thesauri and to the development of Phase 2 search tests during the first year of Phase 2. The final 6 months of Phase 2 would be devoted to conducting search tests, discovering and devising search strategies and procedures, continued thesauri correction and refinement, and preparing for Phase 3 operations.

During the indexing (Section 7.4.2.1.5) existing thesauri descriptors, their explications, rules, and formats are both tested through use and expanded. This feedback is essential for thesauri construction. The directions for the necessary procedures can be found in CAIR, Chapters 7 and 8. Sufficient familiarity with computer-aided supporting functions transforms the perceived user requirements for thesauri refinement. The point, in emphatically pragmatic terms, of such computer-aided support interrelated with the newer thesauri structuring principles is underlined and understood through direct experience. The means can be then supplemented by the will to create thesauri structured in accordance with computer software and vice versa. The resultant pay-off is determined by the search tests and later Phase 3 operations.

However, this glowing picture may not be all that bright. Not every participant group will find their efforts for each of their files completely rewarding. The word "experimental" implies the possibility of at least partial failure. The inability to accomplish the initial construction of a thesaurus for any file of a participant group would be another warning indicator. Before further development, effort, or funds are expended, this warning light must turn green. And that would be indicated by the achievement of agreed upon (by the participant group and project staff) thesauri.

The means, methods, and procedures for thesauri construction are both available and clear. Only through such an implementation program as here described can we be assured of the probability of their accomplishment. Such thesauri are constructable for enough user groups and their files to permit us to consider the remaining Phase 2 efforts.

7.4.2.1.7 DESIGN OF SEARCH TESTS The Phase 2 search tests are part of the continuing effort to build files and refine thesauri. Some information can be expected as to the quality and costs of computer-aided search, however, tests for this specific purpose come later, during Phase 3 operations. Any results obtained during Phase 2 inevitably would be strongly influenced by "shakedown" problems, incomplete systemsware, and the still volatile state of user and project staff learning.

The detailed design for Phase 2 search tests must be accomplished during the first year of Phase 2 itself. Therefore, only the more general characteristics are highlighted here.

We have restricted, perhaps too prudently, file size. One result of this restriction is that we need not go to elaborate means to determine "ideal" search results for the test search requests. The files are small enough for manual inspection and for the resultant determination of just those documents within the files that would, if retrieved, satisfy our test search requests. Thus recall accuracy and relevancy of search results obtained via computer-aided search question formulation can be readily determined. At the same time, such recall accuracy and relevancy as we do find may properly be used only for feedback as to our thesauri, the related computer-aids, and the strategies and procedures based on these. Extrapolation to other or significantly larger files is unreliable. This consequence has been anticipated. We have noted that the primary purpose of Phase 2 search tests is to obtain yet more feedback for thesauri revision and construction.

Undertaking searches involves just another usage of thesauri descriptors and thesauri. Given the computer-aided approach we have followed, we have additional computer support for the processes of descriptor selection in formulating and reformulating search questions. The initial round of search tests also should offer us feedback as to the utility and effectiveness of the procedures and strategies we may use to exploit our computer aids.

In keeping with the general procedures to be followed during indexing, search question formulation should rely heavily on the displayable thesauri for descriptor selection. Focused browsing based on entry of descriptors should be made possible through thesauri formats in which qualifiers are suggested and thesauri rules of association, hierarchical depth, and so on, are offered. As with computer-aided indexing, search question formulation can be enhanced via the computer suggestion of additional potentially useful descriptors to those initially selected. This capability practically insures that even novices who tend to search with one descriptor at a time will be led to other useful descriptors in formulating their search questions.

Last, search procedures and strategies should be the result of participant group and project staff interaction: We are testing; not propounding oracles ex cathedra. Planning groups too often forget this simple fact. There is no reason to resort to "expert" decree. There is every reason why reasonably designed and, for our purposes, valid search tests can be accomplished.

7.4.2.1.8 THE LAST SIX MONTHS Search tests and, if time and spirit remain, additional indexing, should be concluded early. During test and implementation of software for Phase 3 operations (Item 14), consoles will not be available or their usage severely restricted. During system shutdown, while Phase 3 prototype software and equipment are made ready, at least 3 months can be reserved for the following:

a. Print initial thesauri,
b. Produce indexing manuals—indexing strategies and procedures,
c. Produce search manuals—search strategies and procedures,
d. Produce a list of unresolved or newly discovered problems for Phase 3 consideration,
e. Establish file extension goals for Phase 3 accomplishment,
f. Produce documentation for all other systemsware,
g. Produce an Interim Report describing all features, (a through f) generally applicable to all user groups and files. Include in this report a description of all user group or file specific features believed of general interest.

Prior to running out of final digits for section numbers, we shall focus our attention on Phase 2 costs and manpower requirements.

7.4.3 Staff Requirements for Project Phase 2 as a Cost Estimate Basis

The rough categorization of tasks just followed throughout our discussion offers a "natural" appearing indicator of Phase 2 staff assignments. That is to say we have direction, participation in, and monitoring:

1. Soft- and hardware implementation,
2. Participant group file development and construction,
3. Thesauri development and initial thesauri construction,
4. Indexing and search (manual and computer-aided),
5. Documentation and report production.

TOTAL:* Five Senior Project Staff—full-time for 18 months assisted by one skilled programmer/system analyst, one experienced user-oriented analyst, three research assistants, one documentation or report assistant, one project secretary with access to an external typing pool or with one clerk/typist, and a few special consultants.

The task for the programmer/system analyst is obvious. The user-oriented analyst applies his talents to items numbered 2, 3, and 4 with the aid of the three research assistants assigned, respectively, to the three items just noted. The documentation or report assistant's task is obvious also. The project secretary will have more than enough to do. The consultants represent the means to satisfy special needs for information and work pertinent to the informational fields selected and/or participant group requirements and problems (a lawyer if legal matters are of concern in a file or group, a medical doctor if medical matters, etc.).

---

* The special kind of arithmetic used to produce this number has been invented for this book only and pretends to no mathematical credentials. It is another corollary of Burke's Maxim referred to earlier. Burke's Maxim stipulates that the Senior Staff already should know what they have to do. The corollary to this is that no Senior Staff is required, therefore, to discover what the Senior Staff is supposed to do.

What then shall the Senior Staff do?

We offer the following theorem:

By supplying the appropriate assistance to Senior Staff, we can reduce Senior Staff by approximately 50%.* Not everyone need take this theorem seriously; we intend to. The Senior Staff, assuming the assistance just stipulated, can be reduced to three. One Senior Staff member is essential for soft- and hardware implementation direction and monitoring the efforts of the software subcontractor or manufacturer and the hardware supplier. The skilled programmer/systems analyst will assist here, but is primarily responsible for the planning for and preparation of the operational environment. One Senior Staff member is essential to direct, monitor, and participate in the planning and effort involved in seeing that work accomplished under Item 1 and Items 2, 3, and 4 (p.173) fits together. Last, one Senior Staff member is needed for overall project management, for seeing to it that all items (Section 7.4.1) are accomplished on schedule, arranging for needed consultants, and handling problems beyond the scope of any other persons, such as participant group problems, power plays, or dealing with incompetence, arrogance, and the like. Keeping Phase 3 in clear focus despite the quite natural tendency to be overwhelmed by the specific problems of now and here or there, and keeping the overall project goals in mind, are important aspects of this managerial function.

Our arithmetic then produces the following man/year estimate for the 18-month Phase 2 effort:

3 Senior Staff	$4\frac{1}{2}$ man/years
2 system analysts	3 man/years
3 research assistants	$4\frac{1}{2}$ man/years
1 documentation assistant	$1\frac{1}{2}$ man/years
1 project secretary	$1\frac{1}{2}$ man/years
1 clerk typist or equivalent	$1\frac{1}{2}$ man/years

---

* See footnote on p. 173.

Once project location is determined, and assuming a not-for-profit structure, normal costing procedures should enable the determination of a reliable cost estimate for Phase 2. As a plausible guess, a $400,000 limit seems reasonable. Combined with software costs, Phase 1 costs, and the costs of computer time through Phase 2, approximately $1,500,000 is required to begin Phase 3 operations at the Experimental Center for Public Access. Less than $2,000,000 would be a safe overall estimate. Further discussion of such costs is found in Chapter 8; however, we might note that costs through Phase 2 amount to:

a. About 1% of the government-bankrolled loan granted to Lockheed Corporation in 1971 and not yet repaid (11),
b. Much less than 1% of the so-far admitted bribes to foreign governments and persons by industry in the United States or the European Community countries (12),
c. Much less than 1% of the gambling losses in Las Vegas in one week? month? sales of Bavarian beer? replacement of black and white television sets by color . . . ?

To avoid cramping the life styles of television watchers, beer drinkers, gamblers, or legitimate corporate enterprise, we propose half seriously one possible funding source for not only Phases 1 and 2, but 3 and the Center for Public Access' continued existence: Pass legislation to legalize all "pay off," bribes, or broker's commissions associated with foreign sales and to establish a tax of ¼ of 1% of the value of all foreign sales made by United States and EC corporations. A small percentage of the funds resulting from such a tax would cover all plausible expenses of Center operations and further expansion—and maybe implausible expenses as well.

7.5 PHASE 3—EXPERIMENTAL CENTER OPERATIONS

The reliability of either cost estimates or task description for Phase 3 inevitably is less than that presumed for previous phases of our project. We cannot know with assurance even whether the participant groups with which we have started will remain in their entirety for Phase 3. Such participant groups may be replaced with others, or they may wish to expand their participation or files in directions as yet undeterminable. Conflict with project staff and management on these and other related issues may arise, not all of which may be resolvable.

We point to such possibilities because anticipation is one way to avoid their reaching crisis proportions and to indicate additional areas of concern to the Phase 2 project manager.

What is offered then is not only just an outline of Phase 3 tasks. It is the least reliable description of the project so far suggested.

The constructed files, thesauri, and procedures for computer-aided indexing and search are made available to members of the participant groups who have not as yet participated in the project. Prior to this "turn-over," instructional manuals and computer-aided instruction are needed. Such instructional means differ in significant respects from participant group to group and possibly among the files. The production of these instructional materials constitutes perhaps the first critical Phase 3 task.

File extension via additional computer-aided indexing should continue. By this point indexing strategies and procedures should approach average indexing times of 5 minutes per document. Not only should file size increase but also unnecessary document source controls (year of publication, document type, etc.) should slowly be removed. The likely pace of these sorts of expansion of files ought to have been indicated during Phase 2.

The questions associated with eventual restriction of access to special files must be confronted. The participant groups have agreed only to share their files during the first year of Experimental Center operations. Such sharing of files is needed by the participant groups themselves. Each group obtains access to files others have built, thus increasing potential search return values all around. Equally, providing access to members of other groups constitutes a profound test of thesauri and procedures specific to the individual participant groups. Feedback from such expanded access offers us a valuable indicator as to whether significant and further thesauri and/or procedural revisions are necessary. Instructional materials, expanded files, expansion of access for both group members and others will rather well be the initial "story" of Phase 3.

On a more technical level, the most critical problems facing Phase 3 staff probably surround the questions of Center expansion from 5 to 20 consoles, and later or simultaneous external expansion via remote consoles or via otherwise linked external search facilities. An added technical development may be the improvement of the I/O (input/output) consoles themselves. We have touched on both subjects before and do again.

Last, Phase 3 has to conduct an on-going evaluation of this first year of operations. The Phase 3 Final Report should include:

a. An evaluation covering user acceptance, utilization, and system performance,

b. Estimated costs for Experimental Center continuing operations as is,

c. Estimated costs for adding additional participant groups and files and increasing number of available consoles from 5 to 20,

d. Alternate methods of achieving "remote" console operations or links to external search centers and the associated cost estimates,

e. Suggestions for sharing of costs by users.

Further description and discussion of our implementation project certainly is desirable. We hope to have provided a useful basis for such continuing discussion. More significantly for our own and our societies' well-being, we would hope such discussion as there may be will reach our explicit conclusion: The implementation project should be started and the Experimental Center for Public Access created.

To help reach such a conclusion, we next consider two related topics. The project "nationality" and some general questions addressed to funding of the Experimental Center for Public Access; both Phase 3 and continuing operations.

NOTES

1. S. M. Genensky, A. E. Wessel, "Some Thoughts on Developing Future Command and Control Systems," P-2941-1, The RAND Corporation, Santa Monica, California, October 1964.
2. Dr. T. Finley Burke, Associate Department Head, Electronics Division, The RAND Corporation, has been one of my mentors for years. To the extent that I have misphrased him, the responsibility is mine.
3. See also CAIR, Chapters 9 and 10.
4. Seelbach, "IDS" (Kayser Threde).
5. See also CAIR, Chapters 6 and 7.
6. CAIR, Chapters 8 and 10.3.
7. Contract No. 7/75/SDS of 8 July 1975 between Space Documentation Service, European Space Agency, and the author.
8. CAIR, p. 42.
9. Ibid.
10. CAIR, pp. 153–156.
11. *Newsweek,* International Edition, August 18, 1975, p. 36, under "INVESTIGATIONS."
12. W. Michael Blumenthal, President of the Bendix Corporation "which racked up $2.5 *billion* in worldwide sales last year" has argued that such "payoffs, apart from their being illegal . . . grounds enough not to engage in them, *are also singularly ineffective." Newsweek,* International Edition, 11 August 1975, p. 48, under "Interview: W. Michael Blumenthal" (italics added).

Chapter Eight

A Question of
Nationalities and
Costs

Thus far, reasoned argument and rational perception of factual matters have been attempted. Opinion and probabilities were identified, hopefully in clear enough fashion. Even so, errors of fact, perception, and judgment in a discussion the scope of which crosses disciplines and technologies, facts, and values, and excites passions are to be expected. Modesty, pretended or sincere, has not entered into this admission. Such errors as may be found or perceived through the lens of interested observation affect neither the thrust of our argument nor the salient features of our description. The technology and the social context surrounding automated information retrieval and its actual and potential "publics," as discussed in previous chapters, can be taken both seriously and critically.

We now turn to more speculative matters. We have to consider who is to be and who is to pay the piper. We must confront essentially political effects and economic concerns with many long-term features. Accordingly, our time frame is stretched from less than 5 to more than 10 years. Still our speculations need not be empty. We have called attention to the intellectual risks here not to permit unnecessary and useless indulgence but to point to the need for even more care and clarity. We intend to "wipe our glosses with what we know" (1).

Let us start with another admission. The very introduction of the "nationality" question could be seen as unnecessarily involving us in more complexity than an already complex set of problems warrants. Such an objection would be valid if we literally were proposing a binational or international project, or attempting to argue that such a project made more sense than a national one. We propose and argue no such thing. We suggest that many benefits would be derived from an arrangement whereby a simultaneous start of two national projects would permit exchange of staff, experiences, and files. Many features of the procedural developments, the learning from the use of systemsware and files, the resolution of participant group problems, and so on, would be transferable. Also, the option to search through other country files would add to file scope and depth. The software suggested previously makes such extended search plausible. "How plausible?" and "How useful?" are significant questions for which answers could be obtained only by implementing search through other country files. Communications need not be complex here. Simple exchange of file tapes should be added to the above list of suggestions for exchange between national projects. The "nationality" of the projects ought to be mixed or, at the least, binational through these exchanges.

Our solution takes much of the sting from the objection to bi- or international projects; there remain, however, other objections to be considered. Even if on technical and pragmatic grounds (from the perspective of the projects) our suggested exchanges seem appropriate or persuasive, other national interests may intervene. In short, are the politics right?

8.1 THE POLITICS OF THE "EUROPEAN COMPUTER"

In an official "Communication" from the European Commission to the European Council is found:

The Council Resolution of 15 July 1974 on a Community policy for data-processing has provided the groundwork for an industrial policy in this vital sector of the economy. (2)

The Council Resolution gives a European Community orientation to policies that encourage and promote data-processing (3). It then "welcomes the Commission's intention to submit . . . priority proposals (concerning data-processing)" (4). Specifically:

c) the promotion of industrial development projects of common interest involving transnational cooperation." (5)

"Transnational" in the above quote means: *European* nations, not including the United States, as is made clear with the Commission's Initial Proposal:

The Commission has selected as the subject of its first proposal the field of (data-processing) applications . . . The promotion of applications, *notably in the public services,* combines the two main aims of the Resolution: to satisfy user requirements while making economical use of the public resources by joint development and *to create a strong European-based industry.* (6)

There is no question of the intent "to strengthen the competitive power of European industry and broaden its market" (7). The only question for our purposes is whether the sadly parenthetical phrase italicized in the quote (citation 6) may help to balance the also italicized direct phrase that reads, though more politely: AMERICAN INDUSTRY STAY HOME!

Participation even to the extent of our suggested project certainly would benefit the resultant public services. Yet even this weaker form of cooperation for trans-Atlantic projects dealing with advanced data-processing applications will need to be far more persuasive to overcome a Europe-only or America-only perspective. We would have to show that such chauvinistic perspectives are short-sighted and, more to the point, short-sighted where it hurts. There is no question that the notion of the "European Computer" is hurting. We intend to argue that the kind of mixed "nationality" projects we have suggested provides far better medicine for these birth pangs than what so far has come from Brussels. Furthermore, the American data-processing industry could use a similar dose of the very same medicine.

A little recent history is relevant.* In the late 1960s and before England was a member of the Common Market, a decision was made in Germany to catch up with IBM and provide Common Market countries with a third-generation computer system. Siemens AG, through a licensing agreement with RCA, produced the 4004 series of computers known in the United States as the RCA SPECTRA 70 series. It soon turned out in the United States that RCA gave up the SPECTRA 70 in the beginning of the decade for which the SPECTRA was aimed (1970). RCA had found that competition with IBM in this line of large general purpose computers could be left more prudently, if not successfully, to others. Siemens AG was undaunted. In fact, Siemens AG formed a wholly European Alliance (UNIDATA) with Philips (Netherlands) and

---

* As we are speculating and have frankly stated so, the standpoint of the speculator should be of legitimate interest. Our speculator then is American, resident in Munich, Germany, with sympathy for and contracts from both sides of the ocean. As such, the speculator can be regarded as doubly prejudiced, doubly neutral and, therefore, singularly objective.

CII (Compagnie Internationale pour l'Information—France) in July 1973 (8). IBM was not daunted either. It has continued to obtain roughly 60% of the European computer market with UNI-DATA coming in a poor third at 8% after Honeywell's 10%. "All three UNIDATA partners have been losing money heavily on their computer operations" (9). Although some cheer might have been felt concerning IBM's troubles in the United States Courts and its theoretical demonopolization, UNIDATA already has begun to break up. Honeywell and CII, the French UNIDATA partner, have merged through acquisition (10).

Shortly after the Honeywell-CII affair, the *Süddeutsche Zeitung,* one of the better German newspapers (comparable to the Washington *Post,* the Los Angeles *Times,* or the New York *Times* in the United States), reported (4 September 1975) (11) the further dissolution of UNIDATA with Philips N.V.'s withdrawal. According to *Newsweek,* Philips not only is withdrawing from Unidata but also has decided "to get out of the computer business entirely" (12). We question the report that Philips is withdrawing from the computer business entirely. Rather we think Philips is embarked on the minicomputer trail. We agree, however, with *Newsweek's* remarks about American technology in this field: "If Unidata has not been able to meet the American technological and marketing challenge, it is not alone . . . German Bundesbank (figures) show that almost half of all the fees paid by German industry over the last three years for industrial rights and licenses went to the U.S. . . ." (13). We shall darken this confusing picture by one more news item prior to presenting our own views.

An article appeared in the 16/17 August weekend issue of the *Süddeutsche Zeitung.* The shortened and paraphrased translation is offered as it contains some information of great importance in the various strands of our argument to follow. One such strand is that the information in the *Süddeutsche Zeitung* article indeed is important to Europe, a fact we contend is confirmed by the length and prominently placed appearance of the article:

New Computer Memory Highly Condensed

An increase of the component density of semiconductor memory chips by a factor of 10 was achieved by IBM researchers by using electron beam lithography and ion implantation techniques. The experimental '8.192 Bit FET Memory Chip' (an accompanying picture shows a strongly magnified part) has a bit density of 775 000 bits per square centimeter. The memory access time is 90 nano seconds. The high density of the memory circuits on the chips is due to the fact that an electron beam was used to draw the circuit elements on a surface instead of a light beam as this was the case so far. The connecting lines on the chips resulting from this procedure reach 1 to 1.5 micrometers in width. In optical lithography 4 to 5 micrometers are typical. This small size increases the transfer speed. The memory cells were developed by IBM as well: per bit of stored information only one transistor is required. A field effect transistor (FET) charges a condenser (in fact a sequence of semiconductor layers) and thus stores one bit of information. The field effect transistor is of the n-channel type, the transistor zones were produced by ion implantation of arsenic. The control electrodes consist of polycrystalline silicium, the associated oxide layer is about 350 Angström thick. The device contains aluminum conductor elements about 2.3 micrometers wide . . . on which the field effect transistors are located. (14)

We need one more "fact" that is substantiated to date by "qualified" rumor. IBM has spent many many millions of dollars to develop what was to be their fourth-generation, large-scale, computer series. This development and funding seems to have stopped suddenly. It appears that the characteristics of the planned fourth-generation replacement for the IBM 370 series are in flux. We think it worth the speculation that the facts reflected in the *Süddeutsche Zeitung* article just quoted in paraphrase had something to do with the apparent change of course within IBM as to the next step after the IBM 370. We think these same facts have much to say concerning the current plans in Europe for the European Computer as well.

It seems that some very new technology may have produced a radical reorientation of the IBM development plans. The name of this new technology, from the perspective of our argument, can be shortened to the Minicomputer. It appears that both IBM' and

European competitors such as UNIDATA were spending a lot of development money to produce fourth-generation monster computer systems. The minicomputer, in its penetration of the computer applications markets, did not seem to offer a significant threat to these planned fourth-generation monsters. The minicomputer core or working memory was too small to compete with the giant computers for the general purpose applications markets. But then came some new micromemory and minimemory technology, which offered minicomputers the possibility of achieving "massive" capacity cores, while remaining mini in size and cost (15). IBM has, presumably, seen the light. We confidently predict that IBM will enter the competitive fray with an IBM minicomputer series to end all minicomputers. Unidata apparently had not seen this same light, even though Unidata management had access to technological "intelligence" that later became public through the *Süddeutsche Zeitung*. The European Computer is an attempt to produce a competitor to the IBM 370 series and the fourth-generation IBM series that was, but apparently is not, to be. Furthermore, as the minicomputers are being produced by American manufacturers (only one European product comes even close to the variety of minicomputers available through American manufacturers), the continued European development of the monster fourth-generation computer may find that it is competing with a rejected will-o'-the-wisp. Worse it may find its market equally elusive, having been preempted by the newer minicomputers with potentially large enough capacity cores. The Americans, including IBM, the reluctant giant, will have retained their lead.

This consequence, if we are correct in our speculations, should have been expected. We have previously noted that data-processing technology is still very young and that its application to automated information retrieval (in the general sense taken here) is even younger. With the young only the expected is surprising, and certainly we all have learned that with new technology come unexpected consequences. Both IBM and European management had no reasons to believe otherwise. Furthermore, the information was available. The conditioning to understand this information, rather than to reject it as speculative intelligence, might have been assumed. However, both IBM and European management had conventional information retrieval systems to support their decision-making processes. Such management also had the staff support to gather, filter, and "package" the available information. But quite a lot of information was available: good, bad, and indifferent in quality, though impressive in amount. And such information taken as a whole, was contradictory, inconclusive, and mixed with opinion, fancy, emotion, prophecy, and fiction. Conventional information retrieval systems leave such blends of myth and material substance, perhaps smaller and more relevant than otherwise, but, nonetheless, a blend not necessarily composed even in part of all the relevant elements. No one need blame such managements for making poor, ill-considered, or wrong decisions. But we have arrived at one ground for our belief that such managements both in Europe and the United States also would benefit from the same second-generation software (Chapter 6) needed for achieving public access. Such managements could be persuaded that they have their own vested interests in our implementation project (Chapter 7). And if we could resolve the problem of the European Computer, managements on both sides of the ocean might be willing to agree to the kind of participatory exchanges involved in our suggested implementation project. This would require an agreement as to the software and hardware "split" between the implementation projects—a "split" that would result in software and hardware "sharing." Such "sharing" would result in significantly reduced costs as well, a not irrelevant factor.

Another strand of our argument applies to precisely this issue; an acceptable resolution for both Europe and the United States with regard to the European computer. First, we suggest that European computer manufacturers and Brussels seriously consider the broader as well as the narrower meaning of the minicomputer "surprise." The narrower line of thought would be to suggest that

European manufacturers follow IBM and write off their major investments in fourth-generation giants and giant systemsware. Could not European manufacturers make minicomputers too? Certainly they could do just that and again be surprised a few years down the road by American technology in this field. The broader meaning would imply just such a "future shock." American data processing technology is so far ahead in most applications in the data-processing fields that no one is going to catch up in all respects in the foreseeable future (say the next 25 years in this case). Certainly the Russians understand this and realistically attempt to purchase every bit of American data processing technology allowed them.* At the same time, American data processing technology has left a few developments behind in its rush, and American hardware manufacturing managements have not been immune to tunnel vision. European technology in general is sufficiently far advanced that it could achieve a competitive position selectively within the data-processing applications markets. What is needed in Europe is not the European computer but European products that would fill the large number of significant gaps left by American technology and ignored by American managements.

We have mentioned such gaps previously and have explored rather thoroughly one such serious software omission. The hardware gaps are represented by the existing input/output consoles used for interaction with computers by humans. Display screens leave much to be desired. Inexpensive color-coding beyond "black and white," more responsive and less error-prone entry devices, including cursor movements and keyboards, greater screen size and line and part-line identifying capabilities, lower- as well as upper-case letters, and hand-marking capabilities such as bracketing or otherwise indicating textual elements, are, in combination,

---

* The Russian frequently has talked up the Russian computer over the last 10 years and has built a few models, all outmoded as soon as built by "Western standards." The Russians, however, are quite realistic; they talk Russian and buy American or American-derived (West European) whenever they can.

console features that are critically needed given the interactive possibilities opened up by second-generation software. Consoles offering these improved characteristics and flexible usage probably will require their own "buffering computers" as the most efficient links to central data processing computers. One could even envisage certain techniques that would permit the newer consoles to achieve selected, highly efficient processing of data stored in peripheral memories (such as disks) in combination with their small scale buffering computers. This would be a highly interesting approach to the reduction of transfer and access times involved with peripheral storages, which now requires complicated programming techniques. Here is hardware enough for the European data-processing industry. A successful European production of such equipment would find major markets throughout the world. Providing, that is, that European hardware is priced at the admirable and efficient VW or Renault 12 levels and not at the level of the expensive and strangely designed Cadillac. Here too American experience is relevant. We do not claim that because these hardware gaps exist, American hardware manufacturers have never attempted to fill them. They have, but with such faddish conceits as three-dimensional screens. These were quite capable of offering the viewer more complications per cubic inch than, for example, the air-space patterns they were supposed to clarify for air-traffic controllers. Three-dimensional consoles were and are expensive, even if useful in certain scientific, technical, or architectural designing applications (e.g., three-dimensional models of complex organic molecules). Where a third "dimension" (or fourth or fifth, etc.) may be needed or useful, color-coding on a two-dimensional screen might serve as well or better. Consider again the air-traffic controller. Is a compressed three-dimensional copy of a real air-traffic snarl more or less confusing than color codes that would indicate such altitude differences among aircraft whose screen appearance would otherwise conflict? Based on radar data, including height-finding radar, color coding separation via computer analysis would seem more sensible than "eyeballing" a three-dimensional representation. Certainly for our purposes of information retrieval applications, three-dimensional screens are not worth their present cost and complexities. Flexible and more error-free modes for input and output formating on "normal" screens are the sort of improvements needed. If European manufacturers could supply these competitively, they would discover that the market is larger than it might first appear. One need only multiply each American computer by the several or many European consoles and their buffering computers to obtain some notion that selecting this development option is far from limiting European industry to the lesser share of the data-processing markets. Furthermore, the production, marketing, and service facilities built up by first concentrating on what may appear to be the periphery, leaving the main frames to the Americans, might later be useful in taking advantage of on-going main frame technology. That European computer could still make sense, not now but later. One might do well in Brussels and elsewhere in Europe to meditate on the views just expressed.

Such European developed consoles and console buffering computers combined with American main frame or central data-processing computers would have one additional quite profound effect. Minicomputer developments with such equally advanced peripheral products might keep both Europe and the United States sufficiently far enough ahead of the Japanese! Should both Europe and America continue with their current management policies, we confidently assert that the coming Japanese minicomputer systems will outperform and underprice both the American and European product lines. Washington, Boston, and Los Angeles have as much to consider here as do Bonn, Brussels, and Paris.

The lack of second-generation information retrieval software represents the other fundamental omission within the data-processing industry. As previous chapters have indicated, here Europe is already ahead. It would seem that the implementation project hardware and software "nationalities" could turn out to be American minicomputers and large capacity memories of all kinds combined with European consoles, buffering computers, and functional software. Such a "solution" in the terms of our bi- or international implementation program is offered as the preferred mix: beneficial to the projects, the public services rendered, and the data-processing industries in both the United States and Western Europe. We recommend it strongly. Furthermore, we delineate more of the steps to achieve this mix more specifically in Section 8.2.

8.2   PROJECT HARDWARE

Only somewhat vague cost estimates have been given for hardware for our implementation program. These were included in the overall figure (from $1,500,000 to less than $2,000,000) and provided, essentially, for computer time needed for programming development and testing. The hardware configuration needed for the Experimental Center(s), where it shall come from, and how it shall be obtained, must now be considered.

Assuming the special mixture of "nationalities" discussed in Section 8.1, our implementation program would result in two experimental centers: one to be located in Western Europe, the other in the United States. We have stated our belief that the exchanges of information and experience thus made possible make sense. Further reasons to support this opinion have been offered. An additional benefit involving significant cost savings associated with hardware is now explored. As will be obvious, any such benefits depend on the following steps being acceptable to all concerned and appropriately implemented.

To state our initial goal as to hardware: We envisage a hardware configuration from off-the-shelf items for use during Phase 2 and probably through the first year of operations at the experimental centers.

An adequate but small hardware configuration for the initial center operations could be composed of the IBM 360/40 computer system. A 10 station multiuser operation would be possible using

IBM Model 2260/1 Graphic Displays and Model 4766 Alphanumeric Keyboards. An IBM Model 2040H could serve as the central data-processing unit with one Model 2841 Disk Controller, 10 Model 1316 Disk Packs (7MB) and the usual peripheral printers and card readers. Such a configuration is outmoded according to today's standards and probably could be put together from used equipment. A configuration based on the IBM 370 series equipment would present less constraints with regard to expansion and program handling capabilities.

A contemporary hardware configuration for which some of the second-generation software features already have been programmed could consist of the Siemens 4004/150 computer system and would include:

1 Central processing unit 4004/150-J
(This includes a core storage of 524 Kilobytes, with one multiplexer channel and one channel selector)
1 Central control unit 4100
1 Card reader 4239-30
1 High-speed printer 4241-52 and read-only store 45273-1
1 Dual channel tape control unit 4479-208
4 Magnetic tape units 450
1 Disk control unit 581/2
8 Mass disk storage units 580/2
1 Data transmission unit 9685 with 4 line buffers 9608. Up to 20 video data terminals, Transdata 8150 or 8151. Other associated peripheral equipment, such as hard copy printers.

These two configurations represent the lower and upper boundaries of a possible hardware configuration suitable for our implementation program. IBM, Siemens, Control Data Corporation, Honeywell, and other major manufacturers could all supply an appropriate hardware configuration falling within these bounds from off-shelf equipment.

However, this hardware configuration is to be replaced later with a system composed of newer American main frame or minicomputer central data processors, European consoles and console buffering computers. Other peripheral equipment, such as disk packs and printers, would be chosen from the already existent configuration or replaced in accordance with the requirements of the new configuration as then established. Depending on certain developments to be specified below, the newer hardware configuration would come into being during the first year of experimental operations or soon thereafter. A later date would be the more likely alternative and the safer one, permitting us to hedge some quite critical bets.

First, the course and successful outcome of developments associated with minicomputers and large capacity, compact, random-access working storages are important factors requiring our attention during the next 2 or 3 years. Second, these next few years will tell us much concerning the "compatibility" of minicomputers and large-scale disk storage. Last, during this time period we should discover whether the console buffering computers can accomplish a significant amount of "preprocessing" of disk stored data prior to transfer to the computer core for further processing. To some degree, successful accomplishment of the first technological developments for minicomputers will lessen the requirements for successful accomplishment of the latter two. But not entirely! For interactive response times to remain acceptable while providing for the expanded functions of second-generation software, particularly with multiconsole, multiuser operations, these last two developments are far from trivial. Either extremely focused and thus incredibly fast access to disks must be achieved, or significant preprocessing outside of core must be possible on-line in dialogue mode, or both must occur to provide responsive systems. These are the critical developments that may take 3, 5, or more years for their sufficiently successful accomplishment. During Phase 2, or in about 2 years, we shall have more grounds for evaluating our expectations as to these critical technological

developments. At that time it may be possible to shift forward the
schedule for the newer hardware replacements for our experimental
centers.

Should the two experimental centers envisaged materialize, there
are two further requirements to be satisfied in order to allow the
European Center to choose European hardware for the initial configuration, and the American to choose American hardware. One
requirement would be software portability. The software must be
usable with both configurations without significant, if any, adaptation. The other requirement would be an agreement for both
centers to accept the "international" hardware just described as the
newer hardware configuration: American main frame or minicomputer, central data processing units combined with European
consoles, and console buffering computers. This agreement should
apply to all further centers in any future expansions or to any
expansion within the two centers themselves.

Such are our hardware configuration goals. How do we obtain
them?

Let us return to Brussels:

3.8 In regard to *central processors* . . . At the moment, the (European)
Commission does not intend to put forward any proposals in this field. (16)

In accordance with our previous arguments as to central data
processors and continuing American main frame and minicomputer technological leads, such lack of action by the European
Commission is seen here as much the better part of valor. Wisdom
would be indicated by the Commission going all the way on the
negative side and recommending against European central
processor development. In accordance with the Commission's own
views:

3.7 In the hardware sector, the Commission is also considering projects to
be proposed in 1975, *notably in connection with components and
peripherals.* (*17*)

As of summer, 1976 we have not seen the projects under consideration by the European Commission. Concentration on peripherals and components for data processing applications is precisely what we have indicated should be done in Europe. Furthermore, we have called attention to the input/output consoles and their buffers required for taking full advantage of the interactive options to be available with second-generation software. We would recommend strongly that the European Commission establish a project to develop such consoles and their buffers by European data processing industry. European manufacturers might find such a development project to be in their own interests as well. Furthermore, we have suggested an appropriate testing ground for such European consoles as may be developed—the experimental centers for public access to be created under our implementation program. The resultant markets would not be only European. American agreement to use European consoles and console buffering computers in exchange for the use of American main frame or minicomputer central data processing units for both centers opens yet more widely and appropriately the markets in the United States and Europe. We have reason to believe that such an agreement on both sides would be obtainable because of its obvious advantages to each. We recommend that such an agreement be obtained through the auspices of the European Commission and the appropriate United States State Department agencies should the implementation project described above be started.

We now come to our third recommendation. The initial implementation project hardware for both experimental centers should be supplied to the project free of charge by the hardware manufacturers in both Europe and the United States under the following conditions:

a. The European manufacturers be offered development aid in producing the newer consoles and console buffering computers to be used to replace the centers' original equipment. Should such developed consoles and buffers meet the specifications established under the development aid funding, such equipment would be purchased by or on behalf of the experimental centers replacing the equipment "on-loan."

b. The American manufacturer(s) be offered, in addition to the reduction in main frame competition, the right to supply main frame or minicomputer replacements for the central data processing equipment "on-loan" to the centers in Europe and the United States. For American manufacturers also the resultant market would not only be American.

This sort of "political" detail unfortunately is as much part of our planning as was the technical detail considered in earlier chapters. The combination of technical and political detail applies again to the question of software "portability." In addition to projects already established by the European Commission (listed on p. 181), projects for later consideration, for which proposal requests may be sent out, are mentioned. One of these, discussed at some length, concerns us here:

. . . the Commission has found . . . that there is a vitally important area of common interest, namely that of *software portability*. In plain terms, this is the ability to run programmes on different types of computers . . . (18)

The question of software portability is as important as the Commission believes. The costs of incompatibility of software are high. The Commission estimates the cost in Europe during the next 5 years as 1000 MAU (thousands of "Accounting Units" defined in terms of the various EC currencies and approximating $1.20 per unit or DM 3,-) (19). However the technical aspects of this problem are trickier than perhaps the Commission seems to expect. The remainder of the previous quote is as follows:

(the ability to run programmes on different types of computers) without having to worry about the make or the machine language used within the system. (20)

In the quite general terms implied by the Commission, such a goal for software portability is very far away if not effectively impossible to achieve. Developing yet another main frame central data processor in Europe would not help matters any in this regard, nor would it reduce the expected costs in the E.C. countries resulting from the lack of software portability. Standardizing main frame (and at the proper time, minicomputer) central data processing equipment by acceptance of the fact of American continued dominance certainly would help matters. Furthermore, this cost estimate of the Commission could be reduced by developing European consoles and console buffers as a standardized product line for those American central data processors in Europe.

More critical to our purposes, however, is the fact that software portability for the kinds of applications represented by the experimental centers for public access can be built in from the start. The software manufacturer selected would have two potentially different hardware configurations "to worry about."* This is better than being immediately concerned with achieving portability of software for thousands of differing applications, let alone hardware configurations. At the same time the range of generalized information retrieval applications represented by our centers is large, quite large. Software portability is both feasible for our case and meaningful in terms of its potential utility throughout Europe, the United States, and elsewhere.

Last, given the apparent software lead indicated by the Kayser IDS System concept and the earlier Siemens AG PRIMAS, both

---

* It is true that we should consider not only the original hardware to be supplied but also the later hardware configuration that will replace this original equipment. However the latter, in accordance with our programmed mix, would be identical at both centers (or effectively identical). The earlier hardware could certainly be selected in ways that would make the portability of software relatively easy to achieve among the centers. The principal difference would be, perhaps, starting with a Siemens computer at the European center and an IBM at the American. These computers are not that different. As a result the required "translation" program to permit software portability would not be that difficult or add to previous software cost estimates.

European in status, our implementation program might opt for European functional software. (The operational or internal computer systems software, given our assumptions about an American central data processor and European consoles and console buffers, would be mixed but predominantly American in all likelihood.) As American software manufacturers have neither seen fit to nor been much excited about developing computer-aided indexing, thesauri building, and interactive analytic tools, there should be little objection to such a choice at this late date in the United States. If the Americans continue to expend their energies and funds on fully automated textual analysis, the Europeans would have a good 20 years more before American functional software would begin to offer even the computer-aided capabilities now becoming existent in Europe.

This brings us to our fourth and last step or recommendation: European functional software should be selected as it is the closest to the second-generation software required. If Brussels won't fund this next logical developmental step for European functional software, Bonn or Paris should.

Certainly such funding is well within the current expenditures planned at Brussels. The funds for the first 5 projects stipulated by the European Commission, all essentially software developments, total 4,007,500 Accounting Units or $4,809,000 for the next 3 years (21). These five projects, although quite important and socially valuable, are, nonetheless, rather specific in impact. They cover:

1. Data bank for matching organs and blood
2. Data processing systems in import/export, agricultural market organizations, etc.
3. Systems for retrieval of legal information at Community level
4. Requirements for data processing systems in air traffic control
5. Computer-aided design*
   i. Electronics study
   ii. Design-oriented systems (22)

---

* This project is more a feasibility study than a software development at present.

The estimated cost for development of second-generation software for information retrieval capabilities certainly falls within the bounds of such E.C. expenditures. We think it obvious by this point that the social benefits and utility of such software to the general public, private industry, government, and all other users of automated information retrieval are broader and deeper than each and all of the five projects just listed. Furthermore, selection of such European functional software for second-generation information retrieval systems would provide a significant though partial solution to the portability problem. If the European Commission estimate cited above is correct, the costs of developing the suggested standard second-generation software for information retrieval applications would be far less than the costs associated with the lack of such standard software. Thus the fourth, and we think all of the specific action steps recommended in this section, should seem justified and reasonable. Even so, they all hinge on the merits of the case so far made as to the implementation project itself. Granting that the need for public access to information retrieval systems has been established, the technology available or in sight, the costs feasible and the politics right, a deeper look at some alternatives to our implementation project is required. We then can hope to conclude our case.

NOTES

1. James Joyce, "Finnegans Wake," Viking Press, New York, 5th printing, 1947, p. 304. The actual line is, "Wipe your glosses with what you know"—the best operational definition of "to speculate" that we know.
2. Commission of the European Communities, Directorate-General for Industrial and Technological Affairs, Communication from the Commission to the Council, "Initial Proposals for Priority Projects in Data-Processing," Brussels, 7 February 1975, 1191/III/74 E, revision 3, original in French, p. 1.
3. Ibid., p. 1.
4. Ibid., p. 1.
5. Ibid., p. 1.
6. Ibid., p. 1 (italics added).

7. Ibid., p. 1.

8. "French computer plan brings doubts," *TIMES* (London), from their own correspondent, Paris, 13 May 1975.

9. Kenneth Owen, "Honeywell's French connection sends tremors through the European computer industry," *TIMES* (London), 13 May 1975.

10. Ibid.

11. "Philips-Konzern verlässt den Unidata-Verbund" (Philips Trust Leaves Unidata Group) (VWD), *Süddeutsche Zeitung*, No. 202, 4 September 1975, p. 24.

12. "The American Challenge—1975," under the rubric "International Marketplace," *Newsweek*, 15 September 1975, p. 46.

13. Ibid.

14. *Süddeutsche Zeitung*, No. 186, 16/17 August 1975, p. 19 (Wissenschaftsseite—Science Section).

15. We have referred to this possibility at several points in our previous discussions; see also Section 2.2, reference 8; and Section 6.2. 1, reference 11.

16. Commission of the European Communities, "Initial Proposals . . . ," p. 7, italics added.

17. Ibid., p. 6.

18. Ibid., p. 5, with the discussion continued through p. 6. (Italics added.)

19. Ibid., p. 6.

20. Ibid., p. 5.

21. Ibid., p. 9.

22. Ibid., p. 9.

Chapter Nine

Alternatives

9.1 KINDS OF ALTERNATIVES

Attempting to dispose of alternatives is like dealing with the mythical serpent that grows three new heads for each one cut off. As we are more interested in considering than disposing of alternatives, perhaps we shall be able to reach a timely conclusion. The achievement of broader and more equitable access to automated information systems can be accomplished in at least as many ways as there are societies in which the attempts are made. Within these many differing societies, the implementation paths can vary again as a function of the particular public groups admitted to the inner sanctums. We have proposed and described in detail one such feasible method to broaden public access through the development of appropriate software and hardware in conjunction with a participatory implementation program.

One alternative to our approach is based on a claim that the software and hardware will be developed anyway and implemented somehow. Sooner or later, according to this perspective, more and more of us will obtain or be given the benefits of automated information retrieval. Of course, a push here and there might be required. But it will come; access will open up as an inevitable effect of the technological developments. This kind of assumption as to the presumed "random" dispersion of the benefits of technology is a technological version of the well-known economic "trickle down" thesis. It has its merits, and examples of just this sort of distribution of benefits include: a chicken in every pot, an automobile outside of and a television (or two or three) inside of every house.

A second alternative is based on the claim that occasional pushes are not sufficient to turn the trickle into a flow. A good deal of central planning is required and is undertaken by a select few for the benefit of the "masses." Whether the central planners perceive the needs of the many for whom they plan through the "beatitudes" of scientific materialism, idealism, or some other path to wisdom seldom changes one result. The select few retain their power to continue centralized planning and their presumed right to determine for us what shall flow to whom. We intend to call this perspective the "shove down" thesis, independent of whether the shovers are oriented to the political right or left or in between. It too has its merits and examples where bridges, roads, hospitals, schools, and hydrogen bombs were constructed. The fruits of science and civilization have been distributed in many ways.

One other alternative begins with an admission by the establishment that its wisdom is limited and that its power perhaps ought to be. The dangers of assuming enough power and knowledge to force a redistribution of benefits can be summed up in one word: "Totalitarianism." At the same time, the trickle is otherwise too weak and the occasional encouraging pushes too much in the control of already interested and benefited persons and institutions. The resultant distribution of benefits remains badly distorted. The "middle" way then is to turn on (or sometimes off) selected monetary spigots, pumping development and implementation funds into already existing social organizations. By this means the existing technological development and implementation channels can be influenced sufficiently through the carrot of government funding and the related threat of the withdrawal of such funds. In this way, transformations are made to occur within the status quo represented by the already existing organizations and the "inertial system" of the current social distribution patterns. Some of the distortions are to be corrected by selective opening and closing of the monetary spigots. But only *some* of the distortions; the keys to the spigots are retained by the establishment. We shall regard this version of economic pump priming as the "control flow" thesis. It is often difficult to prevent the control flow thesis from degenerating into the trickle down or collapsing into the shove down thesis. But it can be done and has its merits also. Examples exist where this sort of control flow has succeeded, at least temporarily, in putting more social goods into our pockets.

Other alternatives may be worthy of discrimination, but a closer look at these three should place our own approach appropriately and indicate why we prefer it. In so doing we may discover a few other plausible approaches and some insight as to why and how they might work. However, in order to enable a realistic discussion of any alternatives, a brief return to the economics of automated information retrieval is required.

9.2 THE ECONOMICS OF THE "AVERAGE COMPUTER SEARCH"

In previous chapters we have described and emphasized the often hidden and seldom mentioned costs associated with after-search-result staff work. We now intend to look more closely at what is usually included within the average search time costs. A clearer picture of what is involved in such "computer costs" is useful for the discussion of alternative implementation methods in the next section.

The computer time required for search runs is a mere fraction of the time the search console on which the search is initiated has to be connected to the computer. When a figure of $30 per average search is given for the "computer search time," we are actually talking about this console connect time. An average search seems to require about a half-hour of such connect time for the console operations. The typical computer runs per se may be measured in seconds, occasionally minutes. Most interactive search systems permit multiconsole operations. This means that one console initiating the operations for one search need not exclusively tie up the computer during this ½ hour of average connect time. Many such consoles can be so connected, each of which has the required computer run times (in fractions of seconds usually) distributed to it via some "sharing" method. It is important to note at the beginning that our $30 does not mean that we have bought a ½ hour of active computer processing. We have purchased a ½ hour of access to the computer through a terminal or an input/output console. Many other purchasers have access to the computer for that same ½ hour.

It may not have been clear to purchasers of these $30 searches, but a few other things have been included in what they have purchased. What has been purchased for $30 is a ½ hour of access to search through computerized files. This means that such charges have been intended to cover the costs of document indexing and document (identification) entry. These costs and the resultant quality of the document indexing will prove to be as important as and very much related to the costs of after-search-result staff work previously considered.

To one degree or other yet another element has been included in the $30 average search cost. The initial search request formulation is translated into computer acceptable search questions. When one buys a search from INSPEC, for example, someone at INSPEC must translate the search request into a computer acceptable search question(s). (Of course the costs and user time in formulating the initial search request are not included in these costs. Source and search suppliers often provide aids and help for this process.)

Lumping together these essentially manual processes with the costs for computer searches by most search services (INSPEC, DIALIB, etc.) forces us to attempt to unravel them. This must be done in order to understand what really is going on in the determination of search costs. These noncomputer elements are of particular importance to our concerns. For example, such conventional indexing and document entry might be thought to be "inexpensive" or unimportant as a cost factor. But however "cheap" these factors are in themselves, conventional indexing imposes major costs on the other side of the search result. We have already seen that much after-search-result effort must accomplish a good deal of filtering for relevance and analysis of the information obtained, the determination of the completeness and/or suitability of the results obtained, and the usually necessary reformulation of search requests and questions. Conventional indexing just is not good enough to permit reliance on "inexpensive" staff work accomplishing this sort of task. Yet it does not appear that this poor quality, conventional indexing is inexpensive.

Let us make some assumptions, each one of which may error toward the low side. What might the costs be for indexing and document entry for source suppliers of computerized files or for suppliers of searches through the files they have created?

If we assume the cost of conventional indexing and computer entry is $2.50 per document, a file of 100,000 documents would cost $250,000. As we should be considering much larger files, we can start with the assumption that a computerized file containing 1,000,000 indexed documents could be achieved for $2,500,000.

How good an estimate this is will be considered later. However, the argument we now make will not vary too much if our $2,500,000 per 1,000,000 document estimate were one-half or twice as much. Within these boundaries we can begin to form a reasonable picture of the economics involved.

Let us next assume that there are 500 constant users of a search service providing retrospective or special searches. The users of the selective dissemination services will be brought into the picture later. By "constant users" we mean that each such user requests one search per day and that there are 20 working days per month. For the 500 constant users, there would be 120,000 searches conducted per year. At $30 per average search request, $3,600,000 would be paid each year to the search service by constant users alone. If we now subtract the indexing and document entry costs, $2,500,000, from the $3,600,000 obtained from such users for the searches, there is $1,100,000 left over. By applying these left-over funds to the costs of hardware, in about 2 years the computer system would have been paid for, as well as the indexing and document entry costs for the 1,000,000 document file. In addition, new files containing 1,000,000 documents each could be created and paid for perhaps more quickly than it would take conventionally to index them.

Varying these basic figures within the boundaries previously suggested might add or subtract a year or two to the amortization processes. The point is that profitability would soon be reached and maintained as well as continual file growth. The number of constant users also could be reduced from 500 to about 350 and make little change in our calculations as to reaching profitability while continuing the increase of file sizes. Furthermore, additional income would be received through services supplied to "cyclic" users purchasing selective dissemination or special searches. The income from such sources is significant enough to permit the assumed cost of $2.50 per document to be increased to $5.00. Even at $10 per document indexed and entered by including all sources of search income, "profitability" would be attained in about 6 years, perhaps with some slowdown in the growth of the computerized files.

The above analysis offers a fairly good indicator of how the $30 per average search request could be allocated. About $20 of that $30 is allocated to pay for conventional indexing and document entry. The remaining $10 is for the computer connect time and the console operation. Given these assumptions and their stated boundaries of variation, in from 3 to 6 years hardware would be amortized and the number of documents in the computerized files would grow to a few million. Supplying computerized searches looks rather profitable. Is it so?

Unfortunately there is a small problem that cannot be overlooked. As with most "economic models," our analysis may be logical enough but it easily could be dead wrong. Conventional automated information retrieval systems, as we must repeat, do not provide support to the document indexing and entry processes. This neglect means that the assumptions made as to basic indexing and entry costs per document were much too low in many cases. It does not appear that in reality any documentation service, be it INSPEC, DIALOG, RECON at NASA or ESA is able to function without a governmental, institutional, or corporate subsidy. When all the costs of document indexing and entry into computer files are considered (all the man/hours, office space, input equipment and processes, fringe benefits, etc.) a figure of $50 per document might be closer to the real cost than $2.50, $5.00, or even $10. There is probably no valid average indexing and entry cost as the amount of effort involved varies widely from application to application. Yet whether the indexing and entry costs are closer to $50 than $2.50 per document, we have noted quite often that quality or consistently indexed document files do not result from conventional indexing. Still more costly after-search-result processes are required.

These indexing costs alone, however, result in an existing average search cost that severely limits the number of potential users. This fact not only reduces the chances of broadening public access. It also affects "profitability." If the number of constant and cyclic users of search services could be increased, the increase would not have to be very large to reach profitability in spite of high indexing and document entry costs. We have "multiplied" the basic indexing and entry cost by ten, from $5 to $50 per document. Suppose now the same is done with the number of constant users. With 5000 such users and within the framework of our preceding analysis, the "gross" would be $36,000,000 per year. Including revenues from cyclic users, about 1,000,000 documents could be indexed and entered annually at a cost of from $35 to $50 per document. Once again hardware costs could be paid off in a few years and profitability would soon be reached. But the cost for an average search request would have to remain at about $30.

We have now arrived at the heart of the matter. Although some increase in the number of constant and cyclic users may permit search services to become profitable, the number of potential users will remain limited. It is not too difficult to determine just how limited this number will be. For a constant user, as we have defined such, the bill comes to $7200 per year. For this, a constant user can obtain precisely one search per working day during the twelve months of the year. This $7200 annual bill does not cover the often larger costs of the required after-search-result analyses. This figure might have to be multiplied by 2, 3, or sometimes 4 to give us a valid notion of the true annual costs. When the average search cost actually turns out to be $60 or $120 per search, the number of potential users is not going to grow very fast.

One search for information per working day cannot be regarded as "extreme." For many this would result in far too few searches; their informational requirements could not be satisfied. Even should we reduce the requirement for information satisfied by one search per day by one-fourth, one fact stands out clearly: The benefits of conventional information retrieval systems are not going to be dispersed very often very far down within our societies.

This result of our "economic" analysis must be confronted by any suggested approach to achieving broader and more equitable access.

9.3 THE TRICKLE DOWN THESIS

The conclusion reached in Section 9.2 concerning the stringent limitations . to the distribution of the benefits of conventional automated information retrieval does not impose more difficulties on the trickle down thesis than on any other. Conventional information retrieval methods are simply too inadequate or costly to be considered as the means to implement any approach to solving the problems of providing broader public access. Few governments, for example, whether via centralized or decentralized approaches, are willing or able to spend $7200 per year per citizen to provide them with one search per working day. Should some government actually attempt something approaching this, few citizens would be able to pay the additional taxes required and pay as well for the yet higher costs of the necessary after-search-result analyses.

In Section 9.2 we have discovered what the real costs of conventional automated search are likely to be. However, the trickle down thesis could claim that the inadequacies of conventional automated search will be left behind by technological developments that will upgrade conventional systems. This possibility is worth investigation.

The trickle down thesis could be stated as follows: Conventional automated search is inadequate and costly. Technology will have to remove the inadequacies and reduce the costs. This will happen if for no other reason than the fact that existing automated search services cost too much and impose too many burdens on their users. In order to maintain and retain customer satisfaction and to reach profitability by expanding the customer base, technological developments must take place. The "market" demands this. As the only significant way to decrease costs and increase quality, the required developments must focus on the indexing and entry problems and reduce the existing necessity for after-search-result analyses. The relevance and importance of these problems have gradually dawned on the minds of some of the technology managers. As fully automated textual analysis has proved wasteful, the major unresolved problems and the largest costs have now been identified and understood.

In addition, developments that resolve these problems for existing search services and their customers will trickle down to the rest

of us. With reduced costs and reduction or removal of the requirements for intensive staff work, the customer base will grow. More
and more citizens will be able to afford the computerized searches
they may need. Significantly they will also find such computerized
searches much more useful and meaningful.

There are analogies. The "Model T" Ford trickled down after
automobile technology and manufacturing methods made automobiles generally available. Today the Fiats, Renaults, Volkswagens,
and Detroit sub- and compacts provide just about as much "transportation" for the many as the Rolls Royces for the few. In the
same way as cost decreases and utility increases, computer search
becomes available to at least as many people as those having access
to automobiles.*

The following three Barrier/Breakthrough charts represent the
trickle down thesis within a framework of the postulated historical
development of automated information retrieval.

The brief history of electronic data processing applications to
large document files is restricted to an even shorter time span than
the mere 30 years of electronic computers themselves. The period
before 1960 is appropriately labeled "prehistoric" from the
perspective of the kinds of information retrieval we have
considered. As Chart 1 indicates, the number of applications of
automated data processing systems to large document files before

---

* The analogy actually can be made far stronger. Remember that electronic computers are very young and that the first scientific electronic calculator-computer was
born a mere 30 years ago. It then took a good 15 to 20 years before computers
began to offer significant information retrieval capabilities; only recently have we
had automated documentation systems. The first mass produced automobiles, if
memory serves, sold for about $300. Dollars were worth a lot more then than now.
With today's dollars, any one can purchase a fully electronic, programmable, scientific notation, pocket calculator/computer for about the same price of those early
automobiles—$300. It is just a matter then of waiting 15 to 20 years to be able to
buy a pocket automated information system and library for about $300 of yet
cheaper money? How small can very large memories get? Certainly our television
consoles could be connected to such pocket computers as I/O devices. This analogy
and possibility is most intriguing assuming the general availability of computerized
files on tapes.

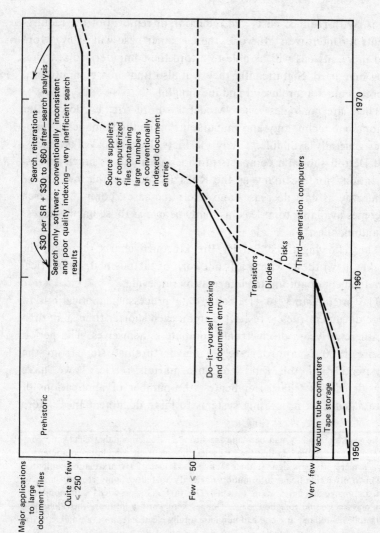

Barrier/Breakthrough Chart 1.

1960 were less than "very few." These predominantly resulted from developments undertaken for military applications. Hardware development then replaced the "tube" computers with diodes and transistors and added disk storage to drum and tape. At this point, anyone with enough money and patience could begin to develop large computerized document files. The number of applications in the early 1960s rose. But as a great deal of patience and money was necessary, only "few" applications were completed. Third-generation computer systems now appeared. Applications increased from very few to few. The basic limiting factor preventing more extensive use of such technology was what we have called "do it yourself indexing and document entry." At about this same time period, however, source suppliers began to make use of third-generation computer systems. They hired large staffs and began conventional indexing of large numbers of documents. Computerized files containing such conventionally indexed documents began to grow rather large—containing millions of documents, as we run off the right side of Chart 1. More organizations could purchase third-generation computer systems and purchase or lease such computerized files. Others could purchase cyclic dissemination or special searches from search services. At the beginning of the 1970s we had "quite a few" applications throughout the world. The barrier now was software; search only software applied to conventionally indexed documents. This combination produced search results so inefficient that costly after-search-result staff analyses were required. Those who could afford the real costs of about $60 to $90 (and sometimes more) per search request could buy automated search. We had now entered the historical period of applications to large document files.

Just as the "prehistoric" Chart 1 took us into the beginnings of historic times for automated information retrieval, Chart 2 extends the historic present just a little into the future. Here we see the first signs of the trickle of applications beginning to grow to a flood. The barrier of search only software applied to conventionally indexed documents began to crumble in the mid-1970s. First of all,

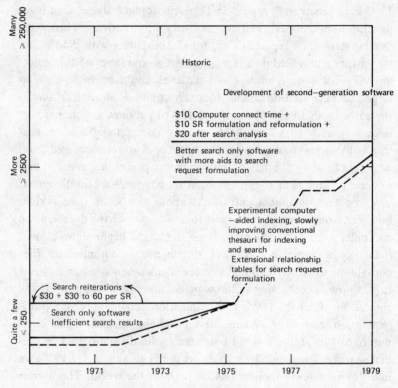

Barrier/Breakthrough Chart 2.

search only software became better, permitting more flexible search question formulation. Descriptor selection for search questions was aided by displayable thesauri, which also began to improve. Perhaps more importantly, computer-aided indexing entered its experimental stages and was applied to "real world" documents in various informational fields. Toward the end of 1975, the concept of extensional relationships was programmed and received its initial test. Even more powerful aids to search question formulation and reformulation seem to have resulted. We can expect the number of applications to rise from "quite a few" to "more" between 1975 and 1977. It appears that computer connect time per search might run as low as $10 with less after-search result staff analysis required. Fewer iterations would be needed. Perhaps the total costs for an average search would range from $30 to $40. Obviously more buyers could afford $30 to $40 per search request than $60 to $90. But not yet enough of us to make the trickle down thesis valid. However, just on the border of the "present" (and running off to the right of Chart 2), a new development begins.

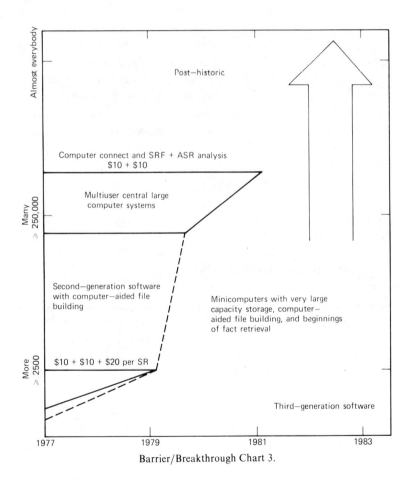

Barrier/Breakthrough Chart 3.

Second-generation information retrieval software is about to permit a break through another barrier.

At some time between 1977 and 1979, second generation software begins to replace search only software. Thereafter, "more" applications become "many." Computer-aided indexing is now generally available to source supplier and user alike, producing significantly better and more consistently indexed documents. Error-correcting document entry is available as well which, combined with computer-aided indexing, builds larger and larger files more cheaply. Extensional relationship methods and other techniques offer powerful computer aids to search question formulation. The quality and efficiency of search results improves to the extent that after-search-result staff costs are minimal and approach zero. The basic cost barrier now is, for the first time, the computer connect time costs. The last barrier is the expensive large main frame computer. Now this is replaced by much cheaper minicomputers after 1979. If not yet "pocket sized" and available in supermarket or chain department store, minicomputers combined with second-generation software sends the applications arrow past "many" to "almost everybody." As time goes on, computer-aided file building becomes commonplace. Computer-aided thesauri construction provides thesauri that are embedded within the computers. Access to the larger and larger files of well-indexed documents becomes, through these methods and techniques, available to almost everyone at the touch of buttons. Then, to suggest that our picture of post-historic times is not stagnant, off to the right border of Chart 3 we see the beginnings of "fact retrieval" and third-generation software. "Now" (around 1983) anyone who can afford to own and adapt a TV and to purchase a few "transistor" minibatteries every so often has the . . . but we have exceeded the time frame of Chart 3.

The trickle down alternative need not adhere exactly to Charts 1, 2, and 3. As a projection of past, present, and near future developments these charts are as reliable, at least, as any others derivable from "expert" opinion. Numbers, dates, and developments could shift within a few years and still support a formidable argument that we need do nothing but wait. The trickle down alternative as such is rather likeable. It suggests somnolence as the best way into the future. By this point certainly it could be claimed that we have done enough homework. We know where and perhaps how to initiate the right amounts of pushes in the right places and times.

Beyond observing, at this point, that Charts 1, 2, and 3 and their plausible "competitors" are easier to draw and talk about than to implement, we shall have only one significant objection to the trickle down alternative. This will involve the question of user participation. However this very same objection, or some version thereof, will be raised in our consideration of the other alternatives as well. We shall first consider these, reserving our critique until later.

9.4 THE CONTROL FLOW ALTERNATIVE

The West German Government has undertaken a major effort begun in 1973 to upgrade and expand the existing information services throughout Germany. From 1974 through 1977, 458.697 million DM has been allocated ($183.48 million) (1); 64.158 million DM ($25.7 million) had already been spent in 1973 (2). Of the 1974 to 1977 funds, DM 186.611 million ($74.64 million) have been spent through 1975 and 125.145 million DM ($50 million) has been allocated for 1976. The bulk of these funds have been allocated to the support and expansion of existing institutional and organizational information and documentation services that are available to the general public. For example, the 1974 through 1977 funding is split up as follows: 258 million DM ($103.2 million) are allocated to transregional information facilities throughout Germany and 114 million DM ($45.6 million) to transregional libraries (3). Relatively little funding is allocated to central planning or technological development. Forty-two million DM ($16.8 million) are allocated to special projects, some of which are developmental; this includes the research program for Information Science within universities and other individual funding measures to support research and development and professional and specialized societies. Additional development funding, to date consisting mainly of study projects, are to be supported through funds, 44 million DM ($17.6 million), allocated to the not yet fully activated Society for Information and Documentation (Gesellschaft für Information and Dokumentation, GID) (4). Under these auspices, a Central Planning Group has been established the members of which include representatives of the organizations being supported. To date, the Central Planning Group primarily has been concerned with the development of a financial allocation plan, analyses of institutional requirements, and, to a much lesser degree, investigations of technological capabilities and the requirements for technological developments.

The breadth of the West German Government program is impressive. A total of 16 disciplinary field information systems and certain other special information facilities have been established. At the end of the government support program the estimates of annual funding requirements for these information systems and special facilities are as follows:*

Disciplinary Information System	DM per Year (millions)
Health, medicine, biology	10–20
Food, agriculture, forestry	5–10
Chemistry	10–20
Energy, physics, mathematics	10–15
Electrical engineering, precision engineering, mechanical engineering	10–15
Metallurgy, materials, metal working, processing	5–10
Extraction and exploration of raw materials; geological sciences	4–6
Transportation	8–12
Regional and city planning, construction	5–10
Consumer goods	8–12

Disciplinary Information System	DM per Year (millions)
Economy	4–8
Law	10–20
Education	8–12
Social sciences	13–18
Liberal arts	5–8
Knowledge of foreign countries	4–6
Ecology	2–4†
Patents	4–8
Development of standards	1–3
Research information	4–10

* These figures may change due to more detailed analyses by the planning groups.
† Does not include the cost of the Environmental Planning and Information System (UMPLIS).

To indicate this spread of funds between already existing information facilities and organizations and potentially new or to be developed facilities a table showing the breakdown of funds allocated among the disciplinary information systems if offered (6):

Disciplinary Information System	Funds Allocated 1974 Through 1977	
	DM	$
	(thousands)	
Health, Medicine, Biology		
Deutsches Institut für medizinische Dokumentation und Information (German Institute for Medical Documentation and Information) Cologne	35,564	14,225.6
Funds allocated to the Verein Arzneimittelinformationsdienst e.V., (Association Drug Information Service) Cologne	668	267.2

Disciplinary Information System	Funds Allocated 1974 Through 1977	
	DM	$
	(thousands)	
Project funds for the construction and development of the disciplinary information system	580	232.0
Food, Agriculture, Forestry		
Subsidies for scientific documentation	9,904	3,961.6
Zentralstelle für Agrardokumentation und -information (Agricultural Documentation and Information Center) Bonn	2,344	937.6
Project funds for the construction and development of the disciplinary information system	2,687	1,074.8
Chemistry		
Project funds for the construction and development of the disciplinary information system	25,000	10,000.0
Energy, Physics, Mathematics		
Subsidies for the Zentralstelle für Atomkernenergie-Dokumentation (ZAED) (Atomic/Nuclear Energy Documentation Center), Karlsruhe, and for suppliers	4,904 (1974)	1,961.6 (1974)
Subsidy for publication and further development of the "Physikalische Berichte" (Physical Reports)	1,545 (1974)	618.0 (1974)
Subsidy to the Mathematical Commission of the Heidelberg Akademie der Wissenschaften (Academy of Sciences) for works on the "Zentralblatt für Mathematik" (Central Journal for Mathematics)	851 (1974)	340.4 (1974)

Disciplinary Information System	Funds Allocated 1974 Through 1977	
	DM	$
	(thousands)	
Funds allocated to the disciplinary information system	34,021	13,608.4
Electrical Engineering, Precision Engineering, Mechanical Engineering		
Project funds for the construction and development of the disciplinary information system [e.g., Zentralstelle Dokumentation Elektrotechnik e.V. (Documentation Center Electrical Engineering), Dokumentation Maschinenbau e.V. (Documentation Center Mechanical Engineering)]	9,800	3,920.0
Metallurgy, Materials, Metal Working, and Processing		
Project funds for the construction and development of the disciplinary information system [e.g., Werkstoff-datenbank (Material Data Bank)]	6,950	2,780.0
Extraction and Exploration of Raw Materials; Geological Sciences		
Documentation of the geological sciences in the Bundesanstalt für Bodenforschung (Federal Institution for Earth Crust Research), Hannover	1,720	688.0
Dokumentationszentrale Wasser (Documentation Center Water) in the Fraunhofer-Gesellschaft	1,607	642.8
Project funds for the construction and development of the disciplinary information system	1,641	656.4

Disciplinary Information System	Funds Allocated 1974 Through 1977	
	DM (thousands)	$ (thousands)

Transportation

Subsidy to the Zentrale Informationsstelle für Verkehr (Information Center for Transportation)	820	328.0
Deutsche Forschungs- und Versuchsanstalt für Luft- und Raumfahrt (German Research and Experimental Institution for Aeronautics and Space) Zentralstelle für Luft- und Raumfahrtdokumentation und -information (Aviation and Space Documentation and Information Center) Munich	12,440	4,976.0
Project funds for the construction and development of the disciplinary information system	4,441	1,776.4

Regional and City Planning, Construction

Subsidy to the cost of documentation activities in the field of housing, construction, and land settlement Dokumentationsstelle für Bautechnik in der Fraunhofer-Gesellschaft (Documentation Center for Civil Engineering, Fraunhofer-Gesellschaft)	2,908	1,163.2
Project funds for the construction and development of the disciplinary information system	3,900	1,560.0

Consumer Goods

Project funds for the construction and development of the disciplinary informa-

Disciplinary Information System	Funds Allocated 1974 Through 1977	
	DM	$
	(thousands)	
tion system [e.g. Zentralstelle für Textildokumentation und -information (Documentation and Information Center for Textiles)]	1,983	793.2
Economy		
Project funds for the construction and development of the disciplinary information system	1,380	552.0
Law		
Cost of the introduction of electronic data processing in the area of justice (legal information system using EDP)	37,200	14,880.0
Project funds for the construction and development of the disciplinary information system	250 (1977)	100.0 (1977)
Social Sciences		
Subsidies to central documentation and information facilities of the social sciences Zentralarchiv für empirische Sozialforschung (Central Archive for Empirical Social Research), Cologne; Informationszentrum für sozialwissenschaftliche Forschung (Information Center for Research in the Social Sciences), Bonn-Bad Godesberg	2,400 (1974)	960.0 (1974)
Cost of electronic data processing for purposes of political documentation	13,319	5,327.6
Bundesanstalt für Arbeitsschutz und Unfallforschung (Federal Institution for		

Disciplinary Information System	Funds Allocated 1974 Through 1977	
	DM	$
	(thousands)	
Labor Protection and Accident Research), Dortmund		
cost of literature documentation in labor medicine		
cost of scientific documentation in the field of labor, safety, and accident research	325 (1974)	130.0 (1974)
Funds allocated to the disciplinary information system	(1975 through 1977) 13,050	5,220.0
Education		
Project funds for the construction and development of the disciplinary information system	250 (1977)	100.0 (1977)
Liberal Arts		
Project funds for the construction and development of the disciplinary information system	(1976 and 1977) 1,080	432.0
Knowledge of Foreign Countries		
Project funds for the construction and development of the disciplinary information system	(1976 and 1977) 600	240.0
Information Facilities for Special Purposes		
Project funds for their construction	2,508	1,003.2
Planning groups for the construction of disciplinary information systems	(1974 through 1976) 7,412	2,964.8

Disciplinary Information System	Funds Allocated 1974 Through 1977	
	DM	$
	(thousands)	
Further project funds for the construction and development of disciplinary information systems	(1975 through 1977) 12,123	4,849.2
Total of federal funds allocated to disciplinary information systems and information facilities for special purposes	258,175	103,270.0

The West German government's program is an impressive illustration of a Control Flow Plan. From our perspective it should be noted that the bulk of funds are being allocated to existing and essentially independent organizations. In addition, not only is there a smaller allocation of funds to central planning functions, but also the central planning group is itself composed of representatives from the major existing and variegated institutions and organizations within the West German social, political, scientific, educational, and industrial structures. As such, control of the informational resources and the methods of structuring information, as well as access to such information, is left pretty much in the hands of a variety of already existing organizations and groups.

We have some further comments to offer here again with particular reference to matters of user participation. But as before, we reserve our critique until we can present it in the context of all the alternative approaches we consider.

9.5 THE SHOVE DOWN THESIS

The technological developments described in the three Barrier/Breakthrough charts could be applied to creating broader public access to automated information retrieval capabilities. The very same technology could also be applied to achieving quite other and opposite prospects for public access within our societies. The question for what we have called the "Shove Down Thesis" is whether any strongly centralized attempt to force both technological developments and implementation programs on a society can result in more and freer public access to the society's informational resources. Less and more controlled access to the informational resources to be made available is at least as likely an outcome of any such strongly centralized attempt.

Theoretically, it may be argued that some benevolent version of the "Shove Down Thesis" could work to the general advantage of the public. In practice, this would depend very much on what is being done to and for the public. In the specific case that we are concerned with, however, there seems to be an inevitable contradiction within the concept of broader and more equitable public access being provided for the public by a centralized elite. To the extent such access as may be provided is significant, the results certainly would tend to diminish the power of the elite in control. Such kinds of strongly centralized planning can provide many social goods, but at a price. The price seems always to be the maintenance if not expansion of the power of the central planners to plan, direct, and implement as they deem fit. Free access to uncontrolled information would seem to be the very kind of social good that such planners can provide only at their peril. The very "right" to information can be held as sacred a right by such central planners as by anyone else. However, as with Plato, central planners tend to regard this sort of "right" as so sacred that it must not be polluted by dispersion among the common people.

There are some quite practical problems as well even to formulate a "Shove Down Plan." We have discovered that many governmental bodies are spending about $3.70 per year per citizen for data automation. Such expenditures are obviously not intended to provide the citizens with access to automated information retrieval capabilities. To date, most such governmental expenditures have been used to apply automated data processing procedures to governmental business operations, book-keeping, and accounting requirements. It takes about $3.70 to enter one citizen's name, address, and a little more information into a data bank. Given the reported levels of governmental expenditures for data processing and the diversion of funds to business and accounting operations, not enough is left over to place all citizens' names, addresses, plus a little more data into all the governmental data banks. Just some of the citizens in some of the data banks!

If there are two things that central planners believe (the first is in central planning) one is in the necessity to have all citizens' names, addresses, and quite a lot of information about them in central data banks in order to do good central planning. It would seem then rather dubious to expect central planners to provide the public with significant access to uncontrolled information before the central data bank has been completed: filled with all the "needed" planning data about all the citizens. Furthermore, one can wonder whether such central planners will find it necessary, not to mention desirable, to bother about giving the public access once the public has been properly and fully accounted for within the central planning data bank. Nonetheless, by changing certain features of the control flow plan just described in Section 9.4, a reasonable version of a Shove Down Plan can be constructed. It would go as follows:

The role of the Central Planning Group would be expanded. The bulk of funds would be allocated to this group. The Central Planning Group would also control the allocation of all funds. Although representatives of the varied existing organizations would have their say, only the Central Planning Group would listen and only they would decide what should be done, when and how and where. A set of "standard" information requirements would be developed, which would specify the extent of the public's need to know. The information to be made available would be determined by the Central Planning Group, which would retain control of information input and description. Similarly a set of "standard" and acceptable search request possibilities would be developed. Search result boundaries would be established as general formats or specific schemata. The allocation of such "search rights" and capabilities among the various public groups would be established by the Central Planning Group. With this accomplished, implementation can then proceed. And so on more or less to suit the particular degree of benevolence and ideology involved. The technology, as we have seen, is becoming available to permit such central planners to achieve whatever versions of an Orwellian 1984 informational world as suits their prejudices.

9.6 THE REQUIREMENT FOR USER PARTICIPATION

We have not so much been describing alternatives to the detailed program in Chapters 7 and 8 as the typical ways technology is developed and implemented within most of the societies we know. Trickle Down, Control Flow, and Shove Down, their permutations and combinations, seem to be the ways technology and its benefits are distributed. It should also be clear to any objective observer that the resultant distribution patterns are seriously distorted although the specific distortions differ from time to time within the various "technological" societies.

One thing these existing technological distribution processes have in common is a lack of significant and direct user participation throughout development, implementation, and subsequent distribution of benefits. User participation is partial and spotty at best; least during development, not enough during implementation, and often irrational during distribution. The implementation program described in Chapters 7 and 8 calls for and requires the direct participation of the user groups concerned throughout these developmental, implementation, and distribution processes. This means specifically that user groups will participate in the analysis and determination of the technological requirements, the functional characteristics of the automated information retrieval systemsware, the selection of the informational fields and the informational files, the description and indexing of such information, the development and test of indexing and search strategies and tactics, and the construction of thesauri permitting access to the files. This kind of user participation pertains to access itself. In fact the only requirement to obtain access is the fulfillment of the commitment of the public groups' participation in these processes. This would apply to other public groups (the late-comers) as well.

To the extent to which Trickle Down, Control Flow, or Shove Down Plans incorporate these specific and significant elements of direct user participation, the essentials of our suggested implementation plan have been accepted. To the extent that the information itself and the means to retrieve it, the "boundaries" for questions and answers, in short the fundamental "rules of the game," are established by the direct participation of the user groups concerned, our implementation plan can be regarded as seriously attempted. To the extent that the user groups directly construct the files, conduct the searches by and for themselves, determine the parameters of utilization and evaluation, and remain free to transform the system capabilities and responses in accordance with their own perceived needs, our implementation program can be regarded as successful.

As described in previous sections, Trickle Down and Control Flow approaches leave such relevant matters in the hands of those already in charge. The West German government's plan essentially leaves the determination of requirements, the rules of access, the information structures, and so on, in the hands of those already with access through existent organizations and institutions. The improvement of information retrieval processes and the partial integration of information collection, file building, and search capabilities will aid those already with access; however, the current patterns of access to information within Germany may be slightly modified but not significantly changed. A few more "representatives" of the public, a few more organized groups perhaps will be admitted to the inner sanctums with access to the national informational resources. This indeed is better than nothing. To some as yet unpredictable degree, access will open up within West Germany as a result. But it will be access to information structured in accordance with the perceived needs and requirements of those with access already.

The Trickle Down process will add a few more percentage points to the population groups with access to the available informational resources. Computer search will become less expensive and more efficient. Less after-search-result analyses will be required as search formulation and indexing aids come into being. This too is better than nothing. Again to some as yet unpredictable degree, access to computerized search will become broadened. More individuals and social groups and organizations will be able to afford computerized search and make use of the search results within all societies. But again this will be access to information structured in accordance with the perceived needs and requirements of those already with the ability to afford such access to the current expensive systems. Such access will remain in accordance with the already established "rules of the game" determined by those now owning or with access to automated information retrieval capabilities.

To arrive at significantly broader and more equitable access to these capabilities, to achieve greater public access to information structured more in accordance with public needs, and to give the public more say as to the search rules, the essentials of our implementation plan would have to be incorporated within either a Trickle Down or Control Flow plan. Given the costs and methods we have previously described, there is no rational ground for not so incorporating our suggested implementation plan. Unless, of course, one does not wish to broaden public access to automated information retrieval capabilities sufficiently to make a significant difference in the existing distribution patterns. Let us consider one new specific alternative example.

We have previously discussed some details of the DIALIB program in Chapter 3. DIALIB makes use of preexistent information collection and distribution facilities; the branch public libraries. There is another group of preexistent distribution facilities with branches located just about everywhere. These facilities concern themselves with the collection and distribution of money, that is to say the banking systems. Banking managements have increased the range and depth of services offered to their customers over the last few decades. Banks have found it profitable to attract more customers by such "customer services." More bank customers means more funds for the banks to "manage" and more profit potential.

Not only are bank branch offices located just about everywhere, most major banks have extensive experience with automated data processing applications. Furthermore, most banks, or the central offices thereof, have extensive collections of monetary, economic, and financial information and data. Most major banks have already automated parts of these data and information collections. A good deal of such information, if properly structured and computerized would be tremendously useful to all bank customers. Making budgets, assessing loan charges, figuring out tax reports, selecting savings programs, evaluating retirement plans, stock or bond purchases begin a long list of potentially valuable applications of such already existent information to customer problems and needs. Developing automated information retrieval technology would make search services through such bank collected and maintained information and data both feasible and inexpensive. A new customer service, a very attractive one at that, could be made available to account holders of the banks inclined to leadership. Charges for such services could be allocated to account holders according to account size or other factors; in any event direct billing through accounts for searches conducted for customers would be a simple matter. Branch facilities could have search consoles permitting access to the computerized files located at central headquarters. File development and maintenance would also be a centralized function leaving branch banks only with the tasks of console operations and local service. Such searches could be offered at little or perhaps no cost. The data is well-structured, the informational fields limited, the search question and search result formats reasonably stable and standard. A little training of selected bank customer search specialists would provide them with sufficient knowledge to achieve a relatively high degree of flexibility in satisfying customer requests within these boundaries. Access to automated information retrieval would open up to a large number of "new" groups and individuals within society; bank account holders. This would be very much better than nothing and the suggestion is offered freely to any banking institution wishing to be the first to offer such services to their customers.

However, note that the central files are owned by the central bank, the control of information input and output resides there as well as does control of access. Pressures from "relatives" in the financial community would keep such information limited or the output of such information to average account holders restricted. Insurance companies, lending institutions, stock salesmen, tax consultants, lawyers, estate planners, and financial advisors wouldn't like too much accurate and inexpensive information to be distributed too broadly. Just how deeply and broadly this new customer service would extend is difficult to guess. But the limits would be real and the access would be to strictly circumscribed information structured and controlled by others, not the public served. The need for the implementation program of Chapters 7 and 8 actually might be emphasized. In fact any such expansion of search services would probably lead to the awakening recognition that precisely the suggested implementation program is critically needed. For this reason alone, there should be only applause for those banks or other institutions seeking to provide even the limited access to the severely restricted information they may have and be willing to make available.

We have yet to further consider the Shove Down approach. For reasons given previously, we intend to give this approach short shrift. It may be that some benevolent variety of this approach could succeed in altering for the better the current distribution patterns of the benefits of technology. It could be that such an alteration would be sufficiently serious as to permit the society involved to do away with the centralized controllers and planners. Presumably this sort of possibility lies behind the Marxist notion of the eventual "withering away of the state." What has been the case to date is that however the distortions are transformed, some distortions seem to be "more equal than others" or more persistent. One such distortion that persists is the overly high degree of the power and control allocated to the central planners. Yet even here, adoption of the essential characteristics of our suggested implementation program by such central planners would be a welcome change. This would mean that direct participation of the publics served would be included within the central planning processes. This would be meaningless unless such direct user participation would be such as to change, influence, and redirect the planned actions. Whether the Shove Down approach and our suggested implementation program could jointly survive under such conditions would remain to be seen. Certainly, however, the attempt would be laudable.

NOTES

1. "Programm der Bundesregierung zur Förderung der Information und Dokumentation" (Program of the Federal Government for the Support of Information and Documentation), Bundesministerium für Forschung und Technologie, Draft, Bonn, 30 October 1974, p. 4. The official report issued later contains only slight revisions to the draft report cited here.
2. Ibid., p. 4.
3. Ibid., p. 2.
4. Ibid., p. 2.
5. Ibid., p. 86.
6. Ibid., pp. 90-96.

Chapter Ten

The Distribution
of Information

Perhaps it is inevitable that some imbalances in the distribution of
resources, wealth, power and the like will persist within any social
order we humans are likely to create. Any social arrangement
seems to involve us in its own skewed distribution of benefits and
goods. Perhaps for many of the social goods we have created and
will create, distortions in distribution patterns may not matter
enough to enough of the people concerned. Or, in any event, the
attempt at rectification may be too problematic, costly, or sacri-
ficial to justify anything other than the acceptance of the inevitability of imbalance.

However, we have been concerned with the distribution of a very
particular kind of social good: information. In an absolute sense
the only thing inevitable about the distribution of information is

that it will always be incomplete. No one has access to complete or perfect information. We all think and act in partial ignorance and error. The distortions in the distribution patterns for information have to do with the relative lack or possession of access.

One of the growingly important dividing lines in this relative sense is that between those groups and persons with access to automated information retrieval capabilities and those without such access. There is nothing inevitable about this dividing line or where and how it is and can be drawn. We may vary widely as to our individual abilities and capabilities, our informational needs and our willingness to satisfy them. We may differ greatly as to what information we wish to use and as to how we shall use it. Such differences will persist and produce variations in the distribution patterns of the available informational resources. But there is neither need nor inevitability as to the persistence of the existing patterns of access to automated information retrieval. Access to computerized files and to search through the information available through such automation could be made available to just about anyone. The means to begin to provide more broadened and equitable access to the information available within computerized files have been described. We also have tried to show that the costs of such an attempt is not excessive. We have indicated and described the appropriate technology and the methods by which it should be implemented. The many valid reasons for the broader public to demand and expect to be given the access through which they can better satisfy their informational needs have been discussed. The remaining questions come down to two:

Do enough of the public seriously want to participate in a more informed manner in the decision making pertinent to their societies?

Do our governments seriously want to have their citizens participate in a better-informed manner in such decision-making?

Should the answers to these two remaining questions be negative, there is little justification for any belief in the continued existence of meaningful forms of what are called the "democratic processes."

Whether in that case the jungle elements of brute force, terrorism, suppression, and violence will increase their encroachments on civilization may be difficult to assess. But it would be reasonable to expect that the conclusion of Chapter 5 would have to be amended. Hypocrisy, self-satisfaction, and short-sightedness can bring forth contemporary Neros with the power to control far deeper and to persist far longer than the Hitlers or Stalins of the computer-less past.

Technology now has brought us computers and automated files. Our present implementation and application policies have not, however, brought us equitable public access to these same technological capabilities. This book began with an open invitation to participate in a discussion intended to transform existing policies and to bring about broader public access to automated information retrieval capabilities. It is hoped that enough will accept this invitation and find it to their advantage to let more of the people know.

Index

Access
  control of, 5
  requirements, Preface, 228
  restriction of, 176
  rules of, 227
  times, 188
  use of, 145
After-search-result
  analysis, 211, 228
  costs, 203, 207-209, 211, 214
  processes, 97, 206
AGRIS (Agricultural Information World-wide-United Nations) file, 31, 42
Air defense, 59
AEG (Allgemeine Elektricitäts-Gesell-schaft)/Telefunken, 91
American central data processors, 196, 197. *See also* United States
American computer, 189. *See also* United States
American hardware, 188, 189, 193. *See also* United States
American industry, 182. *See also* United States
American main-frames, 189, 192, 193. *See also* United States
American management, 187, 189. *See also* United States
American manufacturers, 184, 185, 195, 197. *See also* United States
American minicomputers, 189, 192, 193. *See also* United States
American product lines, 189. *See also* United States
American technology, 183, 187.

  See also United States
Automated information
  access to, 2, 4, 6, 22, 60
  costs, 3
  effectiveness, 3, 4
  see also Information; Information retrieval
Automated information retrieval, 2, 8, 15, 22, 23, 25, 26, 54
  conventional, 27
  costs, 17, 202, 203-207
  development and implementation of, 2
  files, 97
  technological features, 13-17, 18-22
  see also Information retrieval
Automated inventory systems, 18
Automated retrieval, *see* Information retrieval
Automation, *see* Information; Information retrieval
  administrative data flow, 66
  resentments against, 157-159

Bank
  account holders, 229, 230
  branches, 230
  customer services, 229, 230
  managements, 230
  search specialists, 230
BBC (Brown, Boveri & Cie AG), 91
Bibliographic
  categories, 162
  formats, 22
  information, 23